A Will is Not Enough in Texas

2nd Edition

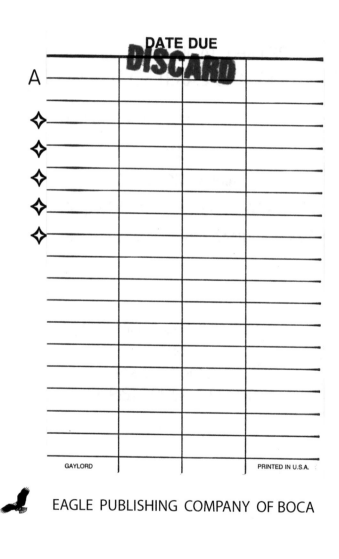

EAGLE PUBLISHING COMPANY OF BOCA

EAGLE PUBLISHING COMPANY OF BOCA
4199 N. Dixie Highway, #2
Boca Raton, FL   33431   E-mail: info@eaglepublishing.com

Printed in the United State of America
ISBN 1-932464-00-X
Library of Congress Catalog Card Number 2004111763

A Will Is Not Enough In Texas

CONTENTS

Introduction

Over the years, as we practiced law, we noticed that the questions people have about Wills, Trusts, powers of attorney, avoiding probate and guardianship, preserving assets, providing health care for themselves and their families, are much the same client to client. Many people are concerned about who will control their finances should they become too aged or too ill to do so themselves. Of even more concern is their health care:

Who will make my medical decisions if I can't do so myself?

How can I pay for my health care?

How much and what type of insurance should I have?

How can I avoid guardianship?

Others worry about the care of family members. Those with minor children worry:

Who will care for my minor child if I become incapacitated or die?

Is there a way to make sure my child has enough money to see him through college?

Those with elderly parents worry:

How can I manage my parent's finances should my parent become too aged or ill to do so?

Can my parent qualify for MEDICAID?

If my parent dies, will I need to go through Probate?

Is there a way to avoid Probate?

We agreed that a book answering such questions would be of service to the general public. We wish to thank all of the clients, whom we have had the honor and pleasure to serve, for providing us with the impetus to write this book.

Christopher J. Pettit, Esq.

CHRISTOPHER J. PETTIT did his undergraduate work in economics, with distinction at the University of Dallas. He earned his Juris Doctor degree from St. Mary's University School of Law in San Antonio, where he was associate editor of The Law Journal.

Mr. Pettit is a founding partner of Chris Pettit & Associates, a full service corporation in San Antonio. The full-service law firm's practice includes helping clients avoid probate, protect their assets, and provide for the security of their loved ones with a well-crafted estate plan in the event of death or disability.

Mr. Pettit taught law at both the San Antonio School of Law and Our Lady of the Lake University. He is also the author of several articles on legal procedure and has authored two books on litigation and estate planning, and has served as briefing attorney to the 14th Court of Appeals in Houston.

Mr. Pettit is admitted to practice before all state courts in Texas as well as the U.S. District Court in the Western District of Texas. He is a member of the American and San Antonio Bar Associations and the Trial Lawyer Associations of Texas. He serves as a Director of the San Antonio Trial Lawyers Association.

In addition to his law practice, Mr. Pettit currently serves as the co-host of "Health, Wealthy and Wise," a radio show on KLUP 930AM on Sunday from 11 a.m to 12:30 p.m.

CHRISTOPHER J. PETTIT also serves as Director of the AMERICAN ACADEMY OF ESTATE PLANNING ATTORNEYS. He regularly provides educational seminars for the public and private groups on the importance of Estate Planning.

About the Academy

The American Academy of Estate Planning Attorneys is a member organization serving the needs of legal professionals concentrating on Estate Planning. Through the Academy's comprehensive training and educational programs on state-of-the-art Estate Planning law and techniques, it fosters excellence in Estate Planning among its members and helps them deliver the highest possible service to their clients. The Academy provides its members with excellent legal education and top notch practice management support. In addition, each member is required to attain thirty-six units of continuing legal education annually.

The American Academy of Estate Planning Attorneys serves law firms in over 150 geographic areas in forty-four states. Clients who choose an attorney who is a member of the Academy can feel confident that they have an attorney who is dedicated to bringing them the highest quality of service.

The Academy is also committed to educating consumers on vital Estate Planning issues that touch their lives. Through its series of publications, educational programs and its consumer Web site, the Academy seeks to create a public armed with the information they need to become wise consumers of Estate Planning services.

 THE AMERICAN ACADEMY OF
ESTATE PLANNING ATTORNEYS
http://www.aaepa.com

Amelia E. Pohl, Esq.

Before becoming an attorney in 1985, AMELIA E. POHL taught mathematics on both the high school and college level. During her tenure as Associate Professor of Mathematics at Prince George's Community College in Maryland, she wrote several books including:

Probability: A Set Theory Approach

Principles of Counting

Common Stock Sense

Ms. Pohl, graduated from Nova Law School in Florida and established an Elder Law practice in Boca Raton, Florida. Over the years she observed that many people want to reduce the high cost of legal fees by performing or assisting with their own legal transactions. Attorney Pohl found that, with a bit of guidance, people are able to perform many legal transactions for themselves. Attorney Pohl utilizes her background as teacher, author and attorney to provide that "bit of guidance" to the general public in the form of self-help legal books that she has written.

With the assistance of an attorney licensed to practice in the given state, Amelia Pohl is currently "translating" this book for the remaining states. Call **EAGLE PUBLISHING COMPANY OF BOCA** at (800) 824-0823 to learn of the availability of this book for other states.

Acknowledgment

Special thanks to JANET SHAFER BOYANTON for her review of the Medicaid section of this book (Chapters 10 and 11) for compliance with Texas law. Ms. Boyanton is an Elder Law attorney with a private practice in DeSoto, Texas, concentrating in Elder Law, Probate, Guardianship and Wills.

Ms. Boyanton is a member of the State Bar of Texas, the Dallas Bar Association, the College of the State Bar of Texas. She is an active member of the National Academy of Elder Law Attorneys. She served on the Public Policy, Managed Care Sub-Committee of the National Academy of Elder Law Attorneys; and she is currently on the Board of Directors of the Texas Chapter of the National Academy of Elder Law Attorneys.

Ms. Boyanton has done numerous presentations, including presentations for the Governor's Conference on Aging and several continuing education courses. She is the author of an article entitled "Nursing Home Litigation" in the Elder Law Reporter. She is co-author of *Texas Elder Law* and *Texas Probate, Beyond the Basics*. Both books were published by NBI in 2002.

THE DESIGN ARTIST

LUBOSH CECH designed the cover of this book. Lubosh Cech is the founder of OKO DESIGN STUDIO located in Portland, Oregon. He designs promotional materials for print and digital media. He has received numerous awards for both graphic design and painting. For more information about Mr. Cech and the OKO Design Studio visit his Web site. http://www.okodesignstudio.com
The photograph on the cover is that of Rio Grande and the Chisos Mountains. The photographer is Jeremy Woodhouse.

Reading the Law

Where applicable, we identified the state statute or federal statute that is the basis of the discussion. We did this as a reference, and also to encourage the reader to look at the law as it is written. Prior to the Internet the only way you could look up the law was to physically take yourself to the local courthouse law library or the law section of a public library. Today all of the state and federal statutes are literally at your finger tips. They are just a mouse click away on the Internet. To look up a statute all you need is the address of the Web site and the identifying number of the statute.

FEDERAL STATUTES
http://www4.law.cornell.edu/uscode
TEXAS STATUTES
http://www.capital.state.tx.us/statutes

The Texas legislature has consolidated their statutes, i.e., laws, into 27 Codes including:

BUSINESS AND COMMERCE CODE ("Bus. & Com.")
BUSINESS ORGANIZATIONS CODE ("Bus. Org.)
CIVIL PRACTICE AND REMEDIES CODE ("Civ. Prac. & Rem.")
CODE OF CRIMINAL PROCEDURE ("Crim. Proc.")
FAMILY CODE ("Family")   FINANCE CODE ("Finance"
GOVERNMENT CODE ("Gov't")
HEALTH & SAFETY CODE ("Health & Safety")
HUMAN RESOURCES ("Hum. Res.") INSURANCE CODE ("Insur.")
PROBATE CODE ("Probate")   PROPERTY CODE ("Property")
REVISED CIVIL STATUTE ("Rev. Civ. Stat.")
TAX CODE ("Tax") TRANSPORTATION CODE ("Transp.")

We will refer to a statute by the title of the Code and the section within that Code. For example, (Family 2.501) refers to Chapter 2, Section 501 of the Family Code. To look up this statute, go to the Texas Statute Web site, locate Chapter 2 of the Family Code, and then Section 501.

If you come across a topic you think is important, you may find it both interesting and profitable to read the law as it is written.

When You Need A Lawyer

The purpose of the book is to give the reader a basic understanding of Texas law as it relates to Wills and other methods of Estate Planning. It is not intended as a substitute for legal counsel or any other kind of professional advice. If you have a legal question, you should seek the counsel of an attorney.

When looking for an attorney, consider three things:
EXPERIENCE, COST and PERSONALITY.

EXPERIENCE

The State of Texas has a certification program for 19 different areas of law including FAMILY LAW, IMMIGRATION TAX, ESTATE PLANNING, CIVIL TRIAL. To be certified by the Texas Supreme Court as a specialist in these areas, the attorney must pass a written examination, demonstrate a high level of experience in the field, be favorably evaluated by other attorneys and judges familiar with their work, and fulfill ongoing educational requirements. You can get information about the different areas of certification at the Texas Bar Legal Specialization at the State Bar Web site.

 THE STATE BAR OF TEXAS
http://www.texasbar.com

The Texas Bar has a Statewide Referral Service. You can call them at (800) 252-9690 and ask for a referral to an attorney in your county who is experienced in the area of law that you seek. The Texas Bar has the name and telephone numbers of Certified Lawyer Referral Services at their Web site.

Certification is just one of the criteria to consider. Many fine attorneys are experienced in an area of law, but the attorney may not have taken the time, effort or expense to become certified as a specialist. If the attorney is not certified in the branch of law you seek, ask how long he has practiced that type of law and what percentage of his practice is devoted to that branch of law.

One of the most reliable ways to find an attorney is through personal referral. Ask your friends, family or business acquaintances if they used an attorney for the field of law that you seek and whether they were pleased with the results. It is important to employ an attorney who is experienced in the area of law you seek. Your friend may have a wonderful Estate Planning attorney, but if you suffered an injury to your body, then you need an attorney experienced in Personal Injury. Before employing an attorney, ask how long he has practiced in that field of law and what percentage of his practice is devoted to that type of law.

COST

In addition to the attorney's experience, it is important to check what it will cost in attorney fees. When you call for an appointment ask what the attorney will charge for the initial consultation and the approximate cost for the service you seek. Ask whether there will be additional costs such as filing fees, accounting fees, expert witness fees, etc. If the least expensive attorney is out of your price range, you can call your local county Bar Association for the telephone number of the Legal Services office nearest you.

The State Bar of Texas has a directory of Texas Legal Services Programs at the FIND A LAWYER section of its Web site, or call them at (800) 204-2222 for the Legal Services Program in your county.

PERSONALITY

Of equal importance to the attorney's experience and legal fees, is your relationship with the attorney. How easy was it to reach the attorney? Did he promptly return your call or did you have to go through layers of receptionists and legal assistants before being allowed to speak to the attorney? If you had difficulty reaching the attorney on your first call, you can expect similar problems should you employ that attorney.

Did the attorney treat you with respect? Did the attorney treat you paternally with a "father knows best" attitude or did he treat you as an intelligent person with the ability to understand the options available to you and the ability to make your own decision based on the information provided to you?

Were you able to understand and easily communicate with the attorney? Was he speaking to you in plain English or was his explanation of the matter so full of legalese to be almost meaningless to you?

Do you find the attorney's personality to be pleasant or grating? If you come away from your first visit feeling annoyed or uncomfortable, then he is not right for you. Find another attorney.

It is worth the effort to take the time to interview as many attorneys as it takes to find one with the right expertise, fee schedule and personality for you.

The Organization of the Book

Many people who have a Will think they have their affairs in order, reasoning that should they die everything will go to the people named in the Will and somehow things will all be taken care of. But this is a simplistic view. There are many more things to consider.

1. What exactly will your beneficiaries inherit?
2. How will your property be transferred?
3. Can you (should you) avoid Probate?
4. Can you avoid a challenge to your Will?

The first four chapters of this book deal with these basic issues. Once you read these chapters you will have an understanding of what will happen to your property should you die, regardless of whether you do, or do not, have a Will. The rest of the book deals with things a Will <u>cannot</u> do, including: appointing someone to make your health care decisions and manage your finances in the event you are unable to do so, help you qualify for MEDICAID should the need arise A Will can't do these things but you will be able to do so once you read these chapters and understand what options are available to you under Texas law.

GLOSSARY

This book is designed for the average reader. Legal terminology has been kept to a minimum. There is a glossary at the end of the book in case you come across a legal term that is not familiar to you.

FICTITIOUS NAMES AND EVENTS

The examples in this book are based loosely on actual events; however, all names are fictitious; and the events, as portrayed, are fictitious.

MALE GENDER USED

Rather than use he/she or himself/herself, for simplicity, we used the male gender.

Your Financial Check-up 1

To understand why *A Will is Not Enough in Texas* you need to know what a Will can and cannot do. One thing a Will can do is make a gift of all you own (your *Estate*). One of the things a Will cannot do is preserve and protect your property during your lifetime. For that, you need to think about risks to your property (poor investments, theft, loss through acts of nature, etc.) and what you can do to minimize or eliminate such risks. In other words, you need an *Estate Plan* for the care and management of your property during your lifetime.

The average person may be thinking "I don't have an Estate — never mind an Estate Plan." But you do. Everyone who owns property, has an Estate Plan. You may not have verbalized your Estate Plan, or even thought about it, but it's there none-the-less. Take the case of the college student purchasing his first car. If his parents bankroll the purchase, the son may offer to hold the car jointly with them. In such case, the son's Estate consists of his car. His Estate Plan is to hold the car jointly with his parents so that they will own the car should anything happen to him.

This may not be the best Estate Plan. Holding the car jointly with his parents may make them liable for injuries or damages should the car be involved in an accident. If the young man's parents are familiar with Texas law, they would be wise to refuse the offer and reassure their son "You can make a Will and make us the beneficiary of your car. But even if you die without a Will, we are your heirs under Texas law. Either way, we will inherit the car. Just make sure to drive carefully and carry enough car insurance."

This is a better Estate Plan. It gives the young man maximum control over his Estate (i.e., his car) during his lifetime. He can sell the car, mortgage it, or trash it, all as he sees fit. If he follows his parents' advice, of driving carefully and purchasing sufficient insurance, his Estate will have maximum protection. If he dies without a Will, and is single and without children, under the ***Texas Laws of Descent and Distribution*** parents will inherit his Estate (see page 17). And that is just the way the son wants things at this stage of his life.

Simple situation, simple Estate Plan. But, for most of us, life isn't all that simple. We may own many items of value and have loved ones who rely on us. At some point in our lives, we need to ask:

> *How can I make sure that my property will be inherited by my choice of beneficiary?*

> *How can I arrange to have my property inherited quickly and at minimum cost?*

> *How can I achieve these goals and yet have maximum control and protection of my property during my lifetime?*

We will explore the different ways to answer these questions so that you can decide on an Estate Plan that is best for you. But before doing so you need to know what property you own; i.e., how much your Estate is worth. If you are married and your spouse handles all of the finances, it may be that you have no idea of the value of your Estate.

That was the case with Kristin. She met Matt when they were both at the pinnacle of their careers, but they had no more insight into their precarious position than fireworks in a summer sky just before self-destruct.

Kristin was a model. Not the best, nor the most beautiful, but she made a comfortable living. She moved in a circle of famous models. She reflected off of their radiance, making her appear more attractive than she actually was.

Matt worked in middle management for one of those high tech companies. Like Kristin, he was not particularly gifted but he happened to be in Silicon Valley just at the time the high stakes investors were showing extraordinary, if not misguided, confidence in the industry. The good times were rolling. It never crossed Matt's mind that this would one day end. He spent the money as fast as it came in.

Kristin was impressed with the lavish gifts Matt gave to her. She, and her family, thought she made quite a catch when she announced her engagement. After the wedding she continued to model, but it took a lot of traveling and Matt resented her time away. Eventually, she agreed to stop working altogether. After all, why should she, the wife of a wealthy man, need to continue with the rigors of a model's life of diet and exercise?

Matt never told Kristin about his financial difficulties. All she knew was that he was drinking quite a bit. Her suspicion that he also was into drugs was verified when he died, suddenly, because of an overdose. Her shock and sadness turned to anger when she discovered that all he owned was mortgaged and he was heavily in debt. He even borrowed money from her family without her knowledge!

Matt's creditors took it all. The house, the boat, the Porsche, everything. If only Kristin had investigated the true state of their finances, she could have arranged to set aside the money she earned prior to her marriage and not end up as she did, a destitute widow, past her prime.

DETERMINING YOUR NET WORTH

Even if you are single you may not know the value of your Estate because you have not taken the time to actually sit down and figure it out. To get maximum benefit from this book, you need to take a few minutes to determine your **Net Worth** i.e. the current value of your Estate.

ASSETS

$_____	Cash (certificates of deposit, bank accounts, etc.)
$_____	Tangible personal property (jewelry, motor vehicles, private art, stamp or coin collections, etc.)
$_____	Cash value of insurance policies
$_____	Securities (stocks, bonds, etc.)
$_____	Cash value of pension plans, IRAs, etc.
$_____	Cash value of a partnership or other business interest
$_____	Real property (residence, time share, lot, condo, cooperatives, etc.)
$_____	TOTAL VALUE OF ASSETS

It may be that you have a loan on your car or home, or any of the above items. You need to subtract away monies you owe to get the bottom line value of what you own:

LIABILITIES

$_____	Private loans
$_____	Mortgage Balance
$_____	Credit card debt
$_____	Car loan or car lease balance
$_____	TOTAL LIABILITIES

A simple subtraction gives you the value of your Estate.

ASSETS — LIABILITIES = NET WORTH

If you are married and hold all property jointly with your spouse, divide by 2 to get the value of your own Net Worth.

Your Net Worth is the value of all that you own, and that is how much your beneficiaries can inherit. Who will inherit your property depends on how your property is *titled* (held or owned).

There are three basic ways to title property:
⇨ IN YOUR NAME ONLY
Property held *in your name only*, and no provision for a transfer to a beneficiary after death will be inherited by the beneficiary named in your Will. If you do not have a Will, the property will go to your heirs according to the Texas Laws of Descent and Distribution.

⇨ JOINTLY WITH ANOTHER
Property you own *jointly with right of survivorship* will belong to the surviving joint owner(s) of that property.

⇨ IN TRUST FOR ANOTHER
Property you hold *in Trust* will go to those you name as the beneficiary of the Trust.

NOTE ⇨ If you are married, your spouse may
have rights in your property,
regardless of the way your property is titled.

We will examine each of these types of ownership in detail so that you can give yourself an Estate Planning check-up, i.e., you can check whether the way you are currently holding your property accomplishes your Estate Planning goals.

There's much to be said about holding property in your name only and not jointly or in trust for another. There's maximum control. You can sell it, trade it, mortgage it, with no one to account to, or ask "may I?" How you protect your assets depends on how much security you require. Again, it's all up to you. As discussed, there are three things to consider when setting up an Estate Plan:

CONTROL How to control and protect your Estate during your lifetime.

BENEFICIARY How to be sure your Estate goes to the beneficiary of your choice.

COST How to transfer your Estate to your beneficiaries at lowest cost.

Holding all of your property in your name only should give you maximum control and protection; but such an Estate Plan may present a problem with the cost of transferring your property upon your death. More than likely it will take some sort of court procedure to transfer that property once you die. The name of the court procedure is **Probate**. In Texas, Probate is conducted in the Probate Division of the County Court (Probate 4). We will use the term *Court* or *Probate Court* to refer to the judge who is presiding over Probate matters. We will refer to property that is transferred to your beneficiaries by means of a Probate proceeding as your *Probate Estate*, and the person appointed by the Court to *settle* your Estate (pay debts and taxes and distribute what is left) as your **Personal Representative**.

Probate can be expensive, so if you keep all of your property in your name only, there could be a significant cost to transfer your property to the beneficiaries of your Estate.

Holding property in your name should not create a problem with having your choice of beneficiary inherit your Estate, provided you have a valid Will. But if you die without a valid Will, the Court will use the Laws of Descent to determine who gets your property. Of course it could be that the beneficiaries of your Estate under the Laws of Descent are exactly who you would have wanted, had you taken the time to prepare a Will. To help you determine if this is the case, we will take a few pages to explain the Law. Those who have a Will might be tempted to skip over the section, but, this information is good to know in the event someone in your family dies in Texas without a Will. Once you read this section you will know whether you have a right to inherit his property.

THE FAMILY'S RIGHT TO INHERIT

The state of Texas recognizes the right of the family to inherit property left by the **decedent** (the person who died); so the Laws of Intestate Succession cover all possible relationships beginning with the surviving spouse. In order for the spouse to inherit property under the Laws of Intestate Succession, the state of Texas needs to recognize the union as a valid marriage.

Who Is Your Spouse?

In this era of people challenging the concept of the family unit, those of a philosophical bent may ponder the meaning of marriage. Is it a union of two people in the eyes of God? Is it even a union? Maybe it is just a contract between two people. The state of Texas does not concern itself with such things. If a person dies without a Will, then the state will distribute the property according to the laws of Texas; and the laws of Texas determine whether two people are married.

There are two types of marriage recognized in the state of Texas: the FORMAL MARRIAGE and the INFORMAL MARRIAGE.

THE FORMAL MARRIAGE

A man and woman are formally married if they have applied for and received a license to marry from the County Clerk; and then within 30 days participate in a marriage ceremony. The Clerk will not issue a license to anyone under the age of 18 unless a parent or guardian gives their consent or there is a Court order authorizing the marriage (Family 2.001, 2.003).

THE INFORMAL MARRIAGE

An Informal Marriage is one in which:
- ⇨ A man and woman, each over 18, agree to be married.
- ⇨ After the agreement they live together in Texas as husband and wife.
- ⇨ They tell everyone that they are married.

If a couple is Informally Married, they can formalize their marriage by going to their local county Clerk and signing a form entitled:
DECLARATION AND REGISTRATION OF INFORMAL MARRIAGE

Once the document is signed the County Clerk will sign a certificate stating the place and time that the Declaration was made. The Clerk will give the couple the original Declaration and send a copy to the TEXAS BUREAU OF VITAL STATISTICS (Family 2.402, 2.404).

If the decedent was Informally Married and signed a Declaration, the surviving spouse has all the rights of a spouse under the Texas Laws of Descent. If a Declaration was not signed, it may take a Court procedure to prove that the parties had a valid Common Law marriage.

Some members of the Texas Legislature have tried to abolish the Informal Marriage. To date their efforts have not been successful, but they did succeed in making it more difficult to establish the existence of an Informal Marriage. Specifically, in 1997, Family 2.401 was amended to require that any Court procedure to prove the existence of a marriage must begin before the second anniversary of the day on which they separated and ceased living together.

To see what is involved in proving the validity of an Informal Marriage read the decision of the Court in (*Lee v. Lee*, 981 S.W.2d 903 (Tex. 1998)).

THE COMMON LAW MARRIAGE

An Informal Marriage is a marriage that occurs without benefit of a marriage ceremony. Many states refer to this as a ***Common Law marriage***. Most states do not recognize a Common Law Marriage as being a valid marriage in their state. Texas will recognize a marriage that took place in another state provided the marriage conforms to Texas law (Family 1.103). This means that Texas recognizes the marriage of a couple who were licensed to marry by another state or country, and who participated in a marriage ceremony in that state or country. Similarly, those who enter a Common Law marriage in another state will be recognized as being married in the state of Texas, provided their union here in Texas satisfies all the requirements of an Informal Marriage.

The state of Texas will not recognize a marriage entered into in another state, regardless of whether it is valid in another state if it does not conform to the laws of the state of Texas. The following marriages are not valid in Texas, even if the marriage is valid elsewhere.

PROHIBITED MARRIAGES

Texas law specifically prohibits the marriage (Formal or Informal) of people who are related as follows:

☒ brother and sister of whole blood or half blood (i.e., share only one natural parent)

☒ a person and his **descendant** (child, grandchild, etc.)

☒ aunt and nephew, uncle or niece

These marriages are prohibited regardless of whether the parties are related through blood (whole or half blood) or through adoption. Notice that the marriage of first cousins is not banned in Texas (Family 6.201).

The marriage of a current or former stepchild and stepparent is not prohibited under Texas statute (Family 6.201). However, when signing a Declaration and Registration of Informal Marriage, the couple must verify that they are not related as above and they are related as stepchild and stepparent (Family 2.004).

☒ BIGAMY

A marriage is *void* (not legal) if it is entered into when either party is still married. The marriage can be made legal, provided the prior marriage is dissolved, and the couple continue living together as husband and wife (Family 6.202).

☒ SAME SEX MARRIAGES

In 1998, the federal government passed the Defense of Marriage Act, saying that for purposes of federal law, marriage is a legal union between one man and one woman (28 U.S.C. 1738C). However, for purposes of state law, whether you can marry, who you can marry; and how you can marry, are determined by the laws of the state in which you live.

There is much variation state to state. California law gives *Domestic Partners* who are registered with the state, the same rights and responsibilities as a married couple. Vermont, Connecticut and New Jersey have approved same-sex *Civil Unions* with the same rights and responsibilities as a married couple. Massachusetts allows gay marriages.

This is not the case in Texas. Under Texas law, a marriage license may not be issued to those of the same sex (Family 2.001). Marriage between those of the same gender or a civil union intended as an alternate to marriage is not valid in Texas regardless of whether that relationship is legal anywhere else (Family 6.204).

Who Is Your Child?

Medical technology has made important contributions to solving the problem of infertility. There are all sorts of solutions, from hormone therapy, to sperm banks that provide donations anonymously, to frozen sperm and/or ova to be thawed and used at a later date, to a woman who becomes a *surrogate* (gestational) mother. Solving a set of medical problems has opened the door to a new set of legal problems.

Used to be, the only question was "Who's the father?" Now it could well be "Who's the mother?

To answer these questions, the Texas legislature passed THE UNIFORM PARENTAGE ACT (Family Chapter 160) effective as of May, 2001. We will examine this law as it relates to the right of the child to inherit property.

CHILD OF ARTIFICIAL INSEMINATION

If a husband agrees to the use of artificial insemination, and a child is born, he is the legal father of that child (Family 160.201 (b)(5)). A child born to a married couple using any other form of assisted reproduction has the same rights as a child conceived the old fashioned way. It is presumed that the husband consented to the assisted conception procedure. If that is not the case, and he is not the father of the child, he can *petition* (ask) the Court to terminate his parental rights and responsibilities. If the husband is successful, the child will not be able to inherit from the husband, nor from his family (Family 160.204).

FROZEN SPERM AND THE AFTERBORN CHILD

Under Texas law a child conceived prior to death and born to the surviving spouse within 300 days from the date of death, has the same right to inherit as any other natural child of the decedent (Family 160.204 (a)(2), Probate 41(a)). But suppose the child was conceived after death?

This question is becoming more of an issue as couples are freezing sperm, ovum or pre-embryo (fertilized cell) for use at a later date. Often the purpose of the procedure is to protect the cell from damage during cancer treatments. If the treatment is unsuccessful, the surviving spouse may decide to go ahead with the pregnancy using the frozen reproductive cell. This raises issues of whether the surviving parent has the right to do that without the written consent of the deceased donor; and whether a child born of such procedure is entitled to inherit from the deceased donor.

The inheritance issue has important consequences, not only on the state level but on the federal level as well. A minor child who has lost a parent is entitled to Social Security benefits, but those benefits are based on the state's *Laws of Intestate Succession*. In Texas, those laws are referred to as the *Laws of Descent and Distribution*. Section 216 of the Social Security Act provides "a child's insurance benefits can be paid to a child who could inherit under the State's intestate laws." Specifically, a child cannot receive Social Security benefits, unless the child is entitled to inherit under the state's Laws of Descent.

The Texas legislature dealt with this issue by passing a law stating that the deceased spouse is not the child's parent unless there is a record that the spouse consented to be the child's parent if assisted conception took place after death (Family 160.707).

It is important for those who decide to freeze their sperm, ovum, or pre-embryo to express, in writing, whether the donor intends the reproductive cell to be used after death and whether a child born of the cell should be entitled to inherit the Estate of the deceased parent.

THE SURROGATE PARENTING CONTRACT

A Surrogate Parenting Contract is an agreement, usually between a married couple (the intended parents) and a woman (the gestational or Surrogate mother), in which the woman agrees to be the birth mother of a child conceived with the sperm of the husband, or the egg cell of the wife, or the embryo of the married couple, or none of these. This means that the husband or wife might be, but is not necessarily, the biological parent of the child born of the Surrogate mother.

Some states such as New York and Michigan consider Surrogate Parent Contracts as being against public policy and have passed laws restricting their use. Other states, such as Florida and Virginia allow a couple to contract with a woman to have their baby, provided it is done according to the law of the state.

In Texas, the mother-child relationship is established by a woman giving birth to a child, so a child born to a Surrogate mother has the same rights as any other child born to the mother (Family 160.201 (1)). After birth, the Surrogate parent can agree to the adoption of the child by the intended (genetic) parents. Adoption is necessary, regardless of whether either (or both) of the intended parents happen to be the genetic parents of the child. If the child is later adopted, the child will have the same status as any other adopted child.

THE ADOPTED CHILD

An adopted child has the same right to inherit from an adoptive parent as does a natural child and vice versa. The adoptive family has the same right to inherit from the adoptive child as they would from any natural child (Family 162.017, Probate 40). The biological relatives of an adopted child have no right to inherit under the Laws of Descent. But here's a surprising thing, and unique to Texas, the adopted child still has the right to inherit from his biological mother (Probate 42 (a)). For example, suppose a woman gives up her child for adoption. If the woman dies without a Will, her adoptive child has just as much right to inherit in the state of Texas, as does a natural child not placed for adoption. An exception to this rule, is the adoption of an adult. In such case, none of his natural (biological) relatives can inherit from him under the Texas Laws of Descent and the adopted person has no right to inherit from his biological relatives (Family 162.507).

THE NON-MARITAL CHILD

A child born out of wedlock has the same rights to inherit from his/her natural father as does one born in wedlock, provided any one of the following are true:

☑   The decedent signed a declaration that the child is his and filed the document with the local registrar of vital statistics (Family 160.204 (a)(4)(A)).

☑   The decedent married the child's mother and the child is born during the marriage or within 300 days after the marriage ends because of death, annulment or divorce (Family 160.204 (a)(3)).

☑   He married the mother after the birth, openly acknowledged the child as his, and voluntarily promised to support the child (Family 160.204 (a)(4)).

☑   During the first two years of the child's life, he lived with the child, and openly admitted that he is the father (Family 160.204 (a)(5)).

☑   A Court determined that his is the father (Probate 42 (b)).

Now that we know who the state of Texas considers to be your spouse, and who is considered to be your child, we can determine how much of your Probate Estate they each are entitled to inherit under the Texas Laws of Descent. However, Texas is a *Community Property* state. If you are married, your surviving spouse may have rights in property that you own — so we must first examine how much of your property can be inherited by someone other than your spouse.

HIS, HERS, THEIRS

If you are a married resident of the state of Texas, the Laws of Descent apply to all of your SEPARATE PROPERTY, and your share of the COMMUNITY PROPERTY.

Separate property is defined to be:

⇨ property owned by you prior to the marriage

⇨ property you received as a gift or an inheritance during the marriage

⇨ money received during the marriage as a result of personal injuries, but not including money received for lost earnings (Family 3.001).

Community Property is all of the property acquired by you and your spouse during the marriage, except for property that is defined above as Separate property (Family 3.002). Money earned during the marriage is considered to be Community Property, with an important distinction. Whoever earns the money has the right to the sole management and control of that money.

Management and Control of Community Property

Each partner has the right to the sole management and control of anything (s)he would have owned if (s)he were single, that is:

⇨ personal earnings

⇨ income derived from Separate Property

⇨ a personal injury settlement

⇨ any increase in value from any of the above

⇨ any revenue received from any of the above

If a spouse mixes his wages, or any of the above property, with the rest of the couple's Community Property, it becomes *Joint Community Property* giving both partners the right to spend and manage that property (Family 3.102).

THE TEXAS LAWS OF DESCENT

Should you die with property titled in your name only, and without a Will, the state of Texas provides one for you in the form of its Laws of Descent and Distribution. The Laws of Descent apply only to your Probate Estate, i.e., property you hold in your name only without any provision for its transfer upon your death. If you are married, your Probate Estate includes:

⇨ all of your Separate Property held in your name only or jointly without a right of survivor, and

⇨ your half of the Community Property.

For purposes of this discussion, we will assume that in addition to having no Will, you and your spouse have no Community Property Agreement to distribute your Probate Estate any differently than as stated in the Laws of Descent and Distribution.

Once your debts, funeral expenses, and the cost of the Probate proceeding is paid, whatever is left (your *net Probate Estate*) is distributed as follows:

✧ SINGLE, WITH DESCENDANT

If you are not married but have children, all of whom survive you, they will share equally in the net Probate Estate. If one or more of your children do not survive you, but your deceased child left surviving *descendants* (child, grandchild, etc.) the descendants inherit the share intended for the deceased child ***per stirpes*** (Probate 43). Per stirpes is one of those legal terms that is best explained through example.

Suppose the decedent was not married and left four children, Ann, Barry, Carl, David. If he dies intestate, and all his children survive him, each will inherit an equal share, namely a quarter of his net Probate Estate.

CHILD WITHOUT DESCENDANTS DIES BEFORE DECEDENT
If Ann dies before her father leaving no descendants, Barry, Carl and David inherit an equal share, namely one third of the net Probate Estate.

CHILD WITH DESCENDANTS DIES BEFORE DECEDENT
Suppose instead that only Carl and David survived their father. If Ann died leaving two children and Barry died leaving one children, the Estate is divided into four shares — one for each surviving child and one share for each deceased child who left a descendant. Carl and David each inherit their 25% share. Ann's two children share her 25% (they each get 12 1/2%). Barry's child inherits the share intended for Barry, namely 25% of the net Probate Estate.

SINGLE, NO DESCENDANT
If you have no surviving descendants, all of your Probate Estate will go to your parents, in equal shares. If only one parent survives you, that parent gets half of your Estate and your siblings inherit the other half, in equal shares, per stirpes. If you have no surviving brother or sister (or their descendants), your surviving parent receives the entire Probate Estate. In the event you are survived by siblings and no parent, they will inherit your entire Probate Estate, in equal shares, per stirpes.

HALF BLOOD INHERITS HALF

Relatives of half blood inherit half as much as a relative of whole blood. For example, suppose you have a brother from the same set of parents, and a sister with the same father and different mother. If you die without a Will and no relatives other than your brother and half-sister, your brother will inherit two-thirds of your Probate Estate and your half-sister, a third. Of course, if you are survived by half-brothers and half-sister only, then they each share equally in your Estate (Probate 41(b)).

✧ NO SPOUSE, CHILD, PARENT OR THEIR DESCENDANT

If you have no child, parent, sibling or their descendants, your Probate Estate is divided with half going to your maternal grandparents (or to the surviving grandparent) and the other half to your paternal grandparents (or to the survivor of them). If both maternal grandparents are deceased, their share is inherited by their descendants in equal shares, per stirpes. If you have no surviving kinsfolk on your mothers side, your entire Probate Estate goes to your paternal grandparents or their descendants in equal shares per stirpes; and vice versa, if no surviving kinsfolk on your father's side, it all goes to your next of kin on your mother's side (Probate 38 (a)(4)).

✧ MARRIED, NO DESCENDANT, NO PARENT, NO SIBLING

If you are married and have no surviving descendant (child, grandchild, etc.) or parent, brother, sister, or descendant of a deceased brother or sister, your spouse inherits all of your net Probate Estate (Probate 38 (b)(2)).

✧   MARRIED WITH DESCENDANT
COMMUNITY PROPERTY

If you are survived by a spouse and descendant, your spouse inherits all of your Community Property — unless you have a descendant who is not a descendant of your spouse. In such case, your descendants inherit your share of the Community Property in equal shares, per stirpes (Probate 45).

SEPARATE PERSONAL PROPERTY

If you are survived by a spouse and descendant(s), your spouse inherits one-third of your separate *personal property* (bank account, securities, car, jewelry, etc.). Your descendants inherit the remaining two-thirds in equal shares, per stirpes (Probate 38 (b)(1)).

You may wonder how your spouse could inherit one-third of tangible personal property such as a your car. In general, your beneficiaries agree on the value of the personal item. Your spouse is entitled to one-third of that value. For example, if your car is valued at $21,000, and you are surviving by a wife and child, they might agree to have your wife keep the car and pay $14,000 to your child, or vice versa — your child takes title to the car and pays $7,000 to your spouse.

If your beneficiaries cannot agree on the value or who is to take possession of the car, the Court will have the car appraised and decide how the inheritance is distributed.

SEPARATE REAL PROPERTY

If you own real property (residence, condominium, vacant lot, etc.), your surviving spouse is entitled to a Life Estate interest in one-third of the real property. Your descendants inherit the remainder in equal shares, per stirpes (Probate 38). This is easy to visualize in the given example, if you leave acreage. For example, if you own 21 acres of land, your child inherits 14 acres. Your surviving spouse is entitled to possession of 7 of those acres for so long as she lives. Any income from the land will go to her. Once she dies, your child inherits the remaining 7 acres, per stirpes.

If you own something that is not divisible, such as a condominium, the parties can have an appraiser use an actuarial table to determine your spouse's life expectancy. The appraiser will use that value to evaluate her Life Estate interest. As with the car, your wife may decide to have your child reimburse your wife for her Life Estate interest and transfer title to the child, or vis-versa, the spouse may buy out the child's *remainder interest* in the property. The remainder interest is equal to the market value of the condo less the value of the Life Estate interest. If the parties cannot agree, the Court will decide how the property is to be distributed.

✧ MARRIED, NO DESCENDANT

If you die without a valid Will and you are survived by spouse, parent, sibling or their descendants, your spouse inherits all of your Community Property, all of your Separate personal property, and half of your Separate real property. Your surviving parents and siblings inherit the other half in the same manner as described on Page 20. If you are not survived by a parent, sibling or descendant of sibling, your spouse inherits your entire Probate Estate (Probate 38 (b)(2)).

TEXAS: HEIR OF LAST RESORT

Property that is either unclaimed or abandoned, goes to the state; so if you die without a Will and you have absolutely no next of kin, the state of Texas "inherits" your net Probate Estate (Property 71.001).

THERE'S MORE TO THE LAW

The explanation of the Laws of Descent is abridged. Even though you may now know more about the Laws of Descent than you ever wanted to know, there is much more to the law. For example, Texas law requires that anyone who inherits property must survive the decedent by at least 120 hours (5 days). If a relative does not survive by at least 5 days, that share is distributed as if the person died before the decedent. This rule is not applied if to do so will result in the State of Texas inheriting the property (Probate 47 (a)).

THE COST OF PROBATE

Holding property in your name only gives you maximum control and protection during your lifetime. If you do not like the way your property will be distributed should you die without a Will, you can control who will inherit your property by preparing a Will. But there is still the question of the cost to transfer your Estate to your beneficiaries. In all probability, a Probate procedure will be necessary. How much of your Estate will need to be spent to Probate your Estate?

TRANSFERRING COMMUNITY PROPERTY

Probate may not be necessary if all you leave is Community Property. Your surviving spouse has the right to settle your Estate without the need for Probate. Your spouse has full authority to use Community Property to pay *Community Debts*,** collect money owed to the Community Estate, and distribute whatever is left to the proper beneficiary. As explained earlier, your spouse inherits all of your Community Property, unless you are survived by a descendant who is not that of your spouse (Probate 45). In such case, once Community Debts are paid and Community affairs settle, your spouse keeps his/her share of the Community Property and your descendants inherit your share of the Community Property (Probate 160 (a)).

** See Chapter 5 for a discussion of Community Debts.

NO ADMINISTRATION

It could happen that Probate is not necessary if there will be nothing left once all of your obligations are paid. Those obligations include providing for the support of your spouse and child for up to a year following your death. Their support payment is called a *Family Allowance.* It can be paid in a single lump sum, or in the form of a monthly allowance. The Probate Court will determine how much is needed by the spouse and/or minor child. The Court will not award a Family Allowance if your spouse and/or minor child have sufficient assets for their own support (Probate 287, 288).

If the amount in your Probate Estate — not counting your homestead or assets that are exempt from your creditors,** is less than the amount your spouse and/or minor child need for their support, a Personal Representative does not need to be appointed. The attorney for the spouse (or minor child) can ask the court to have the Family Allowance distributed and order that no other administration is necessary.

The Probate judge will hold a hearing and if he finds that your funeral expenses and costs of your last illness and the cost of the Court procedure have been paid, and there are no funds available other than that for the Family Allowance, the Court will order that no administration is required and that all of your Probate Estate be given to your spouse and/or minor child (Probate 139, 140, 286).

** See Chapter 5 for a discussion of Exempt Property.

THE SMALL ESTATE AFFIDAVIT

Married or single, the cost of the Probate procedure is also not a concern provided you die without a Will and the value of your Probate Estate (not counting your homestead and Exempt Property) is not greater than $50,000. Your heirs can get possession of your *personal property* (bank accounts, securities, boats, cars, etc.) by filing a SMALL ESTATE AFFIDAVIT with the Clerk of the Probate Court.

The Small Estate Affidavit must be prepared according to Texas statute (Probate 137). Everyone who is entitled to inherit your property under the Texas Laws of Descent must sign the Affidavit in the presence of two witnesses who have no interest in the Will, and the Probate Clerk (or a notary public) stating that all of the following are true:

☑ The decedent died without a Will.

☑ At least 30 days have passed since the decedent died.

☑ No one has been appointed as Personal Representative and no one is in the process of having a Personal Representative appointed.

☑ The value of Probate Estate (not including the homestead or Exempt Property) is not greater than $50,000.

The Affidavit must include a list of all of the assets and liabilities of your Estate.

It is up to the judge to determine whether he will approve the Affidavit. He may decide not to approve it if adequate provision has not been made for the payment of your debts. If the judge is satisfied that the statute applies, and is an appropriate method to distribute your Estate, he will approve the Affidavit. The Clerk will record the Affidavit in the official public records and give a certified copy of the Affidavit to your heirs. Your heirs can get possession of your property by giving a certified copy of the Affidavit to whoever has possession of your property (Probate 137).

The reader may be thinking "You mean all my heirs need to do is go to my bank or my securities broker, give them an Affidavit and they will hand over my personal property?" The answer is "yes, but..."

▶ THE TRANSFER CAN BE REFUSED ◀

The person in possession of the property might refuse to accept the Affidavit from anyone other than a Court appointed Personal Representative. In such case, your heirs can either go through the Probate procedure, or sue the person in possession to compel the transfer. If the Court finds that the person in possession acted unreasonably, then the beneficiary can get the property and be reimbursed for his attorney's fees.

▶ THE HEIR MUST ACT RESPONSIBLY ◀

If someone uses an Affidavit to transfer your property and it is determined that someone else had a superior right to that property, then the property must be turned over to the proper heir. Anyone who knows they have no right to your property, but takes it anyway, can be sued, if not prosecuted for criminal theft (Probate 138).

A Will Is Not Enough In Texas

USING THE AFFIDAVIT TO TRANSFER THE HOMESTEAD

The Small Estate Affidavit cannot be used to transfer real property, with the exception of your homestead. If you die without a Will and the value of your Probate Estate is $50,000 or less, Texas law allows your homestead to be transferred by means of a Small Estate Affidavit. If the judge approves the Affidavit, all the beneficiary needs to do is have a certified copy of the Affidavit recorded in real property division of the county where the property is located. Once the Affidavit is recorded, the person(s) who inherit the property are free to take possession of the property and/or sell it (Probate 137 (c)).

THE FULL PROBATE PROCEDURE

The Small Estate Affidavit is not an option if you have a Will or a Probate Estate in excess of $50,000, or if you own real property that is not your homestead. And the Affidavit may not be a practical choice if there are several heirs who live at a great distance. Still another reason to conduct a full Probate procedure even though your Estate is under $50,000, is to settle disputes about money you may owe. It may be necessary to have a Personal Representative appointed who will have authority to settle claims against your Estate.

The full Probate procedure can be involved and time consuming — not to mention, expensive. Administration of the Estate can take anywhere from several months to more than a year, depending on the size and complexity of the Estate. The first step in the full Probate procedure is to have someone appointed by the court to serve as Personal Representative.

Whoever is named as Executor of the Will is entitled to be appointed for the job of Personal Representative. Texas statute gives an order of priority for appointing a Personal Representative for those who die without a Will, with the surviving spouse having top priority (Probate 77).

Your Personal Representative will take possession of your Probate Estate (Probate 232). Within 90 days of his appointment he must prepare an inventory of the Estate and where necessary, employ an appraiser to evaluate the property (Probate 250). He will make a diligent effort to notify your creditors that they have a right to come forward and file a *claim* (i.e. a demand for payment) for money you owe.

It is the responsibility of the Personal Representative to see that the Probate procedure is conducted properly. If the Personal Representative makes a mistake, he may be responsible to pay for that mistake. For example, if he neglects to collect all of the debts due to the decedent, he may be responsible to pay the beneficiaries of the Estate for such loss (Probate 233).

To avoid mistakes, the Personal Representative needs to employ an attorney to guide him through the process. It then becomes the attorney's job to see to it that the Estate is administered according to Texas law and without any liability to the Personal Representative. The attorney for the Personal Representative is entitled to reasonable compensation as well. There is no statutory value for attorney's fees, however, they generally are much the same as those awarded to the Personal Representative.

THE PERSONAL REPRESENTATIVE'S FEES

The Personal Representative is entitled to reasonable compensation for his efforts. Under Texas statute, the Personal Representative is entitled to a commission of 5% of all of the sums he receives into the Probate Estate. This does not include funds belonging to the decedent in a financial or brokerage account, nor for collecting the proceeds of a life insurance policy. The Personal Representative is also entitled to receive 5% of the sums he pays out in cash — not counting cash he pays to the beneficiaries of the Estate. But the statute sets an upper limit. He is not entitled to more than 5% of the gross fair market value of the Probate Estate (Probate 241).

Fees for the Personal Representative and his attorney are subject to Court approval. The Court can award the Personal Representative and/or his attorney, extra fees for extraordinary services, such as managing a business or a farm . The Court may also award additional fees for services that were performed to settle a dispute. For example, if there is a dispute about whether to pay a creditor's claim or if there is an argument about who is entitled to inherit property, the Personal Representative and his attorney can ask the Court for extra compensation.

THE COST OF A FULL PROBATE PROCEEDING

The Personal Representative and attorney's fees are significant charges to the Probate Estate; but they are not the only charges against the Estate. A Probate proceeding can incur some or all of the following expenses:

- $$ Court filing fees
- $$ The cost of a bond that the Court may order for the protection of your Probate Estate
- $$ The cost of notifying your creditors which may include publishing notice, or mailing notice to them by registered or certified mail
- $$ The cost of an appraisal
- $$ Accounting fees to prepare an inventory, and account for monies spent during Probate
- $$ The cost of transferring property to the proper beneficiary; i.e., recording fees, broker fees to sell securities or real estate (Probate 242).

Once the above costs, Personal Representative fees, attorney fees, taxes and all valid claims are paid, the Personal Representative will distribute whatever is left to the proper beneficiary and then close the Estate.

You may be thinking that Probate is a good thing to avoid. Why should your Personal Representative go through all that effort to settle your Estate? Why should your beneficiaries wait months or maybe years, and pay all these fees to inherit your Estate?

There are ways to arrange your Estate so that your beneficiaries can immediately inherit your Estate without incurring unnecessary costs. In the next two chapters we will examine different methods that can be used to achieve this goal.

Is Probate Necessary? 2

Many people think that only wealthy people need to make plans to avoid Probate, yet each year, beneficiaries of relatively modest estates, spend thousands of dollars to settle an Estate. A bit of Estate Planning could have eliminated most, if not all, of the cost (and hassle) suffered by those families.

It is not difficult to arrange your finances to eliminate the need for Probate if you have a small Estate and only one or two beneficiaries. All you need do is title your property so that it automatically goes to your beneficiaries. There are many ways to arrange your finances to achieve this result. The most common method is to hold property jointly with another. Such an arrangement is the Estate Plan of choice for most married couples. Husband and wife often hold all of their property jointly, so that the surviving spouse has complete and immediate access to their property without any need for Probate.

Holding property jointly may not be the most desirable method for the single person, or for the surviving spouse who is now single. There are other ways to ensure that your property is inherited quickly and without cost to your heirs. In this chapter, we explore the pros and cons of different methods of holding property so that it can be transferred without the need for Probate.

PROPERTY OWNED JOINTLY

Bank accounts, securities, motor vehicles, real property can all be owned by two or more people. If one of the owners dies, the survivor(s) continue to own their share of the property. Who owns the share belonging to the decedent depends on Texas law and how ownership of the property was set up.

THE JOINT BANK ACCOUNT

When a bank account is opened in two or more names, the owners of the account sign an agreement with the bank stating who is to have access to the account during the lifetime of the account owners; i.e. whether each owner has full authority to make a withdrawal, or whether two signatures are required. Ownership of the account is in proportion to the *net contribution* of the owners of the account; i.e., how much each contributed to the account, less how much that person withdrew from the account. If there are two or more surviving owners, the decedent's share is divided equally between them (Probate 438 (a)).

An account can be set up with or without the right of the surviving owner(s) to inherit the monies in the account. In Texas, a joint bank account has no right of survivorship unless the bank document specifically says so (Probate 440). Even a Community Property account between a husband and wife has no right of survivorship unless the account indicates such intent in any one of the following ways:
"with right of survivorship"
"shall pass to the surviving spouse"
"will become the property of the survivor"
"will vest in and belong to the surviving spouse"
(Probate 452).

The benefit of a joint account with right of survivorship is that the surviving joint owner inherits the money in the account immediately and without the need for Probate; but, as with any Estate Plan, convenience needs to be measured against potential problems. For example, suppose all you own is a bank account and you want whatever you have in this account to go to your child should you die. You might think that a simple solution is to make your child joint owner of the account, but first consider risks associated with a joint account.

⊠ OVERREACHING

Making your child a joint owner of the account gives the child free access to the account. Monies may be withdrawn without your knowledge or authorization. You may be thinking that couldn't happen because you would immediately know of the withdrawal, and you could force the child to return the money. That may be true when you are healthy and alert. But in this ever aging society, it is likely that you will live to an advanced age and not be as aware as you are today. And if you have two children and decided to hold your account jointly with them, there may be a problem with how the funds are distributed should you die.

That was the case with Amanda. All she had when her husband died, was a bank account worth $50,000. She wanted to be sure that the money would go to her two sons, Robert and Leon, without the need for Probate. She went to the bank with her two sons and opened a new survivorship account with all three names on the account as joint owners.

Several years passed without incident. As Amanda aged, her health began to fail, and she became more and more dependent on Robert.

She needed his assistance to take her to the doctor, to do her shopping, and of course take care of her finances. Robert had a wife and two children, so it was hard for him to care for his family and his mother as well. Leon was single, yet he never seemed to have the time to help care for his mother. And Robert resented that.

Finally, Amanda died.

After the funeral, Leon asked Robert about the bank account "Didn't Mom have a joint account in our names?"

"Yeah, but I closed it out. There was only a few thousand left, and I used it for her funeral."

Leon thought it strange that all of the money was gone, so he went to the bank and asked to see the record of withdrawals. He found that over the last two years Robert had written several large checks to himself. There was only $7,000 left in the account when Robert closed it out, within a week of her death.

Leon fumed for several weeks before he brought up the subject. Robert's face flushed when Leon asked about the money. Leon did not know if it was from anger or embarrassment. He soon learned that it was both when Robert asked "Where were you for the past two years? You never once helped. Did you know she became incontinent at the end? Who cleaned up? Not you. She blessed me every day. She often said she would have been dead long ago if it wasn't for me. She wanted me to have that money!"

"Mom never said anything to me about wanting you to have the money. She never asked for my help and neither did you. It isn't right for you to throw this up to me now."

The boys never spoke of the money again. But then there were few times that they ever spoke to each other after that.

Overreaching isn't the only problem with a joint account, there is also the problem of liability.

⊠ POTENTIAL LIABILITY

If you hold a bank account jointly with your adult child and that child is sued or gets a divorce, the child may need to disclose his ownership of the joint account. In such a case, you may find yourself spending money to prove that the account was established for convenience only and that all of the money in that account really belongs to you.

Because of these inherent problems, you might want to hold the funds so that your beneficiary does not have access to the monies unless you die while the account is open. You can do so by opening a *Beneficiary Account*.

THE BENEFICIARY ACCOUNT

As explained, the terms of a bank account are established when a bank account is opened. Your agreement gives directions about who can access your account during your lifetime, but it can also give directions about what to do with the account should you die. If you hold the account in your name only and do not give any such directions, then should you die while the account is open, the money in your account will become part of your Probate Estate and will be distributed in the same way as any other item that you own in your name only.

One way to avoid Probate of the account, yet retain full control of the account during your lifetime, is to name one or more persons to be the beneficiary of your account.

There are two forms of beneficiary account. Your contract with the bank can direct the bank to hold your account **In Trust For** ("ITF") one or more beneficiaries that you name; or you can have a contract with the bank that directs the bank to **Pay On Death** ("POD") all of the money in the account to one or more beneficiaries that you name (Finance 34.306 (a)(2), Probate 439).

With both the ITF and POD account, the beneficiary has no right or interest in the account until the owner of the account is deceased.

If you are married, you may want to hold the account jointly with your spouse with directions to the bank to give the funds to one or more beneficiaries that you name. For example,

ELDON CONNORS and LORRAINE CONNORS, his wife
WITH RIGHT OF SURVIVOR
POD SAM CONNORS AND FRED CONNORS

Unless the contract with the bank says differently:

⇨   The children (Sam and Fred) have no right to the account during the lifetime of their parents.

⇨   If either parent dies, the surviving party owns the account, and is free to close the account or change the beneficiary of the account.

⇨   Once both parents are deceased, their sons share the money in the account equally. Should one son die before his parents, the remaining son will inherit the entire account (Probate 439(b)).

THE TRANSFER ON DEATH SECURITY

You can arrange to have a security (a stock, bond or brokerage account) transferred to a beneficiary upon your death. You can instruct the holder of the security to Pay On Death ("POD") or *Transfer On Death* ("TOD") to a named beneficiary.

Many securities are purchased from companies located in other states. The laws regarding TOD accounts are generally are much the same as those of a POD account:

⇨ The beneficiary does not have access to the security until the owner dies. The owner of the security is free to change beneficiaries without asking the beneficiary's permission to do so.

⇨ If the security is owned jointly with right of survivorship, and an owner dies, the survivor owns the security outright. The surviving owner has the right to change the beneficiary of the security.

⇨ If no beneficiary survives the owner, then the security goes to the Estate of the last surviving owner of the account.

When using a TOD or POD designation on a security it is important to verify that all of the above apply.

You can use these Beneficiary Accounts (*In Trust For, Pay On Death, Transfer On Death*) to transfer your bank accounts and securities to your beneficiaries without the need for Probate. More importantly, a Beneficiary Account affords you maximum control and protection of those funds during your lifetime.

REAL PROPERTY OWNED JOINTLY

If you own real property together with another, then who will own the property upon your death depends on how the current owner is identified on the face of the deed. The top paragraph of the deed should identify the person who transferred the property to you as the "Grantor." The person to whom the property was transferred is called the "Grantee." The deed might read something like:

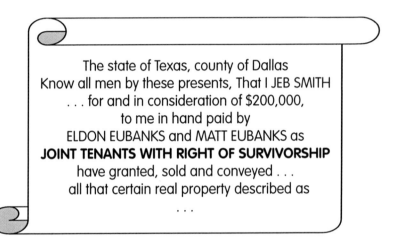

The state of Texas, county of Dallas
Know all men by these presents, That I JEB SMITH
. . . for and in consideration of $200,000,
to me in hand paid by
ELDON EUBANKS and MATT EUBANKS as
JOINT TENANTS WITH RIGHT OF SURVIVORSHIP
have granted, sold and conveyed . . .
all that certain real property described as

. . .

Because this deed clearly states that there is a right of survivorship, should either joint tenant die, the survivor will own the property 100%

Nothing will need be done to establish that ownership, but the name of the deceased joint owner remains on the deed. Should the surviving owner wish to sell or transfer the property, all he needs to do is keep a certified copy of the death certificate to produce at closing to prove that there is now just one owner.

▤ DEED HELD AS TENANTS IN COMMON

You might have a deed that names you and another person as Grantee, followed by TENANTS IN COMMON. Should you die, your share will go to whomever you named as beneficiary of that share in your Will. If you die without a Will, Texas Laws of Descent and Distribution determine who inherits the property (see Chapter 1).

If a deed names two people as Grantee and does not say that they are TENANTS IN COMMON or if the deed says they are JOINT TENANTS, but does not say that there is a RIGHT OF SURVIVORSHIP, the Grantees own the property as TENANTS IN COMMON (Probate 46).

▤ DEED HELD AS HUSBAND AND WIFE

In some states, a deed held as husband and wife, means that the surviving partner owns the property. This is not the case in the Community Property state of Texas. It is presumed that property owned by a married couple is Community Property with each partner owning half. When one partner dies his share is part of his Estate and does not automatically descend to his spouse. If the parties want the surviving partner to own all of the property, the deed needs to state this fact:

TODD AMES AND SUSAN AMES, his wife as
COMMUNITY PROPERTY WITH RIGHT OF SURVIVORSHIP

The surviving spouse will own the property 100% and will be free to sell or transfer the property as (s)he sees fit (Probate 451). As with the survivorship tenancy, all the surviving spouse needs to do is keep a certified copy of the death certificate to produce at closing.

As explained earlier, a Life Estate interest in real property means that the person who owns the Life Estate has the right to live in that property until (s)he dies. You can identify a Life Estate interest by examining the face of the deed. If somewhere on the face of the deed you see the phrase RESERVING A LIFE ESTATE, the Grantee cannot take possession of the property until the owner of the Life Estate dies. For example, suppose the granting paragraph of the deed reads:

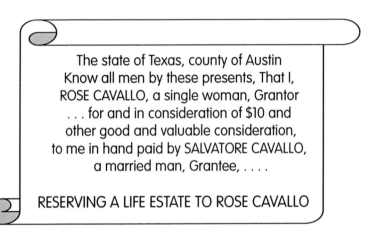

The state of Texas, county of Austin
Know all men by these presents, That I,
ROSE CAVALLO, a single woman, Grantor
. . . for and in consideration of $10 and
other good and valuable consideration,
to me in hand paid by SALVATORE CAVALLO,
a married man, Grantee, ...

RESERVING A LIFE ESTATE TO ROSE CAVALLO

Rose is the owner of the Life Estate. Salvatore is the owner of the **Remainder Interest**. Rose has the right to occupy the premises during her lifetime or to rent it out and receive the income from the property. During Rose's lifetime, Salvatore has no right to the possession of, or the income from, the property. Once Rose dies, Salvatore will own the property and is free to take possession of the property and to lease, sell or transfer it, as he sees fit.

If you are an owner of the Life Estate interest, upon your death, no Probate procedure will be necessary to transfer the property to the owner of the Remainder Interest.

THE INVISIBLE LIFE ESTATE

A married owner of a Texas homestead is free to leave his home to whomever he wishes, however Texas law gives the surviving spouse the right to continue to live in that home for the rest of his/her life. The beneficiary of the homestead will not be able to take possession of the property before the spouse dies, unless the surviving spouse decides not to continue to live there. If the owner of a Texas homestead is not survived by a spouse, but by a minor child, the parent or Guardian of the child has the right to ask the Probate court to allow the child to occupy the property until the child is an adult (Probate 283, 284, 285).

TRANSFERRING TEXAS REAL PROPERTY

No Probate procedure will be necessary if you hold property in Texas:
- ⇨ as the owner of a Life Estate - or -
- ⇨ as a Joint Tenant with right of survivorship - or -
- ⇨ as Community Property with right of survivorship.

As explained in Chapter 1, your homestead can be transferred without a Probate procedure, provided you die without a Will and the value of your Probate Estate is not greater than $50,000 (Probate 137). If you own other property in Texas that is in your name only, or as a Tenant In Common, it will probably take a Probate procedure in order to transfer property to the beneficiary of your choice.

The laws of the state determine who inherits real property within that state. The inheritance of real property located within the state of Texas is determined by the laws of Texas, and this is so regardless of whether you are a resident of this state or whether you live in another state and own property here. The laws of each state are similar, but not the same. In general, property held as Joint Tenants With Rights of Survivorship belongs to the surviving joint owner, but states differ in how the deed needs to be worded. In some states, just the term "Joint Tenants" means that there are rights of survivorship. In other states, "Joint Tenant" without a stated right of survivorship is a Tenancy In Common.

In some states, such as Florida, there is a right of survivorship whenever the deed identifies the Grantees as being married. For example, a deed that identifies the couple as "husband and wife," or a deed that identifies the couple as "Tenants by Entirety" is similar to a Joint Tenancy With Right of Survivorship. When one party dies, the surviving spouse owns the property 100%.

If you are married, and own property in your name only, you need to be aware that your spouse may have rights in your property, regardless of how the deed is worded. That is the case in Community property states, but in other states a surviving spouse may have Dower rights or other statutory rights. In the next chapter, we will discuss the statutory rights of a surviving spouse in real property located in Texas. But if you are married and own property in your name only in another state, you need to determine the rights of your spouse in that state as well.

TRANSFERRING OUT OF STATE PROPERTY

Still another concern is whether a Probate procedure will be necessary to transfer out of state property that you own to your beneficiary. Each state is in charge of the way real property located in that state is transferred. Most state laws are similar to Texas, namely, property you hold as a Joint Tenant with right of survivorship or property in which you hold a Life Estate interest are transferred without the need for Probate. Property you own as a Tenant In Common or in your name only may require a Probate procedure in order to transfer the property to your beneficiary.

If you own property in your name only in this state and in another state, upon your death it may be necessary to have a Probate proceeding in Texas, and an *ancillary* (secondary) Probate proceeding in the state where the property is located. This can double the cost of Probate.

Another problem with out of state property is the matter of taxes. Some states have an inheritance or transfer tax. Taxes may be due in the state where the property is located as well as in Texas. It may be necessary to file a tax return in two states. In addition to increased taxes, this can significantly increase the cost of accounting fees.

If you own property in another state, it is important to consult with an attorney to learn the answers to all of these questions, namely:

Who will inherit my property under the laws of the state where it is located?

Will a Probate procedure be necessary to transfer that property to my beneficiaries?

What taxes will need to be paid in that state?

THE COST OF AVOIDING PROBATE

If you find that Probate will be necessary to transfer real property that you own in Texas or elsewhere, you may decide that the cost of Probate is too expensive. You may be tempted to go for the quick fix of having the deed to the property changed so that you are joint owners with the intended beneficiary of the property; or you may decide to transfer the property to your intended beneficiary and keep a Life Estate for yourself.

This will avoid Probate, but it may not be the best Estate Plan because you will not have maximum control over the property during your lifetime. If you hold real property as a Joint Tenant or as the owner of a Life Estate interest, you will not be able to sell that property during your lifetime without getting permission from your beneficiary. And if the beneficiary gives permission and the property is sold, the beneficiary will have the legal right to share in the proceeds of the sale.

You may be thinking "I can make my son joint owner of my home and avoid any need for Probate. I trust him to do what I want with the property. If I decide to sell, I know he won't ask for any part of the proceeds regardless of his legal right to those funds."

And all that may be true, but it may cost you more in taxes to sell your property than if you kept the property in your name only.

Under today's law, you can sell your home without paying a Capital Gains Tax, provided you lived there for 2 of the prior 5 years and the Capital Gains on the sale is not greater than $250,000 ($500,000 if married). If you sell your home after making the Life Estate transfer (or making your child a Joint Tenant), unless your child occupies the home as his primary residence, his share of the property is subject to a Capital Gains Tax.

If your son does not take his share of the proceeds, then why should he pay any Capital Gains Tax?

In such case, you'll be the one to pay the tax on your son's share of the proceeds.

Is there a better way to avoid Probate?

Maybe. Read on.

How To Avoid Probate 3

TRUE OR FALSE?
(   )   If you have a Will, then Probate will be necessary.
(   )   Probate will be necessary if you don't have a Will.
(   )   Probate is necessary if you own property that is worth more than $50,000.

If you answered false to all of the above, you are either a lawyer, or you carefully read the last chapter.

All of these sentences are false because all of your property may pass to your beneficiaries automatically, without the need for Probate, such as property held jointly or in a Pay On Death account. The point we were trying to make is:

> Whether Probate is necessary has nothing to do with whether there is a Will, or even how much money is involved. The determining factor is how the property is titled (owned).

There are three basic ways to title property:
- ✧   in your name only
- ✧   jointly with another
- ✧   in trust for another

In Chapter 1, we examined the pros and cons of holding property in your name only, with the biggest "con" being that Probate may be necessary.

In Chapter 2, we noted that holding property jointly with another solved the Probate problem, but at the sacrifice of the control and protection offered by keeping property in your name only. In this Chapter, we examine another option which may be the solution to these problems, namely the REVOCABLE LIVING TRUST (also known as an *Inter Vivos Trust*).

A Revocable Living Trust is designed to care for your property during your lifetime and then to distribute your property once you die without the need for Probate. You may have been encouraged to set up such a Trust by your financial planner, attorney, or accountant. Even people of modest means are being encouraged to use a Trust as the basis of their Estate Plan. But Trusts also have their benefits and drawbacks. Before getting into that, let's first discuss what a Trust is and how it works.

HOW A TRUST IS CREATED

To create a **Revocable Living Trust**, an attorney prepares a Trust Agreement in accordance with the client's needs and desires. The "Agreement" refers to the fact that the person creating the Trust (the client) is contracting with someone to be the **Trustee** (manager) of property placed in the Trust. By signing the Trust Agreement, the Trustee agrees to manage the Trust property according to the directions given in the Trust Agreement.

The person who creates the Trust is referred to as the *Settlor* or *Grantor* or *Trustor* (Property 111.004(14)). We will refer to the Revocable Living Trust as the "Living Trust" or just the "Trust" and the person who sets up and funds the Trust as the **Settlor**. Usually the Settlor appoints himself as the initial Trustee so that he is in total control of property that he places into the Trust. In that case he signs the Trust Agreement as the Settlor and also as the Trustee who agrees to follow the terms of the Trust Agreement (Property 112.009). The Trust Agreement also appoints a **Successor Trustee** to take over the management of the Trust property should the Trustee resign, become disabled or die.

Once the Trust document is properly signed, the Settlor can transfer property into the Trust. The Settlor does this by changing the name on the account from his individual name to his name as Trustee. For example, if Susan Clark sets up a Trust naming herself as Trustee, and she wants to put her bank account into the Trust, all she need do is instruct the bank to change the name on the account from Susan Clark to:

SUSAN CLARK, TRUSTEE OF THE SUSAN CLARK
REVOCABLE LIVING TRUST
UNDER AGREEMENT DATED JUNE 12, 2007.

If Susan wants to put real property that she owns into the Trust, she can have her attorney or a title insurance company prepare and record a new deed with the owner of the property identified in the same manner, i.e.

SUSAN CLARK, TRUSTEE OF THE SUSAN CLARK
REVOCABLE LIVING TRUST
UNDER AGREEMENT DATED JUNE 12, 2007.

The Trust Agreement states how property placed into the Trust is to be managed during Susan's lifetime. Susan, as Trustee, controls the Trust property. For example, money she keeps in a Trust bank account can be withdrawn or added to in the same manner as if the account were in her name only.

During her lifetime, Susan is free to *amend*, i.e., change the terms of her Trust or even *revoke* (terminate) the Trust altogether and have the Trust property placed back into her own name. If Susan does not revoke the Trust during her lifetime, once she dies the Trust becomes irrevocable. Her Successor Trustee is required to follow the terms of the Trust Agreement as it is written. If the Trust says to give the Trust property to certain beneficiaries, the Successor Trustee will do so; and in most cases without the need for Probate. If the Trust directs the Successor Trustee to continue to hold property in Trust and use the money to take care of a member of Susan's family, the Successor Trustee will use the Trust funds to care for the family member in the manner described in the Trust Agreement.

A Living Trust has many good features.

☆ AVOID PROBATE

As discussed in Chapter 1, Probate can be time consuming and expensive. Both the Personal Representative and his attorney are entitled to payment for their services. These fees can be significant. It may be necessary to hire accountants and appraisers, as well. If you have property in two states, then two Probate procedures may be necessary (one in each state). That could have the effect of doubling the cost of Probate. If the Trust is properly drafted and your property placed into the Trust, there should be no need for Probate. Upon your death, your Successor Trustee can transfer property, in this or any other state, to the beneficiary of your Trust.

☆ AVOID A CHALLENGE TO YOUR ESTATE PLAN

A Trust operates much like a Will because it provides for the distribution of your Estate when you die. Unlike a Will, it is not subject to Probate, so no Court is charged with the duty of "proving" that your Trust is valid. Your Successor Trustee can distribute your property as you direct, without asking anyone's permission to do so, and without giving the Court or any outside party an opportunity to examine the document. This does not mean that your Estate Plan cannot be challenged; but if the Trust is drafted according to Texas law, and not with the intent of ripping off your creditors, or cutting off your spouse's right to inherit, it will be very difficult for anyone to challenge the document.

☆ PRIVACY

Your Trust is a private document. No one but your Successor Trustee and your beneficiaries need ever read it. When opening a bank account in the name of the Trust, the bank might ask for a copy of the Trust Agreement, but all they need is basic information about the Trust such as the date of execution of the Trust; the Trust tax identification number; the identity of the Settlor, the current Trustee, the identity of Successor Trustee and the beneficiaries of the Trust, etc. You attorney can prepare a *Certificate of Trust* to give to the bank that contains this basic information (Finance 34.306).

If you have a Will, once it is admitted to Probate it becomes part of the Court records. Anyone can examine the Court records, read your Will and see who you did (or did not) provide for. Other Probate documents such as the inventory of your Probate Estate, creditor's claims, etc. are also open to public scrutiny. In some states, Court records are now available on the Internet!

LEASE SAFE DEPOSIT BOX AS TRUSTEE

Another privacy issue is what happens to the contents of your safe deposit box, should you become disabled or die. Under Texas law, if you hold a safe deposit box in your name only, once the bank (or other safe deposit box lessor) learns of your death, access to the box is restricted. The Court may appoint someone to serve as *Court Representative* to look at the contents of the box under the supervision of an officer or employee of the company. The bank will allow the Court Representative to take possession of the Will or a deed to a burial plot. They will also allow the beneficiary of an insurance policy to take possession of the policy. Other than the Will, deed and insurance policy nothing else can be removed from the safe deposit box without an order from the Probate Court (Probate 36B).

Other than these items, nothing can be removed from the safe deposit box without authorization from the Probate Court. That authorization is usually in the form of *Letters* issued to the person appointed as Personal Representative of your Estate.

By leasing the safe deposit box in your capacity as Trustee, you can arrange to have your Successor Trustee enter the box and remove any and all of the items from that box in the event of your death or incapacity. Not only will this avoid Probate, it will prevent the bank officer, or anyone other than your Successor Trustee, from examining the contents of your safe deposit box.

☆ CARE FOR FAMILY MEMBER

You can make provision in your Trust to care for a minor child or family member after you die. If your family member is immature or a born spender, and you are concerned that he may spend, within months, what it took you a lifetime to earn, you can have your attorney prepare a Trust that will spread the inheritance over an extended period of time. Your Trust can direct the Trustee to give a certain amount of money every 5 or 10 years; for example you can direct the Trustee to give part of the gift when the beneficiary reaches 25, another amount when he reaches 35, and then 45, etc.

If your beneficiary has a creditor problem, you can set up a *Spendthrift Trust*. You can direct your Successor Trustee to use the Trust funds for your beneficiary's health care, education, and living expenses, and nothing else. With a properly drafted Spendthrift Trust provision the Trust funds should be protected from the claims of the creditors of the beneficiary (Property 112.035).

An important exception is money owed by the beneficiary for alimony or child support. The Court may order your Trustee to make alimony or child support payments from the amount to be distributed to the beneficiary. If your Trust does not require the assets of the Trust be distributed to the beneficiary, the Court may order child support payments from the income of the Trust but not from the Trust principal (Property 154.005).

NO CREDITOR PROTECTION FOR SETTLOR
Although you can set up a Spendthrift Trust for the benefit of a family member, you cannot set one up for yourself. Property you place in your Revocable Living Trust is freely accessible to you. It is likewise accessible to your creditors both before and after your death (Property 112.035). If you die owing money, your creditors can have a Personal Representative appointed to locate funds to pay those debts. The Personal Representative can require that your Trust property be used to pay for those debt.

☆☆ AVOID GUARDIANSHIP
Once you have a Trust, you do not need to worry about who will take care of your property should you become disabled or too aged to handle your finances. The person you appointed as Successor Trustee will take over the care of the Trust property if you are unable to do so. If you do not have a Trust, and become incapacitated, a court may need to appoint a Guardian to care for your property. The cost to establish and maintain the guardianship is charged to you. As we will see in Chapter 9, such legal procedures can be expensive; and once established cannot be terminated unless you die or are restored to health (Probate 694).

With all these perks, you may be ready to call your attorney to make an appointment to set up a Trust, but before doing so there are a few things you need to consider.

THE CONS

⊠ COMPLEXITY

A Trust is a fairly complex document, often more than 30 pages long. It needs to be that long because you are establishing a vehicle for taking care of your property during your lifetime, as well as after your death. Your Trust may be written in "legalese," so it may take you considerable time and effort to understand it. It is important to have your Trust document prepared by an attorney who has the patience to work with you until you fully understand each paragraph of the document and are satisfied that what it states is what you really want.

⊠ COST

Because of the thoroughness of the document and the fact that it is custom designed for you, a Trust will cost much more to draft than a simple Will. In addition to the initial cost of the Trust, it can be expensive to maintain the Trust should you become disabled or die. Your Successor Trustee will be responsible to manage the Trust according to the terms of the Trust Agreement, and according to Texas law. He may need to employ an attorney to be sure he is administering the Trust according to the Texas Trust Code (Property Title 9B).

Your Successor Trustee has the right to charge for his duties as Trustee, as well as to charge for any specialized services performed (Property 114.061). A financial institution can charge to serve as Successor Trustee, and also charge to manage the Trust portfolio.

If you decide to have a financial institution serve as Trustee, then it is important to compare the fee schedules of different institutions.

You can choose an attorney, or an accountant, or a financial planner, to serve as Trustee, but this may create a conflict of interest because the professional can use his position as Trustee to generate fees for himself or his firm. If you decide to appoint a professional as Trustee you should have a fee agreement stating what will be charged for his duties as Trustee and what will be charged for professional work done on behalf of the Trust. The fee agreement should be included in the Trust document with a provision that whoever accepts the job of Successor Trustee, agrees to accept the fee as provided in the Trust document.

You may decide to appoint your spouse or a family member as Successor Trustee, who may want little, or no compensation. Regardless of who you choose to be Successor Trustee, you need to come to a fee agreement. The agreement can be for a set amount or a percentage of the value of the Trust, or other method to be used to determine his compensation.

If you make no provision for fees in your Trust Agreement, your Successor Trustee has the right to take a reasonable fee from the Trust property (Property 114.061). If the beneficiaries of the Trust do not think the fee reasonable, they can ask the Court to set the fee. But that will probably trigger a legal battle. It is better that you set the fee. Hopefully, that will head off unnecessary legal fees.

⊠ ☆ THE TRUST IS LEGALLY ENFORCEABLE

Any beneficiary of the Trust can petition the Chancery Division of the Superior Court to settle a dispute arising out of the administration of the Trust. For example, if the Trustee is not properly administering the Trust, the beneficiaries can petition the Court to remove the Trustee and appoint another to serve as Successor Trustee (Property 113.082).

We gave this section a cross and a star, because the right to have a Trust enforced or administered by a court is a double edged sword. It is great to have the Court protect the rights of your beneficiaries, but the cost of a Court battle could be greater than using Probate to transfer your Estate. Worse yet, your beneficiaries are at a disadvantage because the Trustee can charge the legal expenses to your Trust, while the beneficiaries must pay for their legal battles out of their own pocket. Even if the beneficiaries win the argument, the Trustee's legal fees are paid from the Trust, so there is just that much less for the beneficiaries to inherit.

⊠ YOU MAY NEED YOUR SPOUSE'S PERMISSION TO TRANSFER PROPERTY INTO YOUR TRUST

Most married couples prepare a Trust as part of their overall Estate Plan. Sometimes a married person has a Trust that was prepared prior to the marriage, or he may decide to create a Trust to care for children from a previous marriage. The Settlor is free to place any of his Separate Property and his half of the couple's Community Property into his Trust but he may not place his spouse's half of the Community Property into the Trust (or anywhere else not accessible to his spouse) without the spouse's written consent (Family 3.102).

If you are married and make a transfer of Community Property into your Trust without your spouse's permission; and that transfer results in your spouse not having a half interest in the Community Property, your spouse can petition (ask) the Court to undo the transfer and return his/her share of the Community Property.

⊠ PROBATE MIGHT STILL BE NECESSARY

The Trust only works for those items that you place in the Trust. If you own property in your name only, then upon your death, a Probate procedure might be necessary in order to transfer the property to your beneficiary. For example, if you purchase a security in your name only, without a "Transfer On Death" designation to a beneficiary or to your Trust, a Probate procedure may be necessary to determine who should inherit the security.

The attorney who prepares the Trust usually creates a safety net for such situations. He prepares a Will for you to sign at the same time you sign the Trust. The Will makes your Trust the beneficiary of your Probate Estate. If you own anything in your name only, should a Probate procedure be necessary, the Will directs your Personal Representative to make that asset part of your Trust by transferring the asset to your Successor Trustee. Your Successor Trustee will add that asset to your Trust (Probate 58(a)). The Will prepared by the attorney is called a **Pour Over Will** because it is designed to "pour" any asset titled in your name only, into the Trust

Having a Pour Over Will ensures that your property will go to the beneficiaries named in your Trust. But the downside of holding property in your name only is that a full Probate procedure may be necessary just to get that asset into your Trust. If avoiding Probate is your goal, holding property, in your name only, defeats that goal.

TAXES AND YOUR TRUST

Putting property into a Revocable Living Trust does not shield that property from taxes. All of the property held in a Revocable Living Trust is taxed as if the Settlor were holding that property in his own name. If the property earns income, income taxes will be due, and at the same rate as the Settlor would have paid if he had no Trust. Once the Settlor dies, both the federal and state government have the right to impose an *Estate Tax* on property transferred to a beneficiary as a result of the death.

All the property owned as of the date of death becomes the decedent's *Taxable Estate.* This includes *real property* (residential lots, condominiums, etc.) and *personal property* (cars, life insurance policies, business interests, securities, IRA accounts, etc.). It includes property held in the decedent's name alone, as well as property that he held jointly or in Trust. It also includes gifts given by the decedent during his lifetime that exceeded the *Annual Gift Tax Exclusion.* Up to the year 2002 that value was $10,000 per person, per year. The Annual Gift Tax Exclusion was adjusted for inflation in 2002 to $11,000 and again in 2006 to $12,000 (26 U.S.C. 2503(b)). For most of us, this is not a concern because no federal Estate Tax need be paid unless the decedent's Taxable Estate exceeds the federal *Estate Tax Exclusion* amount. That value is currently two million dollars and is scheduled to go even higher.

YEAR	ESTATE TAX EXCLUSION AMOUNT
2007-2008	$2,000,000
2009	$3,500,000

Under current law, the federal Estate Tax is scheduled to be phased out in the year 2010, but reinstated once again in the year 2011 with an Estate Tax Exclusion Amount of $1,000,000 — unless lawmakers change the tax law once again.

THE TEXAS "PICK-UP" ESTATE TAX

The Texas Estate Tax is based on the federal Estate Tax. The federal government imposes a tax on all property transferred because of the death, with certain exceptions for transfers made to a U.S. citizen spouse and to qualified charities. The federal government then grants an Estate Tax exclusion so that no federal Estate Tax need be paid unless the amount transferred at death is greater than the federal Estate Tax Exclusion amount. See the prior page for the current value of the Estate Tax Exclusion amount.

The Texas Estate Tax is called a "pick-up" tax, because the state collects the tax that would have gone to the federal government had it not been the federal Estate Tax Exclusion value. The federal government then allowed a credit on the federal Estate Tax return for Estate Taxes paid to the state.

The Economic Growth and Tax Relief Reconciliation Act of 2001 amended the Internal Revenue Code to provide that an Estate cannot claim a credit for state death taxes for those who die after December 31, 2004.

The amount of Estate Taxes paid to Texas are based on the federal Estate Tax credit (Tax 211.052). Because no credit is allowed for state death taxes on the federal Estate Tax return, there is no Texas Estate Tax for the years 2005 through 2010 (Tax 211.051, 211.055).

In the year 2011, and beyond, the federal Estate Tax exclusion is scheduled to be $1,000,000, with the state credit for federal Estate Tax restored. If there are no changes to the law, Texas will, once again collect a portion of the federal Estate Tax.

A TRUST TO REDUCE ESTATE TAXES

Under current law, Estates of those who die in 2010 are exempt from federal Estate Taxes, but in 2011, the Estate Tax is scheduled to be reinstated and Estates worth more than $1,000,000 will once again be subject to a sizeable Estate Tax. A couple with an Estate in excess of a million dollars can reduce the risk of an Estate Tax by setting up "His and Her" Trusts, so that each person can take advantage of his own Exclusion Amount.

For example, if a husband and wife own two million dollars, they can separate their funds into two Trusts each valued at one million dollars. The Trusts can be set up so that a surviving spouse can use the income from the deceased partner's Trust for living expenses. In this way, their standard of living need not be reduced by separating their funds into two Trusts.

If they do not wish to separate funds, they can set up a single Joint Trust that separates into two Trusts once one partner dies. Again, the surviving spouse is free to use the income from both Trusts. Once both partners are deceased, the beneficiaries of their respective Trusts will inherit the funds, hopefully with no Estate Tax due.

If the couple make no Trust provision, and they hold their property jointly, the last to die will own the two million dollars with only one Estate Tax Exclusion available. If lawmakers do not change the tax law, and the surviving spouse dies in 2011, or later, everything over one million dollars will be subject to federal Estate Taxes. A Revocable Living Trust is a relatively simple way for a married couple to reduce, if not eliminate, the need to pay Estate Taxes. However, there is still the problem of the federal Gift Tax and the Capital Gains Tax.

THE UN-UNIFIED GIFT TAX

As explained, up to 2002, the federal Annual Gift Tax Exclusion was $10,000. It increased to $11,000 in 2002, and then to $12,000 in 2006. The IRS keeps a running count of amounts you give to someone that exceed the Annual Gift Tax Exclusion that is effective in the year of the donation.

Although you are required to report a gift that exceeds the Annual Gift Tax Exclusion, no tax need be paid unless that running total is more than the federal lifetime Gift Tax Exclusion. That amount is currently one million dollars. If your running total does not exceed the Gift Tax Exclusion amount during your lifetime, once you die, the cumulative value of gifts you reported to the IRS will be added to your Taxable Estate.

Until the Estate Tax law was changed, the Gift and Estate Tax were unified. No Gift Tax needed to be paid unless the total value of the taxable gifts exceeded the federal Estate Tax Exclusion amount. In 2004 that changed. The Estate Tax Exclusion amount went up to $1,500,000, but the amount for the Gift Tax Exclusion remained at $1,000,000, so they now are no longer unified.

To summarize:
If you make a gift to anyone that is greater than the Annual Gift Tax Exclusion for that year, you must report the gift to the IRS. The IRS keeps a running count of gifts you made in excess of the Annual Gift Tax Exclusion. If that sum exceeds $1,000,000, you will pay a Gift Tax on any amount that you give that is over the Annual Gift Tax Exclusion. The Estate Tax is scheduled to be repealed in 2010, but not the Gift Tax.

Texas does not have a Gift Tax at this time.

The current federal Estate tax is scheduled to be phased out in the year 2010, but a new Capital Gains Tax is scheduled for 2010 that may prove even more costly than the Estate Tax. The new Capital Gains Tax is related to the way inherited property is evaluated by the federal government. Real and personal property is inherited at a "stepped-up" basis, meaning that if the decedent's property increased in value from the time he acquired it, the beneficiary inherits the property at its fair market value as of the decedent's date of death. For example, if the decedent bought stock for $20,000 and it is worth $50,000 as of his date of death, the beneficiary will take a step-up in basis of $30,000; i.e., the beneficiary inherits the stock at the current $50,000 value. If the beneficiary sells the stock for $50,000, he pays no Capital Gains Tax. If the beneficiary holds onto the stock and later sells it for $60,000, the beneficiary will pay a Capital Gains Tax only on the $10,000 increase in value since the decedent's death.

Up to 2009, there is no limit to the amount a beneficiary can take as a step-up in basis. But in 2010 caps are set in place. The decedent's Estate will be allowed a 1.3 million dollar step-up in basis, plus another 3 million for property passing to the surviving spouse (26 U.S.C. 1022(b)). The new law could result in significant Capital Gains taxes that the beneficiary must pay. For example, suppose in 2010 you inherit a business from your father that he purchased for $100,000 and it is now worth 2 million dollars. There is a capital gain of 1.9 million dollars, but you are allowed a step-up in basis of only 1.3 million. If you sell it for two million dollars, $600,000 of your inheritance will be subject to a Capital Gains tax.

We will discuss methods of reducing the Gift Tax and the Capital Gains Tax in Chapter 7.

MAYBE A WILL IS BEST AFTER ALL

Although many methods can be used to transfer property without the need for Probate, it may be each method has a downside that is objectionable to you. Maybe you don't have enough money at this time to warrant the cost of setting up a Trust. Holding property jointly with another may raise issues of security and independence. Holding property so that it goes directly to a few beneficiaries in a Pay On Death account may not be as flexible as you wish. This may be the case if you want to give gifts to several charities or to a minor child.

For example, you can hold all your property so that it goes directly to your son without the need for Probate. If you ask him to use some of the money for your grandchild's education, it may be that your grandchild gets none of the money because your son is sued or falls upon hard times. If you keep your property in your name only and leave a Will giving a certain amount of money to your grandchild, the child will know exactly how much money you left and the purpose of that gift.

After taking into account all the pros and cons of avoiding Probate, you may well opt for a Will and a Probate procedure. If you make such a decision, it is important to keep in mind that Estate Planning is not an "all or nothing" choice. You can arrange your Estate so that certain items pass automatically to your intended beneficiary, and other items can be left in your name only, to be distributed as part of a Probate procedure. By arranging your finances in this manner, you can reduce the value of your Probate Estate, and that in turn should reduce the cost of Probate.

In the next chapter, we discuss the Will as an Estate Planning tool.

Those of you who have a Will may be thinking that there is no reason to read the Chapter, but does your Will:

- Make provision for the amount to be paid to your Personal Representative?

- Make gifts of your personal property? (jewelry, car, etc.)

- Name a Guardian to care for your minor child?

- Make adjustment for gifts or loans that you gave to the beneficiaries of your Will?

- Give specific instructions about how your bills and taxes are to be paid; i.e., which of your beneficiaries will have his inheritance reduced in order to pay your debts and taxes?

Has your Will been prepared so that it will be difficult for anyone to challenge it?

Have you stored your Will so that it is safe AND easily accessible to you during your lifetime and to your Personal Representative after your death?

If you answered "Yes" to all of the above questions, then you can skip over to Chapter 5.

Your Will– Your Way 4

Many people decide that the Will is the best route to go but do not act upon it, thinking it unnecessary to prepare a Will until they are very old and about to die. But according to reports published by the National Center for Health Statistics (a division of the U.S. Department of Health and Human Services) 2 of every 10 people who die in any given year are under the age of 60. Twenty percent may seem like a small number until it hits close to home as it did with a young couple.

Alex and Cathy were an old-fashioned couple in a modern world. When they married, they knew they wanted a large family. There was no question that Cathy would stay home and raise the children while Alex went to work. Luckily he did very well as one of the managers of a string of restaurants. Better yet, he enjoyed his work. He loved to cook and would even take over the kitchen when he returned from work. That suited Cathy just fine because she had her hands full raising their three boys.

Cathy couldn't help thinking how lucky they were that morning as she fixed breakfast. A nice house. Healthy, if not rambunctious, boys. All in all, a comfortable marriage. Her only concern that day was the fact that Alex was flying off on a business trip. All this terrorist news made her nervous about flying. Alex reassured her that it was only an hour's flight, and besides he was flying the company plane and not a commercial airliner.

But it was not terrorists that brought down the plane, just a malfunctioning rudder.

THINGS A WILL CAN DO

Though we all agree that one never knows, still people put off making a Will, figuring that if they die before getting around to it, Texas law will take over and their property will be distributed in the manner that they would have wanted anyway. The problem with that logic is the complexity of the Texas Laws of Descent. It isn't too difficult to figure out who will inherit your property, if you are survived by a spouse, child, parent or sibling. But if none of these survive you, the ultimate beneficiary of your property may not be the person you would have chosen, had you taken the time to do so. Why chance having your property go to someone you may not like or even know? Best to prepare a Will and have your property inherited by the person of your choice.

Others may think that it is not necessary to have a Will because they have arranged their finances so that all of their property will be inherited without the need for Probate. But money could come into your Estate after your death. This could happen in any number of ways from winning the lottery and dying (of happiness, no doubt), to receiving insurance funds after your death. For example, if you die in a house fire, the company that insures your home may need to pay for damages done to the property. In such case, the funds will need to be paid to your Estate. A Personal Representative may need to be appointed and the insurance funds distributed according to Texas law.

If you die without a Will, your Estate may be distributed differently than you would have wished. And there are other important reasons to make a Will.

APPOINT PERSONAL REPRESENTATIVE

The Court will give top priority to the person you name as Personal Representative of your Will. Without a Will, the Court will use the following order of priority to decide who will serve as your Personal Representative.

1st   your surviving spouse

2nd the principal beneficiary of your Estate

3rd any beneficiary of your Estate

4th next of kin as determined by the Texas Laws of Descent and Distribution

5th a creditor of your Estate

6th anyone of good character who lives in the county

7th anyone the Court thinks is qualified and will do a good job (Probate 77).

Usually, the family decides among themselves who should serve as Personal Representative, but if two people have the same priority and there is disagreement over who should serve, the judge will make the decision. If you die without a Will, the Personal Representative may not be the person you would have chosen.

ADMINISTRATION MAY BE AFFECTED BY YOUR CHOICE OF PERSONAL REPRESENTATIVE

As explained in Chapter 1, if you do not own Separate Property, your surviving spouse may use Community Property to settle your affairs without the need to go through Probate (Probate 160). However, if you use your Will to appoint someone other than your spouse to serve as Personal Representative, that person may ask the Court to be appointed and to conduct a full Probate proceeding (Probate 76).

🗐 SET PERSONAL REPRESENTATIVE'S FEE

Once you decide on a Personal Representative, you need check with that person to be sure that he is willing to serve in that capacity. And if so, then you should come to an understanding about how much compensation he will receive to settle your Estate, If you make no provision for his fee, he is entitled to receive the amount as allowed under Texas law, namely up to 5% of your Gross Probate Estate (Probate 241).

PERSONAL REPRESENTATIVE MAY SEEK MORE MONEY

You can put the amount of agreed compensation in your Will; however your Personal Representative can reject that amount and ask for the amount allowed under law. To avoid the problem, you can have your attorney draft an Agreement that you and your Personal Representative sign and attach it to your Will. Having a separate fee Agreement will not stop your Personal Representative from asking for more money, but with such an Agreement, the Court will not agree to the increase unless something unusual occurs (such as a law suit) causing much more work than the ordinary Probate procedure.

You also need to keep in mind that the Personal Representative's fee is just to administer the Estate. It does not include payment for professional work he may do while settling the Estate. For example, if you appoint your attorney as Personal Representative, he can agree to the amount stated in the Will for his role as Personal Representative, and then ask the Court to award him attorney's fees as well (Probate 242).

The same goes for any other professional. If you appoint your accountant to serve as Personal Representative, he is entitled to receive compensation for his work as Personal Representative and also for any accounting work he does such as preparing and filing tax returns; preparing an inventory and doing an accounting for the beneficiaries. A financial planner who serves as Personal Representative may be compensated for his management of the Estate property (buying and selling securities, taking care of rental property, etc.) in addition to his fee to administer the Estate.

But the main problem with appointing a professional as your Personal Representative is the same as appointing a professional to serve as the Successor Trustee of your Trust; namely, that it creates a potential conflict of interest. The professional can use his position as Personal Representative to generate fees that might have been avoided had someone else settled the Estate.

When choosing a Personal Representative, consider the relationship of the Personal Representative to the beneficiaries and determine whether it would be better to appoint a non-professional for the job.

If you decide to appoint a professional for the job, have your compensation agreement state what will be paid for duties performed in the administration of the Estate as Personal Representative and what monies will be paid as compensation for any professional service he may perform.

🗐 MAKE GIFTS OF YOUR PERSONAL PROPERTY

Another benefit to making a Will is that you can make provision for who will get your personal property (computers, antiques, securities, boats, snowmobiles etc.). When making a Will consider making provision for your car. If you make a *specific gift,* i.e., a gift to a named beneficiary of your Will, it will be relatively simple for your Personal Representative to transfer the car to your beneficiary. If you do not make a specific gift of your car, your Personal Representative will decide what to do with it. He may decide to sell it and include the proceeds of the sale in the Estate funds to be distributed as part of the Probate Estate; or he can give the car to one beneficiary of your Estate as part of that beneficiary's share of the Estate.

CAUTION YOU CAN'T GIVE WHAT YOU DON'T HAVE

You need to give considerable thought whenever you make a specific gift to someone. It could be that you no longer own the item at the time of your death. This could happen with property or money. For example, suppose you leave all of your Estate to your son, with a specific gift of $10,000 to each of your three grandchildren. Your son is the *residuary beneficiary* of the Probate Estate, meaning he gets whatever is left once all of the bills are paid and all of the specific gifts made. If the cost of your last illness leaves your Probate Estate with only $30,000 to distribute, would you want the grandchildren to get their gifts and your son nothing? The simple solution is to make all of them residuary beneficiaries by leaving each a percent of your Estate. For example, instead of making a specific gift to each grandchild you could leave 70% to your son and 10% to each grandchild.

GIFTS OF COMMUNITY PROPERTY

You can give only those items you own. If you are married, unless you have an Agreement that states otherwise, personal property you acquire during your marriage is Community Property (Family 3.002). You can make a gift of Community Property, but only with the consent of your partner.

NON-PROBATE ASSETS

Property held in a Pay On Death Account, a Transfer On Death Security, the proceeds of a life insurance policy, Trust property, joint property with right of survivorship and IRA accounts are all *non-Probate* assets because they will be inherited by your named beneficiary without the need for Probate. You are free to change the beneficiary of a non-Probate asset during your lifetime, but once you are deceased, the gift is made (Probate 450). Unless your Estate is the beneficiary of a non-Probate asset, it should not be mentioned in your Will. If you make provision in your Will for the inheritance of a non-Probate asset that is different from the arrangement made during your lifetime, it will, at the very least, cause confusion. At worst, it will trigger a law suit to determine who should inherit the property.

CONTENTS OF REAL PROPERTY

Property located within a building is personal property. Under Texas law, a gift of real property with a building or home located on that land does not include the items located within the structure, unless you leave a Will saying to give that personal property to the beneficiary of that property (Probate 58(c)). If you do not leave such instructions, the contents of the building become part of your Probate Estate to be distributed by your Personal Representative to the beneficiaries of your Will.

GIFTS OF PERSONAL EFFECTS

Many who have lost someone close to them report that the distribution of small personal items caused the greatest conflict. If you arrange your finances so that no Probate procedure is necessary, your next of kin will need to decide among themselves how to distribute your personal effects. Without guidance from you and no Personal Representative with authority to make decisions, there could be disagreement and hard feelings over items of little monetary value, but much sentimental value.

If you make a Will, you can make gifts of your *personal effects* (clothing, books, record collection, radio, etc.) by making a list of these gifts and attaching it to your Will. Your Personal Representative will distribute your personal effects according to that list. Of course, it is not possible to make a list of each and every item you own; but you can instruct your Personal Representative to allow certain family members to take their choice of items not mentioned in your Will. If two or more family members want the same item, instruct your Personal Representative to use an appropriate lottery system (coin toss, high card in a cut of a deck of cards, etc.) to decide who "wins."

MAKE PROVISION FOR YOUR CHILD

A Will maker can "cut" a child out of his Will by indicating in his Will that he intentionally makes no provision for that child (Probate 58(b)(1)). If you wish to disinherit your child, simply omitting any reference to the child, may not be the way to go. Your child may challenge the Will saying that you "forgot" to include him as a beneficiary. The better approach is to discuss the problem with your attorney. He will be able to suggest several provisions that can be included in your Will to avoid such challenge to your Will.

▤ MAKE ADJUSTMENT FOR PRIOR GIFTS

With a Will, you can make adjustments for gifts or loans given during your lifetime. For example, if you have loaned money to a family member and do not expect to be repaid, you can deduct the loan from that person's inheritance. Of course, it may be that you are not concerned with inequities. That was the case of an aged woman who had three children, Paul, Rita and Frank, her youngest. Frank always seemed to need some assistance from his mother. She often "loaned" him money that he never repaid.

Her other children were responsible and independent. Paul was married and had children of his own. He decided to purchase a house but was having trouble accumulating the down payment. His mother agreed to lend him the money. Paul and his wife offered to give his mother a mortgage on the property. The mother said a simple promissory note from Paul was sufficient, and she would have her attorney draft the note.

The attorney drafted the note but was concerned about the inequity. "You never made a Will. Were you to die, each of your children will inherit an equal amount of money. If Paul still owes money on this promissory note, he will either need to pay the balance to your Estate, or have it subtracted from the amount he inherits. All of the money you gave to Frank will not count towards his inheritance unless you make your intentions clear that you considered the money you gave to Frank to be an advancement of his inheritance. You can do this by making an adjustment in a Will, or by having Frank give you a promissory note for any outstanding debts." (Probate 44).

"It's O.K." replied the mother "I love all my children equally . . . some are a little more equal than others."

MAKE PROVISION FOR PAYMENT OF DEBTS

Most Wills contain an instruction to the Personal Representative to ". . . pay all the expenses of my last illness, funeral expenses, costs of administration, taxes and just debts. . . " Under Texas law, paying all of your debts does not include paying off a loan on a gift made to a beneficiary (Probate 71A) For example, if you leave your car to a beneficiary, and you have a loan on the car, you need to specify whether you want the loan to be paid from your Probate Estate and your beneficiary inherit the car free and clear, or whether you want your beneficiary to be responsible to pay off the loan. If you make no provision in your Will, your beneficiary will inherit the debt along with the gift.

MAKE PROVISION FOR PAYMENT OF TAXES

Taxes are another concern for those Estates large enough to be subject to Estate Taxes. State and federal law require that Estate taxes be paid by the beneficiaries of the Estate in proportion to the value received, unless the decedent made some other arrangements to pay for the taxes (26 U.S.C. 6324 (a)(2)).

If you make no provision for the payment of taxes, whoever inherits your property will pay a percentage of the taxes based on the amount they receive. The beneficiary must pay his share regardless of whether he inherits the property through a non-Probate transfer (joint owner, beneficiary of a Trust, Pay On Death account, life insurance policy, etc.) or as the beneficiary of your Probate Estate. If a beneficiary refuses to contribute his share of the taxes, whoever is responsible to make payment (usually the surviving spouse or Personal Representative) can ask the Court to order the beneficiary to contribute his share of the taxes (Probate 322 A).

CHOOSE A GUARDIAN FOR YOUR MINOR CHILD

If one parent dies, it is the right, and duty, of the surviving parent to care for the child (Family 151.001). But it could happen that both parents become incapacitated or die before the child is grown. If you have a minor child, you can use your Will to appoint someone to serve as the Guardian of your child in the event that both you and the other parent are deceased (Probate 676). You can even include a Trust in your Will, naming someone to serve as Trustee to care for property that you leave to your minor child. See Chapter 7 for more information about how to make provision for the care of your minor child in the event of your incapacity, or death.

INCLUDE SAFEGUARDS FOR YOUR BENEFICIARIES

It is a fairly common practice in Texas to include a provision in the Will directing that the Personal Representative be allowed to conduct the Probate independently and without Court supervision. The Will maker may include the waiver of the right to a *Supervised Administration* because he is trying to make the job easier for his Personal Representative; or maybe he is concerned with the cost of the Probate procedure.

Allowing the Representative to act independently can save the Estate money, but the downside is that without Court supervision the Personal Representative can do some serious mischief. He can do all of the following without asking permission from the beneficiaries or from the Court:

⇨ distribute Exempt Property and Family Allowance (Probate 146 (4)).

⇨ settle claims against the decedent's Estate (Probate 146 (3)).

⇨ distribute the Estate (Probate 151).

With an *Independent Administration,* the Personal Representative can close out the Estate without consulting with Court or beneficiaries. This is not the case with a Supervised Administration. Your beneficiaries can raise any concern they have about the way the Probate is conducted, or about the way the Personal Representative intends to distribute the property. The Court will conduct a hearing on the disputed matter. The Estate will not be closed until all issues are resolved.

BENEFICIARY CAN SIGN HIS OWN WAIVER

Some Will makers may want their Personal Representative to have sole authority in the Probate proceeding. They see no need to have input from the beneficiaries during the Estate Administration. That is often the case with a married couple. Each names the other to be Personal Representative and sole beneficiary of the Estate. But suppose the couple die simultaneously in a car accident. Would the Will maker have wanted the alternate Personal Representative to have such authority over the beneficiaries of the Estate?

The thing to keep in mind is that once you direct an Independent Administration in your Will, you are taking a right away from your beneficiary, namely the right of a Court review of the Probate proceeding. Your beneficiaries are always free to sign their own waiver of a Supervised Administration. If they are comfortable with the Personal Representative, they can ask the Court to allow an Independent Administration (Probate 145).

The same reasoning applies to a bond. No bond will be required if you waive the requirement in your Will (Probate 195). However, your beneficiaries are always free to ask the Court to waive bond if they feel that the Estate funds are safe (Probate 194).

PREPARING YOUR WILL

After reading the last few pages, those who do not have a Will may decide that a Will is a good thing to have and decide to sit down and write one out. And you can, because in the state of Texas, you can prepare a Will in your own hand, without the assistance of an attorney (Probate 59). Such a Will is called a *holographic* Will.

But preparing a Will is like figure skating. It is harder than it looks. A Will needs to be clearly worded. A sentence that can be read in two different ways can lead to a dispute over what you intended; and that could lead to a long and expensive Court battle.

Texas allows an unwitnessed holographic Will to be admitted to Probate provided the signature and the material parts of the Will (the "who" gets "what") are in the Will maker's own hand. However the problem with an unwitnessed Will is its authenticity. If no one sees you sign the Will, how do they know you actually wrote it out? It could be a forgery, or maybe someone was forcing you to sign it. The problem of authenticity can be solved by later attaching an Affidavit to your Will in which you state, under oath, that at the time you signed the Will, you were

> ➢ of sound mind – and -

> ➢ at least 18, or if less than 18, married, or a member of the U.S. armed forces - and -

> ➢ you have not revoked your Will (Probate 60).

Under Texas law, once you attach this Affidavit to your Will it becomes **self-proved**, meaning that the Probate Court can accept your Will into Probate without the need for a witness to come to Court and testify as to its authenticity (Probate 84).

Even if you sign the Will in the presence of two disinterested witnesses, it could be that the Will is challenged because someone is accused of pressuring you into giving him/her most if not all of your property. Texas courts have ruled that there is **undue influence** whenever someone exerts influence over the Will maker causing the Will to be prepared according to the wishes of the person exerting the pressure and not those of the Will maker (*Estate of Graham*, 69 S.W. 3d 598 (Tex. 2001)).

The Estate of Graham is an interesting case to read because it sets out all of the factors that the Court used to determine whether the Will maker was of sound mind and whether anyone used undue influence.

HOW TO AVOID A CHALLENGE TO YOUR WILL

As discussed, there are any number of ways someone can challenge your Will. If this is of concern to you, then it is important that you consult with an attorney who is experienced in Estate Planning. Your attorney can prepare the Will according to your directions. He will see to it that your Will is signed and witnessed in the presence of two disinterested witnesses — usually members of his staff.

Once signed in this manner it will be difficult for anyone to say that you did not know what you were doing when you signed the Will. If anyone challenges your Will, your attorney will be able to present proof to the Court that the Will was prepared exactly as you wished, and that you had full capacity when you signed the Will.

You can even have your attorney include a *no contest* provision in your Will stating that if your Will is challenged, whoever makes the challenge gets none of your Probate Estate. Such a provision is called an *In Terrorem Clause* because it is designed to cause fear (if not terror) in the heart of your beneficiary.

Some states will not enforce such a clause, because they want people to have the right to challenge a Will, and let the Court decide whether that challenge is proper. Texas courts have upheld In Terrorem Clauses, but reluctantly. It is the goal of the Texas Court to carry the directions of the Will maker, but whenever possible they will avoid having the beneficiary forfeit his inheritance.

Texas Courts have refused to uphold an In Terrorem Clause unless it is clear that the action of the beneficiary is in direct violation of the In Terrorem Clause as written in the Will (*Estate of Newbill*, 781 S.W.2d 727 (Tex. 1989)). This being the case, to be upheld in the state of Texas, an In Terrorem Clause must be clearly written and unambiguous in its meaning.

STORING YOUR WILL

Once you sign your Will, you may wonder where to store it. If an attorney prepared your Will, he may suggest that he place it in his vault for safekeeping. By doing so, he ensures that your family will contact him when you die. Once notified of your death, he will forward the Will to the Clerk of the Probate Court (Probate 75). Forwarding the Will to the Court does not mean that your family is required to employ him should Probate be necessary. It only means that he has an opportunity for future employment.

But there are problems with such an arrangement. The Will could be lost or mistaken for another Will. That happened in at least one case. The attorney prepared Wills for two people with the same name and similar family circumstances. When one person died the attorney submitted the wrong Will to Probate. Luckily the error was quickly discovered. The decedent had a distinctive signature. The family challenged the validity of the Will based on the unfamiliar signature and the way the property was to be distributed. They knew the decedent would never have distributed his property in the manner stated in the Will.

If you decide to allow your attorney to store the Will, you need assurance that the attorney will be responsible for the document. You should get a receipt and something in writing that says:

⇨ The attorney accepts full responsibility for storage of the Will. Should it be lost or damaged, he will replace the document at no cost to you; and if you are deceased, he will, at no cost to your beneficiaries, present sufficient evidence to the Court to accept a valid copy of the Will into Probate.

⇨   There will be no charge to you, or your heirs, for the storage and retrieval of the document.

⇨   Should he sell his practice, retire, or die, he or the successor to his practice, will return the original document to you.

THE SAFE DEPOSIT BOX, SAFE BUT . . .

You might consider placing your Will in a safe deposit box that you lease at a bank. The only problem with the bank safe deposit box is convenient access. If you hold a safe deposit box in your name only, should you die, the bank will restrict access to the safe deposit box. Under Texas law, the bank may allow any of the following people to inspect the contents of your safe box

▷   your spouse

▷   your parent

▷   your adult child or grandchild

▷   whoever you named as Executor, i.e., Personal Representative, of your Will.

The statute requires that a company officer be present when the safe deposit box is opened (Probate 36D).

Your family can access your safe deposit box for the limited purpose of retrieving your Will, or deed to a burial plot, or life insurance policy (Probate 36E). Nothing else may be removed from the safe deposit box until a Personal Representative is appointed who is authorized by the Probate Court to take possession of your property. If you arranged your finances to avoid Probate, it is self defeating to have entry to a safe deposit box trigger a Probate procedure.

For those who are happily married, the solution to the problem of accessing the safe deposit box after death, may be to lease the box jointly with your spouse such that each of you has free access to the box. However, this may not be the best choice if you think your spouse will be unhappy with certain provisions made in your Will. Some Wills never see the light of day for this reason. In such case, it may be better to keep the safe deposit box in your name only, with instructions to the bank to allow only your Personal Representative to retrieve the Will.

As explained in the previous Chapter, those who have a Trust can solve the problem by giving their Successor Trustee joint access to the safe deposit box.

If you are single and do not have a Trust, you can lease the box jointly with a trusted family member. Of course, if privacy and security are important to you, that may outweigh any concern for the convenience of your beneficiaries.

DEPOSIT IN PROBATE COURT
Perhaps the best place to store your Will is with the Probate Court in the county of your residence. The fee for doing so is nominal ($3 as of the year 2007). You are free to retrieve the Will from Probate Court in the event that you move or decide to change your Will (Probate 71).

Regardless of where you choose to store your Will, let your Personal Representative know that you have a Will and how to retrieve it in the event of your death.

I thought you said a Will is not enough

After reading this chapter, you may be thinking that the book is poorly named. After all, look at all the good things a Will can do:

❋ choose the person you want to settle your Estate

❋ arrange to have your Personal Representative settle your Estate for a reasonable fee

❋ give your personal items, including your car, to the person of your choice

❋ choose a Guardian for your child

❋ discourage a challenge to your Will.

But that is not all there is to an Estate Plan. A Will cares for your property when you are deceased, but it cannot provide for the care of your property in the event you become disabled. A complete Estate Plan provides for the care of your property during your lifetime and for the care of your person as well.

In these days of extended old age, many of us will need assistance with our health care and/or finances as we age. It is important to arrange to have someone manage finances and make medical decisions in the event that we are too aged or too ill to do so ourselves. These topics are covered in Chapters 8 and 9.

And a Will may be effective to transfer all that you own upon your death, but it cannot help your family pay for your debts. It may be that you have so many debts that your family is left with little or nothing. A complete Estate Plan provides for the financial well being of your family once you are deceased; and that is the topic of the next chapter.

Arranging To Pay Bills 5

You can think of your Estate Plan as being composed of two separate parts, a Lifetime Plan and an Inheritance Plan. Your Lifetime Plan provides for the care of your property during your lifetime, with the goal being maximum control and protection. Your Inheritance Plan provides for the inheritance of your property, with the goal being minimum cost and hassle to your beneficiaries. You could consider your Estate Plan to be a master plan that balances the goals of the Lifetime Plan with those of the Inheritance Plan.

When people consider their Inheritance Plan, they are mostly concerned about giving their possessions away. Many do not take into account how the bills they have accumulated will be paid once they are deceased, or even who will be responsible for paying those bills. Most of us do not worry about providing for the payment of our debts, thinking "I'll have that paid off long before I die." But with easily available credit, many are maintaining a high debt balance as a way of life. Paying off all of their loans is not a priority. Many will live their lives without ever being free of debt.

This does not imply that people do not know how to manage their funds. For many people (and corporations), it makes good sense to use other people's money to carry on business. In fact, great debt is a badge of honor for the wealthy. If a bank will lend you a million dollars, it means you have the means to repay that amount. Banks will not lend much money to those with few assets. Rich or poor, we all need to think about how our debts will be paid once we are gone.

Suppose you die without funds, and owing money. Does the debt die with you or is someone else responsible to pay what you owe? If you are married, the first person the creditor will look to, is your spouse. To understand the basis of this expectation, you need to know a bit of the history of our legal system.

Our laws are derived from the English Common Law. Under English Common law, a single woman had the right to own property in her own name and also the right to contract to buy or sell property. When a woman married, her legal identity merged with her spouse. She could not hold property free from her husband's claim or control. She could no longer enter into a contract without her husband's permission.

Once married, a woman became financially dependent on her husband. He, in turn, became legally responsible to provide his wife with basic necessities — food, clothing, shelter and medical services. If anyone provided basic necessities to his wife, then, regardless of whether the husband agreed to be responsible for the debt, he became obliged to pay for them. This law was called the DOCTRINE OF NECESSARIES.

In the United States, a series of Married Women's Rights Acts were passed giving a married woman the right to own property. Under Texas law, a married woman has the same right to contract, own property and run a business in the same manner as any single woman (Family 1.105).

As Married Women's Rights laws were passed, states had to decide whether the Doctrine of Necessaries still applied— especially in light of the equal protection under the law. Specifically, if a husband is responsible to pay for his wife's necessities, shouldn't his wife be responsible to pay for his necessities?

Some states decided that the law was obsolete and that neither husband nor wife should be responsible for the other's debts, unless they contracted or agreed to do so. Other states decided that each partner is responsible to provide basic necessities for his spouse. Texas took the latter approach, Anyone who provides necessities for a married person in this state has the right to demand payment from the spouse — whether or not the spouse agreed to be personally liable to pay for the necessities (Family 2.501).

COMMUNITY PROPERTY DEBTS

Texas is a Community Property state, so in addition to each spouse being liable to pay for the family's necessities, the spouse may be responsible to pay for his partner's debts from Community Property that they own, but with restrictions. As explained in Chapter 1, Community Property is property acquired by either spouse during the marriage, not counting gifts, inheritances, or monies from a personal injury (Family 3.002).

A spouse can keep money he earns during the marriage, separate from his partner. The earning partner can manage, control or spend any of the Community Property funds that are held separately (Family 3.102). These separately managed Community Property funds are available to pay money owed by the earning spouse, but not money owed by his spouse (Family 3.202).

Should the earning partner mix his income with that of his spouse, those funds become Joint Community Property. Both partners have the right to manage, control and dispose of Community Property held jointly. Joint Community Property is available to pay monies owed by the either spouse, regardless of whether that debt was incurred before or after the marriage.

The Separate Property of a spouse, and Community Property that is held separately, is not available to pay for the debts of his/her partner, with an important exception, all Community Property (held separately or jointly) is available to pay for a tortious act committed by either party during the marriage (Family 3.202 (a)). A "tortious act" is a broad legal term. It includes an act that causes harm or loss to person or to property, such as trespass, slander, assault and battery, etc.

In the event that one of the partners has a judgment against him, the judge can determine the order in which Separate or Community Property should be used to pay for that judgment. The judge will consider all of the facts, but in general the judgment will be paid in the following order:

1st   The Separate Property of the spouse who committed the act.

2nd   Community Property held separately by the spouse committing the act.

3rd   Community Property held separately by the other spouse.

4th   Joint Community Property (Family 3.203).

CONVERTING COMMUNITY PROPERTY

A Texas couple can agree, in writing, to convert Community Property into Separate Property, provided, this is not done to protect assets from a creditor. Similarly, the couple can agree, in writing, to convert Separate Property to Community Property (Family 4.102, 4.202). Texas statute (Family 4.205) contains a form that can be used to convert Separate Property to Community Property. You can download the form from the Texas statute Web site. http://www.capital.state.tx.us/statutes.

You may be wondering why anyone would want to change Separate Property to Community Property. Why give up control of Separate Property and make it available to the creditors of your spouse? But for those who do not anticipate a creditor problem, changing Separate Property to Community Property makes sense for tax reasons. Under current tax law, when a spouse dies, property owned as Community Property gets a step-up in basis (26 U.S.C. 1014(b)(6)). The couple's Community Property is valued as of the decedent's date of death and that value becomes the new basis for the surviving spouse.

If a married couple own Separate Property, or even as Joint Tenants With Right of Survivorship, only the decedent's share is stepped-up in basis. For example, suppose the couple own a parcel of land as:

JOINT TENANTS WITH RIGHT OF SURVIVORSHIP

should one die, the surviving spouse will inherit the property, 100%, but only the decedent's share in the property takes a step-up in basis. If the surviving spouse sells the property at that time, there might be a Capital Gains Tax on the increase in value of the half of the property owned by the surviving spouse.

If the married couple owns the same parcel of land as:

COMMUNITY PROPERTY WITH RIGHT OF SURVIVORSHIP

there is a step-up in basis on the entire parcel of land. Under current law (i.e., in the year 2007), the surviving spouse can sell the property at that time with no Capital Gains Tax due.

Whichever way a married couple decide to hold their property, it is important to keep a clear record of the status of that property. Should a married person die, his creditors can demand payment from the decedent's share of Community Property even if the surviving spouse now owns the property without any need for Probate.

For example, suppose the couple acquired an expensive painting during their marriage. That painting now belongs to the surviving spouse. No Probate procedure is necessary to establish that ownership. But if the decedent owed money, and was without Separate Property, his creditor can demand that the surviving spouse use the decedent's half of the value of the painting to satisfy that debt.

Which brings us to the question of whether the painting really is Community Property. If the wife can prove that the painting was purchased with monies she owned prior to the marriage, then the painting is her own Separate Property and it is not accessible to pay the decedent's debts. But if the painting was purchased with monies she earned during the marriage, then it is Community Property and half of the value of the painting will go toward payment of the decedent's debt.

A Will Is Not Enough In Texas

This example illustrates the need for keeping a record that identifies Separate Property. It may not be an issue where all of the property owned by the couple is Community Property, but it is a different matter should there be a significant difference in the amount each person brings to the marriage; or receives as a gift or inheritance during the marriage.

The reader may be thinking that it is easy enough to identify Separate Property by titling property in one name only. But if one party buys a car or real property and does not put the name of his/her spouse on the title to the property, it does not necessarily mean that the property is Separate Property. It could be Community Property under the sole management and control of the partner who holds title.

To identify Separate Property, there needs to be a paper trail showing that the car or residence was purchased with money owned by the buyer prior to the marriage; or from a gift or an inheritance. An accountant, financial planner, or attorney can help you set up a record that can be quickly produced should a creditor demand payment for your spouse's debts.

That record is especially important should one of you die without a Will. As explained in Chapter 1, the Laws of Descent apply to the decedent's half of the Community Property, and all of his Separate Property. Having a record that identifies Community Property and Separate property will make it easier to Probate the Estate.

With or without a Will, there can be a problem if a married person dies with much debt and no Separate Property. Theoretically, if the decedent came into the marriage with nothing and contributed little to the marriage, there may be little, if any, Community Property available to pay his debts. No doubt a creditor will not see things that way. The creditor knows that there could be property held in the name of the surviving spouse that is really Community Property.

The creditor has the right to ask the Probate Court to order an accounting to determine whether any of the property held by the spouse is Community Property (Probate 156, 461). Having good financial records will make it easy for the surviving spouse to identify his/her Separate Property. It might even head off the need for an accounting.

JOINT DEBTS

A *joint debt* is a debt that two or more people are responsible to pay. Usually the contract or promissory note signed by the borrowers makes them *jointly and severally liable* for the debt. This means they both agree to pay the debt and each of them, individually, agrees to pay the debt. A joint debt can also be in the form of monies owed by one person with payment guaranteed by another person. If the person who owes the money does not pay, the *guarantor* (the person who guaranteed payment) is responsible to pay the debt. And as just discussed, if a married couple own Joint Community Property, the debts of either partner can be considered to be joint debts regardless of whether they both agreed to pay for the debt.

Should you die, your hospital bills, nursing home bills, funeral expenses, legal fees for the Probate of your Estate, are all debts of your Estate. For a single decedent, they are not joint debts unless someone guaranteed payment for the monies owed.

JOINT PROPERTY BUT NO JOINT DEBT

Suppose you are single and you have a joint bank account with right of survivorship with your son. If you have a credit card in your name only, should you die, can the credit card company require that your share of the joint funds be set aside to pay the debt? The answer to the question is "yes," but only if there is not enough money in your Estate to pay for that debt. Your creditor will need to make a written demand for payment. The Personal Representative can then ask the surviving joint owner of your bank account to contribute as much as he inherited from the account to pay the bill (Probate 442).

This same rule applies if you are married. If you own a joint account with someone other than your spouse, if there are no other assets available to pay your debts, or if there is not enough to pay for the Family Allowance, the Personal Representative can demand your share of the bank account be used to settle your Estate

BANK CAN TAKE MONEY OWED FROM ACCOUNT
In 1992, the Supreme Court of Texas ruled that a bank has the right to take money owed to them by a decedent depositor from the depositor's account without going through a Probate procedure — even if the debt is not yet due and payable (*Bandy v First State Bank Overton Texas*, 835 S.W.2d 609 (Texas 1992)). In light of this ruling, you may want to borrow money from one bank, but keep your savings account and Certificates of Deposit in a different bank.

LOAN INSURANCE

Many mortgage companies offer mortgage insurance to their borrowers. Those who have a relatively low mortgage rate might consider having mortgage insurance on the life of the primary wage earner of the family. Even those with a higher rate might want to make the effort to purchase mortgage insurance if they are raising children. With such insurance, the family can inherit the homestead free of debt. The monthly insurance charge may be a small price to pay to ensure that the children can continue to live in their own home until they are grown.

Car loan insurance is still another thing to consider. If a married couple purchases (or leases) a car, and one of them dies, it may be a struggle for the other to pay off the loan. This was the case with Eva and Howard. Both had to work to support their three children. They owned two well used cars. It seemed that one car or the other was always in the shop. When they saw an advertisement for a *NO INTEREST* new car loan, they decided the offer was too good to pass up.

The monthly payments were high, but it was their only luxury. With both their salaries, they were able to make the payments. When Howard had his first heart attack, he was out of work for several weeks so they struggled to keep the payments current. Howard worked in construction, and was anxious to return to work. The doctors advised that such work might be too strenuous for his weakened heart. Construction work was all Howard knew, and the pay was good, so he ignored the warning and went back to his old job.

The second heart attack was fatal, leaving Eva as the sole means of support for her family.

With Howard gone there was no need for two cars. Eva could not afford the payments on the new car anyway, so she decided to sell it. Unfortunately, what she could get for the car was significantly less than the balance owed. Once she fell behind in payments she decided to surrender the car rather than have them repossess it. She was sure they would understand, considering all that she had been through these past several months, not to mention that she was a widow with three small children.

They didn't understand.

The company took the car and then sued for the balance of monies owed. The judge was sympathetic, but under the law there is no "life is tough" defense. He ruled that Eva had to pay the monies owed; and, as per the terms of the loan agreement, she even had to pay the fees for the company's attorney and all court costs. What an emotional and financial nightmare!

The pity was, it all could have been avoided, had they worked payment of debts into their Estate Plan. Howard was the primary driver of the new car and the primary wage earner. All he had to do was put the loan in his name only, and take out loan insurance. Eva would have inherited the car, debt free. She could have kept it or sold it as she saw fit.

PURCHASING LIFE INSURANCE

The good part of purchasing loan insurance — be it credit card insurance, mortgage insurance or car insurance, is that you can usually purchase the insurance without taking a medical examination. The down side is that companies generally do not offer such insurance to those over the age of 65; and for those under 65 the cost of the insurance is a factor. It usually costs more to purchase loan insurance than a life insurance policy. Those in fairly good health need to comparison shop. If it is your goal to have insurance cover all of your outstanding debts, then the cost of a single life insurance policy may be much less than purchasing several loan insurance policies. If you want the insurance funds used to pay your debts, you can name your Estate as the beneficiary of your policy.

The Estate Planning strategy of purchasing life insurance to pay off all of your loans works best if you are married and your spouse is jointly liable for your debts. If you name your spouse as beneficiary of the life insurance policy, (s)he can use the life insurance funds to pay off all monies owed.

If you name your spouse (or anyone else) as beneficiary of your insurance policy, and that person has no legal obligation to pay your debts, none of your creditors can ask your beneficiary to use the insurance funds to pay your debts (Insur. 1108.051).

There are a few exceptions to the rule, such as money you owe for back child support (see page 99). However, in general, if you want someone to inherit money after you are gone, and you do not want those funds reduced by the cost of Probate or to pay off your debts, naming that person as beneficiary of the insurance proceeds should accomplish your goal.

If you want the insurance funds used to pay your debts, then you need to name your Estate as beneficiary of your policy. If you want someone to inherit money after you are gone, and you do not want those funds reduced by the cost of Probate or to pay off your debts, then naming that person as beneficiary of the insurance proceeds should accomplish your goal.

With or without debt, you may be wondering about life insurance — should you have it? How much is enough? The answer to these questions depends on the "sleep at night" factor, namely how much insurance do you need so that you won't worry about insurance coverage when you go to sleep at night? It is often more an emotional than a financial issue.

Some people have an "every man for himself" attitude and are content to have no life insurance at all. When they die, whatever they have, they have. And that is what their heirs will inherit. Others worry about how their loved ones will manage if they are not around to support them, and decide to purchase enough insurance to maintain their dependents in their accustomed life style. The same person may have different thoughts about insurance coverage as circumstances change — from no coverage in his bachelor days to more-than-enough coverage in his child rearing days to just-enough-to-bury-me in his senior years.

Insurance companies recognize that people's needs change over the years. Many companies offer flexible insurance coverage. As with any consumer item, it is a good idea to shop around. In addition to the problem of how much life insurance to carry, there is the concern of how the monies will be spent. Leaving a large sum of money to a person who is less than prudent, may lead to a spending spree.

ANNUITIES TO SPREAD THE INHERITANCE

Most beneficiaries go through their inheritance within two years. For many, the reason the money is gone so soon, is that there just wasn't much money to inherit in the first place. But for others, it's a spending frenzy. Luckily, people are fairly consistent in their spending habits, so you probably know in advance whether your intended beneficiary will "go wild," or prudently invest the monies he inherits.

If you want to leave an insurance policy benefit to someone you love, but the intended beneficiary is immature, or a born spendthrift, then a simple solution to the problem may be to purchase an *Annuity* rather than a life insurance policy with a single lump sum payment. You can purchase an Annuity from an insurance company so that upon your death (the *Annuitant*) receives money on a regular basis (monthly, quarterly, yearly) rather than one large payment. Hopefully, this regular source of income will encourage your beneficiary to think ahead, and learn to budget his finances.

In addition to spreading out the inheritance, you can protect some of the monies from the claims of the creditors of your beneficiary. In Texas, monies received by your beneficiary under an Annuity contract is exempt from the claims of his creditors — with the exception of a judgment for back child support payments (Insur. 1108.051, 1108.052). This means that the creditor cannot force the insurance company to pay the Annuity to the creditor instead of the beneficiary. Of course, once the beneficiary receives the annuity, he can use some, or all of it to pay monies that he may owe.

SOME THINGS ARE CREDITOR PROOF

The next question to consider is whether you can leave property to your family free of the claims of your creditors. We already noted that if you are married, all of your Separate Property and your Joint Community Property is available to pay your debts. Your spouse is personally responsible to pay for your necessities, but not for any other debt you may owe.

Even though you may die with more debts than money, there are still things that can be inherited by your spouse (and others) free from the claims of your creditors:

✧ INSURANCE AND ANNUITY PROCEEDS ✧

The beneficiary of the proceeds of your life, health or accident insurance policy, including annuity or benefit plans, takes the proceeds free from the claims of your creditors, and the creditors of your beneficiary. There is no limit on the value of the policy (Insur. 1108.051). However, there are a few exceptions.

⇨ back child support

The insurance proceeds are available to pay a judgment for back child support.

⇨ policy used as collateral

If you or your beneficiary used the insurance policy or its proceeds as collateral for the payment of a debt, the proceeds are available to pay that debt.

⇨ purchase to defraud creditors.

The exemption does not apply if you purchased the policy to defraud your creditors, i.e., you used the money to buy insurance instead of paying money that you owed (Insur. 1108.053)

✧ PENSION PLANS ✧

All government retirement plans and annuities, and those retirement plans as described by Section 403(b) or 408A of the Internal Revenue Code of 1986, including IRA accounts are creditor proof (Gov't 811.005, Property 42.0021).

Monies received by a beneficiary of such plans are protected from the decedent's creditors with the exception of income taxes.

NO EXEMPTION FOR TAXES

In general, income taxes are not paid when money is placed in a retirement plan. Taxes are paid when the monies are withdrawn from the account regardless of whether the monies are withdrawn by the retiree or the person he named as beneficiary of the retirement plan. If your beneficiary inherits money from your pension, retirement allowance, or annuity, he may need to pay federal income taxes on those monies.

Texas law does not allow another state to place a claim on your retirement plan for income taxes owed in that state. This means that another state will not be able to collect income taxes from your retirement plan or from any other property you own that is located within the state of Texas (Property 44.003).

✧ THE HOMESTEAD EXEMPTION ✧

The constitution of the state of Texas extends creditor rotection for the primary residence of a resident of Texas (Texas Constitution Article XVI, section 50). The extent of creditor protection depends on whether the property is located in a rural or urban area. An *urban homestead* is one located within the limits of a town or city. Creditor protection extends to up to 10 acres of land adjacent to the urban homestead. The extent of creditor protection for a rural homestead depends on whether you are single or married. Creditor protection, for a single adult person extends to up to 100 acres of rural land and up to 200 acres for the married homeowner (Property 41.001, 41.002).

The *Homestead Exemption* is unlimited, meaning that even if your home is worth a million dollars, a creditor cannot force the sale of your home. However, there are exceptions to this rule. For example, creditor protection does not extend to delinquent taxes, mortgages or mechanic's liens.

The Homestead Exemption continues after your death provided you are survived by a spouse, minor child or an unmarried adult child living with the family. In such case, the beneficiary of the homestead will inherit your homestead free from the claims of creditors (other than taxes, mortgages and/or mechanic's liens). The beneficiary of your home does not need to be your surviving spouse or child. Texas Courts have ruled that creditor protection continues, no matter who inherits the homestead, just so long as the decedent is survived by a spouse, minor child or single adult child living with the family (*Nat'l Union Fire Insur. v. Olson*, 920 S.W. 2d 458 (Texas, 1996)). Of course, if you are not survived by any of these family members, once you die, your creditors can demand that your homestead be sold to pay your debts.

✧ PERSONAL PROPERTY EXEMPTION ✧

In the state of Texas, certain personal items are exempt from the claims of creditors. Unlike the homestead exemption, there is a limit on the value of the protected items. For a single adult, the protected amount is $30,000. For a family, the amount is $60,000 (Property 42.001). Exempt personal property includes:

⇨   home furnishings, including family heirlooms

⇨   clothing, tools, books, boats

⇨   two firearms

⇨   athletic and sporting equipment, including bicycles

⇨   a motor vehicle for each family member who drives

⇨   jewelry, not to exceed 25% of the protected amount

⇨   pets and certain farm animals.

Creditor protection does not apply to money owed on a given item, for example, a car loan must be paid, or the creditor can take the car (Property 42.002).

This personal property exemption does not continue after the owner is deceased, however if the decedent was married, the exemption of these items continues for the surviving spouse.

The surviving spouse is also entitled to take his/her Family Allowance free from the claims of creditors, with the exception of up to $15,000 for the payment of the decedent's funeral and last illness. Specifically, the first $15,000 must be used to pay for the funeral and cost of the last illness. Second in line is payment for the Family Allowance. No other bill can be paid until the surviving spouse and/or minor child have received the amount awarded by the Court for their Allowance (Probate 322).

AN ESTATE PLAN FOR THE BANKRUPT

You may think the above title to be an oxymoron (a contradiction in terms). If a person is bankrupt, why plan for an Estate he doesn't have? But facts are, that people who file for bankruptcy are often quite wealthy and that is their downfall. Because they have substantial income or property, banks and people are willing to lend them money. If more money is borrowed than can be repaid, the unhappy result is bankruptcy. In the event you are concerned about meeting your responsibilities as parent or spouse, yet you enjoy a life style of financial brinksmanship, consider investing in items that are "creditor proof."

That's exactly what Alan decided to do. Alan was astute, well aware of his strengths and weaknesses. He enjoyed his work and knew he had the capacity to earn large sums of money. But he also knew he was a gambler. Not the Las Vegas type, but a gambler in business ventures. "No risk, no gain" was one of his favorite sayings.

If you charted Alan's net worth over the years it would look like the peaks and valleys of the NASDAQ. Lots of high highs and low lows. Unfortunately, he married a woman who did not share his adventurous spirit. His wife became increasingly intolerant of their financial instability. She came to realize that this was his life style and things would never change. "All gamblers die broke," she said as she walked out the door with their 5 year old daughter in tow.

That, and the fact that he had to declare bankruptcy, brought Alan up short; and he began to be concerned about his future and that of his family.

Alan talked things over with his bankruptcy attorney "I am a good businessman, but not a clairvoyant. There was no way to predict the turn of events that led to this situation. But I know I will bounce back, and it will just be a matter of time before I earn my next fortune. I also know that I am an entrepreneur and not a 9 to 5 type guy so this could happen again. What concerns me is how to provide some security for my child in case something happens to me before she is grown."

"There are many items here in Texas that are creditor proof. Your Homestead Exemption is unlimited. You daughter can inherit your home free from the claims of your creditors. You could put money into a federal retirement plan such as an IRA or Keogh account, and your daughter can inherit that free of your debts.

Alan didn't think that would work. "I am my own boss, but I don't have the self discipline to put money aside each month for my retirement."

The attorney suggested "You could purchase a life insurance policy and your daughter will inherit the proceeds free of your debts. I don't recommend you buy the policy right now. If you purchase the policy when you are insolvent (i.e., you owe more than you own), and then die, your creditors can demand that the monies paid for the policy (plus interest) be given to them and not to your daughter (Insur. 1108.051, 1108.053). But only the premium (what you paid for the policy) is at risk. If the premium is just a small part of the proceeds, then maybe this is not of concern to you."

Alan mentioned that he had separated from his wife and was thinking of moving out of state.

The attorney cautioned "There is much creditor protection here in Texas, but many other states have little protection."

Alan was curious "What do people in those state do to protect their property?"

"Well some — the very wealthy — set up Offshore Trusts."

How does that work?"

"They put their money into a Trust. When they do so, they essentially give up control of that money."

Alan was skeptical "Oh come now. Why would anyone put his money where he can't get to it?"

The attorney explained "The Trust can be set up so that funds are available for whatever the millionaire wants. Usually funds are made available to support his family. Trust funds can be used to maintain the family home or yacht. Monies from the Trust can be used to pay for travel or for an expensive vacation. And of course the Trust would provide for the transfer of the property to the millionaire's beneficiaries, once the millionaire dies. What the millionaire can't do is be the Trustee of the Trust, because if he were, he would have control over the money, and his creditors could take legal action here in the United States to force him to use his Trustee powers 8 to use that money to pay his creditors."

"How can they force the issue? Why couldn't he, as Trustee, just refuse?"

"Remember, that as long as the millionaire is a citizen of the United States, and he is physically present in the states, he is subject to the laws of this country. If a creditor goes to Court and wins, the U.S. judge could order the millionaire, as Trustee, to use Trust funds to pay that debt. If the millionaire-Trustee refused, the judge could put him in jail for contempt of Court. No, for an Offshore Trust to work, the Trust must be a foreign Trust, that is, drafted according to the laws of a foreign country, Trust property must be located outside of the United States, and the Trustee cannot be a citizen of the United States."

Alan said "Well I guess the millionaire might have a relative who is not a U.S. citizen to manage the Trust."

The attorney agreed "Yes, or he could use a financial institution that does not do business in the U.S., to manage the funds. But there are other problems with an Offshore Trust. There's the safety factor. Trust funds are kept outside of the United States. If the funds are kept in a foreign bank and the country suffers an economic collapse, then those funds could be lost."

Alan wondered "Isn't that much the same risk as money in a U.S. bank? Only $100,000 of the cash in a U. S. bank account is insured. If the bank fails, any money in that bank over $100,000 could be lost."

The attorney disagreed "Our U.S government is stable, and we trust that they will regulate U.S. banks and keep our money safe. But that is not the case with other small countries. The government of a small country could collapse and the banks along with it."

"But why keep money in a bank? Most millionaires have their funds invested in stocks and bonds, or in real property."

The attorney agreed "True, but real estate could be risky. If your Trust contains real property located within the United States, your creditor could go to a U.S. court and take that property."

Alan wondered "Couldn't the creditor take the overseas property as well?"

"He could, but it would be hard. For one thing he would need to find the property. And the Trustee is not about to tell him where it is, unless the creditor sues, and the laws of that foreign country require the Trustee to tell. Even if the creditor locates Trust property, whether it is stocks, bonds, or real estate, most Offshore Trusts are established in countries that are not creditor friendly. For example, if you set up an Offshore Trust in the Cook Islands, they will not accept a judgment that a creditor won in the United States. The creditor will need to employ a Cook Islands attorney to sue you all over again in the Cook Islands. That's expensive. And the Cook Islands have a higher standard of proof. Here in the U.S., all your creditor need do is show that you owe the money *by a preponderance of the evidence.* That's lawyer talk for "the jury must be more than 50% sure you owe the money." In the Cook Islands, the creditor's attorney must prove you owe the money *beyond a reasonable doubt* (Cook Islands, International Trusts Act of 1984 Section 13B(1)). That standard is the one we use here in the U.S. for criminal cases. In addition, the foreign country usually has a short Statute of Limitations, so if your creditor does not sue you in that country within that period of time, he cannot sue you at all."

Alan said "I can see why Offshore Trusts are so popular."

The attorney cautioned "But there are other problems. The U.S. considers transfers into and/or out of the Trust to be taxable. The IRS requires special tax returns to be filed for all foreign Trusts. In addition, the IRS looks closely at Offshore Trusts to determine whether they are fraudulent transfers, designed to avoid U.S. income taxes or U.S. Estate taxes. The IRS wants to be sure that the creditor the millionaire is avoiding isn't Uncle Sam!"

Alan said "Yes, but if you pay your taxes, that shouldn't be a problem. If I ever get to the point where I am that wealthy, I'll come back to discuss setting up an Offshore Trust."

The attorney refused "No, I'm just a country lawyer. If you want to go that route, you need a specialist — someone who has overseas connections, and who has experience in writing such Trusts. If you are serious about setting up an Offshore Trust, let me know and I will recommend someone to you."

"O.K. I will."

The attorney offered a final word of caution "If you are able to accumulate a significant amount of money, don't risk it all in a business venture. Limit the amount of money you can lose to just the money that you invest in business. Keep your personal funds separate and protected from your business debts. If you want to start a business, make sure that you cannot be personally liable for your business debts. You can avoid personal liability by forming a corporation, or a Limited Partnership, or a Limited Liability Company.** Stay away from a sole proprietorship or a business partnership."

** These topics are discussed in the next chapter.

Your Business Estate Plan 6

It would take a very thick book to do justice to the topic of Business Estate Planning. Estate Planning issues must be discussed for each type of business:

CONTROL	How to control and protect your business during your lifetime.
BENEFICIARY	How to be sure your business goes to the beneficiary of your choice.
COST	How to transfer your business to your beneficiary quickly and at lowest cost.

With just one chapter to devote to the topic, we can only provide the reader with an overview of the subject. Hopefully, the overview will give the reader some ideas that can later be pursued with a financial planner, or an attorney.

We have written this chapter for the reader who listed a business value as part of his Net Worth on page 4. People who are self employed, but who do not think of themselves as owners of a business, may profit from the information covered in this chapter, as well.

This chapter should also be of interest to someone who has the possibility of inheriting a business interest, such as the child of a small business owner, or perhaps the spouse of someone who is self employed. Even those who are thinking of starting a business, may find it worthwhile to take a few minutes to read this chapter.

Those who have no present business interest may want to skip this chapter and go on to Chapter 7.

Your business is your property, and as such it is included as part of your overall Estate Plan. But owning a business isn't as simple as just holding title to a tangible item such as a car or parcel of real estate. For example, if you own a business in your name only, i.e. as a **sole proprietor**, there may be no single document that indicates ownership of your business property.

If you are doing business under a name other than your own, you probably filed an *Assumed Business or Professional Name Certificate* with the Office of the County Clerk stating the name of the business and identifying you as the owner of the business (Bus. & Com. 36.10). However, that Certificate does not identify your business property. You could own a truck, computer, copier or other expensive business equipment. Title to that property is probably in your personal name.

Your business bank account may be in your name only, or in the Trade Name of the business with you alone as signatory on the account. Charge cards and business loans are either in your name only, or in the Trade Name with your name as guarantor.

If you want to leave your business to your son, how do you do it? Do you leave him the equipment used in the business? If you are doing business under your own name and not a registered Trade Name or Trade Mark, how do you give him that name? And how do you handle business related loans? If you leave him the business, will he agree to be responsible for outstanding business debts?

In addition to providing for the transfer of your business, you need to make provision for its operation in the event of your incapacity or death. If you do not make such provision, a Court may need to make that decision for you. In particular, if you become incapacitated, it may be necessary to have a Court appoint a Guardian to operate your business (Probate 693). If you die, and have not provided for the transfer or continued operation of the business, the Court may need to authorize your Personal Representative to operate the business until it can be transferred to the proper beneficiary (Probate 234).

A partnership can be even more complicated, unless there is a written Partnership Agreement that says how the business is to be transferred in the event one of the partners dies. Even the transfer of a corporation can be a major headache if there are several shareholders and no shareholders' agreement to say how shares should be transferred in the event of the death of a shareholder.

For these reasons, it is important to think about an Estate Plan for your business. You need to ask yourself:

How can I have maximum protection and control over my business during my lifetime?

How can I ensure that my business continues to operate in the event of my incapacity?

How can I structure my business so that it can be transferred quickly and at minimum cost to my beneficiaries?

We will examine each type of business ownership as it relates to these questions.

Those who read the first five chapters know us well enough not to expect a definitive answer to the above question. Our job, as we see it, is to explain the rules of the game (i.e., Texas law) to the reader. Once you know how things work in Texas, you can make an informed decision as to the type of business ownership that best accomplishes your goal.

> ## SOLE PROPRIETORSHIP
> ## Maximum control — Maximum liability

You are the boss if you do business in your name only, but you take full personal responsibility for any loss suffered by the company; and as explained, you may need to consult with an attorney if you want to make arrangements for someone to take over your business should you become incapacitated or die.

Because of this personal liability issue, many people think it best to form a corporation as soon as they start their business. That may not be the best strategy. It takes money to form a corporation. You may need to pay an attorney to set up the corporation. Each year you need to file an annual report and pay a Franchise Tax** to the Comptroller of Public Accounts (Tax 171.001, 171.202).

** However, as of January 1, 2008, the Franchise Tax and annual report will extend to all companies doing business in the state of Texas.

There may be additional accounting fees associated with doing business as a corporation. Each year you will need to file a separate corporate income tax return.

You do not need to pay a filing fees to form a sole proprietorship, and you do not need to file a separate income tax return. You can include your business income as part of your personal income tax return and not go through the cost and hassle of filing a separate corporate return.

Another reason to start business as a sole proprietorship is the risk of failure. Although every new business owner thinks his venture must surely culminate in riches, research conducted by the Brandow Company shows that only 55% of new businesses get to celebrate their third birthday (see their data at www.brandow.com). You can always form a corporation should your business succeed. If the business does not succeed, then at least you didn't waste time, effort and money to form a corporation.

But What About My Personal Liability?

Many people seek to limit their personal liability by forming a corporation, however, that doesn't always work in the real world. For example, if you wish to rent a store front or office space, an experienced landlord will allow you to lease the space in the corporate name, but he will require you to sign as a guarantor. Should the business fail, he will have the right to sue you, personally, for the full value of the lease. Once you have established a successful business, the landlord may agree to just hold the business liable; and in that case having a corporation instead of a sole proprietorship will limit your personal liability.

Regardless of what form of business ownership you choose, you can be held personally liable for any fraudulent or negligent act that you commit. The way to avoid personal liability for fraudulent acts is not to willfully (deliberately) deceive or cheat anyone.

Most of us are honest folk, but negligence is another matter. We all make mistakes. The way to limit your liability for negligence is to purchase insurance that provides protection for mistakes and accidents. For example, if you open a title insurance business, you can purchase an Errors and Omissions insurance policy to cover a loss caused by a mistake you might make in a title search. If you have a business involving the care of a person (adult or child day care center, nurse practitioner, etc.), it is important to have coverage for an injury to a client due to accident or negligence.

If you have a business location (a storefront or office) consider purchasing a comprehensive business insurance policy to cover injury to anyone who visits your business, as well as damages to the premises. For example, if you open a flower shop you can get insurance to cover an injury to a customer who slips and falls. The same policy can cover vandalism to your shop, such as a broken plate glass window. You can be compensated for loss should a storm cause the electricity to go out and your shipment of fresh cut flowers wilt for lack of refrigeration.

The purpose of any business insurance policy is to shift the risk of a business loss from your pocket to that of the insurance company.

And the downside is . . .
The problem with insurance is the greater the risk, the greater the cost. We all would like 100% insurance coverage, but few of us can afford the premium. What holds true for life insurance holds true for business insurance. The right amount of insurance coverage for you is the amount that allows you to sleep at night.

BUSINESS PARTNERSHIP
Shared control — Maximum liability

A business partnership is much like a marriage. You can both start out with the best of intentions, only to find that you are hopelessly incompatible. The break-up of a business partnership can be just as bitter and hotly contested as the breakup of a marriage. A properly drafted Partnership Agreement is a must — not only to set the terms of a dissolution, but to clearly state what is expected of each partner; i.e., how much each will contribute to the business venture in terms of effort or financing.

The Partnership Agreement should cover what will happen to the partner's share in the event of his incapacity or death. Most Partnership Agreements provide for an appraisal of the business and the buy out of the deceased (or disabled) partner's share. The Partnership Agreement may need to be backed up with financing. For example, you could sign a Partnership Agreement that requires the company to buy out your partnership interest should you become disabled or die. But what good is the Agreement if there is not enough cash in the company to pay for the buy out?

You will have better protection if the Partnership Agreement requires the company to maintain disability and life insurance to pay for the buy out. Many insurance companies offer Key man insurance. The policy is designed to compensate the company for the loss of someone who is essential to the continuation of the business. If sufficient insurance is purchased, the proceeds of the policy can be used to cover any loss suffered by the company and to buy out the share of the company that was owned by the deceased or disabled partner.

The sole proprietorship and the partnership are the earliest type of business organization. Texas laws governing these types of business organizations have their roots in English Common Law. Common law requires the sole proprietor and each business partner to take full personal responsibility for the debts of the company. As people became ever more litigious (lawyer talk for "sue happy") businessmen sought to limit their liability and prevailed on the legislature to create a form of business ownership to limit that liability.

Legislatures in each state responded to that need by giving businessmen the right to create a company (the corporation) with an identity separate from the owners of the business. By doing business as a corporation, the businessman's liability is limited to the money he invests in the company. A person can sue the corporation for business debts, but not the owners of the corporation.

This does not mean that a corporate owner can use the corporation to do things that are fraudulent. If he does, he can be held personally liable. The owner of the corporation cannot use the corporation as a "veil" to cover his wrongdoing. The Court of Appeals of the state of Texas ruled that Courts in Texas have authority to "pierce the corporate veil" and hold officers, directors and/or shareholders personally liable whenever justice demands that they be held accountable for wrongful acts (*Weaver v. State,* 652 S.W. 420 (Tex. App. 1982)).

THE CORPORATION
flexible control — limited liability

Whoever forms a corporation (the *incorporator*) has maximum control over the corporation. He decides how the company will operate by having the Articles of Incorporation and the company By-laws prepared according to his specifications. He can keep full control of the company as the only shareholder, or he can distribute shares and give up as much control as he wishes. Transferring corporate ownership is simple. It is a matter of signing a stock certificate transferring the shares of stock in the company. You can have a Transfer On Death ("TOD") designation to a named beneficiary.

If you own shares of stock in your name only, without a TOD designation, your Personal Representative will transfer the shares to the proper beneficiary. But keeping shares in your name only may not be the best way to go if you own a majority of shares and operate the business yourself. If Probate is necessary, it may take several months before the shares are transferred to the proper beneficiary, meanwhile, someone needs to continue to operate the business. If you do not leave directions for the continuation of the business, the Personal Representative (or the Probate Court) may decide it is best to just sell the company and give the proceeds of the sale to your beneficiaries.

The better route is to have your attorney prepare a Revocable Living Trust and transfer the shares into the Trust. The Trust document can give your Successor Trustee specific instructions about how the business is to be managed or transferred should you become incapacitated or die. Still another important benefit is to avoid the need to Probate what may be your only valuable asset.

THE LIMITED PARTNERSHIP

Just as a sole proprietor can limit his liability by forming a corporation, the partners of a general partnership can limit their liability by converting the partnership to a *Limited Partnership*. As with the corporation, the Limited Partnership is a creation of the legislature and is regulated by Texas law. The name of the Limited Partnership must identify it as a Limited Partnership (Bus. Org. 5.055). A Certificate of Limited Partnership must be filed with the TEXAS SECRETARY OF STATE (Bus. Org. 153.104, 153.105).

The structure of a Limited Partnership differs from a general partnership. In a general partnership, each partner has full authority to conduct business on behalf of the partnership. Each partner is personally liable for monies owed by the partnership, regardless of whether that partner actually incurred the debt. The Limited Partnership has *General Partners* and *Limited Partners*. Only a General Partner has authority to conduct partnership business and only a General Partner is liable for company debts. A Limited Partner has no control over the management of the company and has no personal liability for company debts.

But even a General Partner can avoid personal liability by forming a corporation, and then letting the corporation serve as the sole General Partner. An unpaid creditor of the Limited Partnership can sue the corporate General Partner, but not the shareholders of the corporation. Liability can be limited to the amount of money invested in the business venture. None of the owners will have personal liability. Of course, as with the corporation, all parties can be held personally liable for fraudulent or criminal acts performed in their partnership capacity.

The astute reader might be wondering "Why would anyone form a corporation (and pay all of the costs to set up the corporation) and then make the corporation the General Partner of a Limited Partnership (after paying all that money to set up the Partnership)? If limited business liability is the goal, why not just form a corporation?"

Answers to those questions are many and in fact, far removed from the original goal of limiting the business risk of the partners to just the money they invested in the business. The Limited Partnership can be used as a means of transferring a family business to the children with some significant tax benefits. For example, suppose Mom & Pop run a small, highly profitable, rapidly expanding, gourmet chocolate shop. They have two children, both in college. Right now, the business is worth about $500,000, but they figure that by the time they retire, the business could be worth millions. If their children inherit the business at that time, there could be significant Estate Taxes due. Also, because they are making lots of money right now, they are paying very high income taxes.

Both problems can be solved with a Family Limited Partnership. Mom and Pop can be the General Partners of the company and retain total control. They can make each child a Limited Partner by transferring shares of the business worth less than the Annual Gift Tax Exclusion. In the year 2007, each parent may gift up to $12,000. Together Mom and Pop can gift shares of the partnership up to $24,000 per child, per year. By gifting a percentage of the business each year, the parents can eventually transfer all of the business to the children. When the parents die, there will be no Gift or Estate Tax because the children already own the business. Of course there is still the problem of the Capital Gains Tax should the children decide to sell the business.

Regardless of how much of the company they give away, Mom and Pop can keep total control of the company because they are General Partners. When the parents are ready to retire, one or both of the children can take over as General Partner — but if making chocolate is not their thing, the parents can arrange to have a corporation manage the Limited Partnership and the children continue to receive income as limited partners. As for the current income tax problem, the children, as limited partners, are entitled to receive income from the business. Income paid to the children and their parents is generally taxed at a lower rate than the taxes to just Mom and Pop. For example, suppose the company earns $100,000. Mom and Pop will pay a high rate of income tax if they are the only two partners in the company. If the children become partners, then each partner can earn $25,000 and the overall bill for income taxes will be smaller.

Still another important advantage of the Family Limited Partnership over the corporation is creditor protection for the children's partnership interest. For example, suppose one of the children becomes a dentist, gets sued for malpractice, and loses the case. If Mom and Pop had incorporated the business and given the children most of the shares of stock in the company, the creditor could take the shares to satisfy the judgment. The creditor could wind up owning the company! Not so, with a Limited Partnership interest. A judge could order that the income from the Limited Partnership be used to pay the judgment, but he could not order the Partnership share itself to be given to the creditor unless the Limited Partnership Agreement allows for such transfer or they all agree (Bus. Org. 153.253, 153.256). Not likely with Mom and Pop as General Partners. They might even decide to use company income to pay themselves salary and not distribute anything to the hapless creditor!

We used an actual business as an example to explain how the Limited Partnership worked. It didn't take Estate Planning attorneys long to figure out that the "family business" could be just income producing items (such as stocks and bonds) that Mom and Pop placed into the Limited Partnership. The family "business" could be just the business of earning income. In other words, the Family Limited Partnership (or even a Family Partnership) could just be a type of an Estate Plan created solely for the purpose of transferring assets to the children to avoid paying Estate Taxes, and to pay less in income taxes.

It didn't take the IRS long to challenge this method of Estate Planning. A series of IRS rulings and court cases followed, with the main issue being whether a bona fide business partnership existed.

There is a common sense rule of evidence that says "If it looks like a duck and walks like a duck, and quacks like a duck, it must be a duck." In 1946 the Supreme Court decided that whether a family partnership is really a business partnership for tax purposes, should be determined on a case by case basis; and that the IRS should use the "walk and quack" test. Only the justices said this in proper legal terms. They said to determine whether a partnership exists depends on ". . .whether the partners really and truly intended to join together for the purpose of carrying on a business and sharing in the profits or losses or both. And their intention in this respect is a question of fact, to be determined from testimony disclosed by their agreement, considered as a whole, and by their conduct in execution of its provisions" (*Commissioner v. Tower*, 327 U.S. 280 (1946)).

THE LIMITED LIABILITY COMPANY

The IRS continues to take a close look at family partnerships, and will challenge any tax break if the family partnership (limited or not) does not meet the basic requirement of being a bona fide business partnership. Perhaps in response to IRS challenges, in the 1990s each of the 50 states, and even the District of Columbia, passed laws enabling residents of their state to form a new business entity called a *Limited Liability Company* ("LLC").

This new entity is not required to be a profit making venture. In Texas, an LLC can be formed to carry on any lawful business (Art. 1528n Rev. Civ. Stat. Art. 2.01). A Texas LLC is formed by filing a *Certificate of Formation* with the Texas Secretary of State (Bus. Org. 101.051). The LLC combines the better features of the Limited Partnership and the Corporation. Like the corporation, it can be formed by a single person who sets the rules of the company when he forms the corporation (Bus. Org. 101.101). The set of rules is called an *Operating Agreement*.

The LLC can be run by a manager (who is not a member of the company) or it can be run by a member or members of the company (Bus. Org. 101.251). As with a corporation, all members have limited liability, regardless of whether that member happens to be managing the company (Bus. Org. 101.113). As with a Limited Partnership, a creditor cannot take possession or control of a share of the company owned by a member unless the company regulations allow for such transfer or all members agree (Bus. Org. 101.111, 101.112). In the absence of these, the most the creditor can do is get a court to assign income generated by that share to the creditor (Bus. Org. 101.110).

Now Mom and Pop can form a LLC, give away some or all of the shares of the company during their lifetime, and still keep control of the company, and with no more personal liability than a non-managing member of the Limited Liability Company.

Transfers into the Limited Liability Company can be made so that there are no Estate or Gift Tax consequences. Income can be distributed to the children, or not, as Mom and Pop see fit.

The skeptic is probably thinking "Maximum control, limited liability, easily transferred to my beneficiaries, no Estate Tax. This is too good to be true. There must be a catch somewhere."

And so there is. It's called the Capital Gains Tax. If you transfer property during your lifetime, that property is valued by the IRS as of the date of transfer. If you gift a share of the Limited Liability Company during your lifetime, your beneficiary will take your basis in the property (i.e., the value that you paid for your interest in the Company). If you sell the share to your beneficiary, the basis is the fair market value of the share as of the date of purchase. Either way, once the beneficiary decides to sell the property, there may be a significant Capital Gains Tax due.

An experienced Estate Planning attorney should be able to suggest any number of ways to solve the problem, including purchasing life insurance to pay the tax.

Regardless of what form of business ownership you have, you need to think about what will happen to your business in the event of your incapacity or death. And in particular, how company debts will be paid. If your business is highly leveraged (business talk for "owes lots of money"), you also need to consider how those loans will be paid should you become disabled or die. One solution is to purchase Key man insurance. As explained earlier, Key man insurance is protection for the company against the loss of a valuable employee. The company purchases the policy and the proceeds are paid to the company to compensate it for the loss; but ultimately the policy benefits those who inherit the business.

Taxes are still another concern. Your business may be worth millions on paper, and your Estate Taxes will be based on that value. Your heirs might be forced to sell the company just to pay the taxes, but without your leadership they may get only a fraction of the value of the company.

Even if the federal government decides to eliminate federal Estate Taxes, the state of Texas, or any other state where you have a business location, may decide to levy its own Estate or Inheritance Tax.

And there is still the problem of the Capital Gains Tax. No one in Congress is talking about doing away with the Capital Gains Tax — and that tax could be sizeable. One solution to the problem of an unknown Estate Tax and/or Capital Gains Tax is to purchase life insurance that can be used to pay for any Estate Tax that may be due upon your death and any Capital Gains Tax that may be due when your beneficiary sells the property he inherits.

That may sound like a good, simple, solution, but you need to think things through before calling your insurance agent. The first question being:

How much insurance should I purchase?

That is a tough question. If you are in good health, who knows what will happen before you die. Will your business increase in value or go bust? Will the federal government really do away with Estate Taxes or will they do nothing and allow the tax to be reinstated in 2011?

The last question is particularly troublesome. Under today's tax law, if you purchase a life insurance policy, or even control the benefits of the policy, all of the proceeds of the policy will be counted as part of your taxable Estate. You may be buying insurance just to pay more in taxes to Uncle Sam.

You don't need a soothsayer or psychic to solve the problem. A financial planner with access to computer generated models can predict your life expectancy, how much your business will be worth when you retire and even the probability that the economy will require Estate Taxes to be reinstated!

Suppose your financial planner predicts that Estate Taxes will be reinstated and that your heirs will probably need to pay one million dollars in federal and state Estate Taxes. If you purchase a million dollar insurance policy, the proceeds of the policy will be included in your Estate. If there is an Estate Tax of 40% your heirs will net only $600,000 of the million dollar policy, with the rest going to pay for Estate Taxes on the policy itself. Your heirs will need to come up with an additional $400,000 to make up for the original million dollars predicted as being necessary to pay your Estate Taxes. A solution to this dilemma is the IRREVOCABLE LIFE INSURANCE TRUST.

THE IRREVOCABLE LIFE INSURANCE TRUST

An *Irrevocable Life Insurance Trust* can be designed to provide money to pay any tax that may be due after your death. To be sure that the IRS does not count the proceeds of the Trust as part of your taxable Estate the Trust must meet the following requirements:

⇨ The Trust must be irrevocable.

⇨ You cannot be Trustee.

The Trust can be set up for the benefit of your child. In such case, the child can be Trustee of the Trust. The child, as Trustee, will purchase an insurance policy on your life. You may need to file a Gift Tax return if you give your child a large sum of money to purchase the policy. It is better to have the child purchase a policy that is paid in quarterly or annual premiums instead of a single lump sum payment. You can give the child an amount each year up to the Annual Gift Tax Exclusion ($12,000 in the year 2007) to pay for the premium. If you are married, you and your spouse can gift up to $24,000 per year without the need to file a Gift Tax return.

As tax laws change, the child/Trustee can use as much of the gift as is needed to purchase sufficient insurance to cover the taxes. The Trust can be set up to cover Estate taxes or Capital Gains taxes, or both. For example, the Trustee can purchase an insurance policy that pays a million dollars upon your death. Those insurance funds can be used to pay your Estate taxes. Should it happen that no Estate taxes are due, the Trustee can keep the monies invested until the business is sold. The Trust funds can be used to pay any Capital Gains Tax that may be due at that time. If monies are left over once all taxes are paid, they can be distributed to the named beneficiaries of the Trust.

Your attorney can design an Irrevocable Insurance Trust in any number of ways to meet the special needs of you and your family. For example, an Irrevocable Insurance Trust can be set up to solve problems described in the last Chapter. Alan wanted to leave insurance proceeds for his child but was concerned that the cash value of the policy could be taken by his creditors. A properly drafted Irrevocable Insurance Trust can solve such problem, because the Trust, and not Alan, is the owner of the policy.

Of course, it costs significant money to set up and maintain an Irrevocable Insurance Trust. Those who do not have concerns about creditors may wonder whether it's necessary to go through all that cost and bother if there will be no more Estate Taxes in the future. After all a simple life insurance policy can cover any Capital Gains Tax that may be due. But, as explained, the tax law as passed in 2001 reinstates the federal Estate Tax in 2011. If lawmakers take no further action, the Estate of anyone who dies on January 1, 2011, and thereafter is subject to a federal Estate Tax for an Estate over one million dollars.

Someone with an active imagination could envision the following scenario:

It is New Year's eve, 2010. A 97 year old lies sleeping, at his home, surrounded by his four grandchildren who are his sole heirs.

"He looks so peaceful."

"Yes. Surprising, considering that he has terminal cancer, failing kidneys and heart. His doctor says he can't last more than a few days. The doctor left a supply of morphine so that we can keep Gramps comfortable over the New Year's holiday. The doctor gave him a shot just before he left."

"The doctor said not to give Gramps another shot unless he was in pain. His heart is in such a weakened condition, he could easily overdose on morphine."

"Yes, of course."

"Too bad he didn't get a chance to do some Estate Planning before he had that stroke last year. "

"I thought his attorney took care of all that."

"His attorney suggested he set up an Irrevocable Insurance Trust to pay for any Estate Tax, but Gramps felt sure that Congress would pass a law that would permanently repeal the Estate Tax."

"I can't imagine Gramps coming to that conclusion. The economy is down and the government needs to raise taxes. It is easier for legislators to leave the law as written back in 2001, than take some affirmative action."

"Gramps was always a sharp business man, but in his later years his mind wasn't as clear as when he earned his five million dollars."

"Is that what we are going to inherit?"

"Not unless he dies before midnight. After midnight the Estate Tax is reinstated, and at a rate of 45%. Between state and federal taxes, we'll be lucky to come away with half a mill each."

"Gramps moved. I think he may be in pain."

"Yes, he does look uncomfortable."

"It isn't right to let him suffer like this."

"Yes, of course."

Continuing To Care

There are any number of reasons that people give for wanting to continue on with their lives. For the lucky ones, their main reason for living is that they are having a great time and don't want it to end. For many, it is more a sense of responsibility. During child rearing years the concern of the parent is what will happen to the child should the parent suddenly die. Once a child is grown, the roles often reverse, and it is the child worrying about what will happen to his parent if the child were not present to see to the care of the aging parent. Even pet lovers worry about what will happen to their pet should the owner no longer be around.

There is little that can be done to prepare those who depend on you for the loss of your companionship and emotional support; but there are many things you can do to provide financial support for those who rely on you. Even people of modest means can make financial provision so their loved ones will have an easy transition from being dependent to becoming self sufficient.

This chapter explains the many simple, and relatively inexpensive, things you can do to provide care for your loved ones should you not be present to do so yourself.

It doesn't happen very often, but both parents could die or become incapacitated before their child reaches adulthood. Most parents don't want to think about, much less prepare for such a happening. But in this age of postponing parenthood, many parents are in their fifties and sixties and still raising children. The probability of a life threatening illness increases with age, so parents need to understand the importance of planning ahead.

Parents with dangerous occupations also need to provide for the care of their minor child in the event of the disability or death of both parents. It is surprising to think of how many of us are employed in high risk occupations. Construction workers, military personnel, firemen, state and federal law enforcement agents, and in this day and age, even postal workers face hazards on a daily basis.

Regardless of the parent's age or occupation, planning for the care of a minor child should be part of every parent's Estate Plan, not only because it is the responsible thing to do, but also because it is relatively simple and inexpensive to do.

A child must be cared for in two ways, the *person* of the child and the *property* of the child. To care for the person of the child, someone must be in charge of the child's everyday living, not only food and shelter but also to provide social, ethical and religious training. Someone must have legal authority to make medical decisions and see to the child's education. To care for the child's property, someone must be responsible to see that monies left to the child are used for the care of the child and that anything left over is preserved until the child becomes an adult.

A Guardian will need to be appointed to care for the person and property of the child in the event that both parents become incapacitated or die before the child is grown.

USING A WILL TO APPOINT A GUARDIAN

As explained in Chapter 4, each parent can name someone in their Will to serve as Guardian of their minor child in the event that both parents are deceased. It is a good idea for both parents to name the same person to serve as Guardian. If the parents appoint different people for the job and then die simultaneously, it will be up to the judge to decide who is best suited to be Guardian. The Court will give top priority to the person named in the Will of the last parent to die.

USING A DECLARATION TO APPOINT A GUARDIAN

The problem with using a Will to appoint someone to be your child's Guardian, is that for the appointment to be effective, the Will must be admitted to Probate; i.e., the Court must determine that the Will is valid; and the person you chose as Guardian needs to file a petition to be appointed as the child's Guardian. It might take several weeks before that person has the legal authority to care for the child. A better solution is to sign a separate document entitled:

DECLARATION OF APPOINTMENT OF GUARDIAN FOR MY CHILDREN IN THE EVENT OF MY DEATH OR INCAPACITY

Texas Probate statute 677A gives a form that can be used to name someone to serve as the child's Guardian in the event both parents are deceased or incapacitated. You can copy the statute from your nearest law library, or you can download the statute from the Internet.

http://www.capital.state.tx.us/statutes

Each parent can sign a Declaration naming someone to serve as the child's Guardian and an alternate Guardian to serve in the event the other parent is incapacitated or deceased. Once the Declaration is properly signed and witnessed, it needs to be stored in the same place as other important documents.

The parent should notify the proposed Guardian of the appointment and the location of the signed Declaration. Should it ever be needed, the Guardian can file the Declaration with the Court. The Court will appoint the person chosen by the parent to serve as the child's legal Guardian, unless for some reason the chosen Guardian is unable or unwilling to serve (Probate 677A).

If you make no provision for the appointment of a Guardian for your minor child, should you and the other parent become incapacitated, or die, the judge will give priority to the child's grandparent. If there is no grandparent, but a surviving great-grandparent, that person will have priority to be appointed as Guardian. In the event there is no grandparent (or great-grandparent) who is willing or able to serve as Guardian, the judge will appoint the nearest next of kin. If there are two or more relatives with priority who wish to serve as Guardian, it will be up to the judge to decide who is best suited for the job. His primary concern will be whatever is in the best interests of the child (Probate 676).

It is simple and inexpensive to make your choice of Guardian known to the Court. All you need do is sign a Declaration and tell your choice of Guardian where to find the Declaration should it be needed. If you do not take the time to do so, the Guardian appointed by the Court may not be the person you would have chosen to raise your child.

THE BEST CHOICE OF GUARDIAN

Many parents never get around to appointing a Guardian for their minor child because they cannot come to an agreement as to the best choice of Guardian. "I think my mother should be Guardian. After all she raised me, and I turned out fine" can signal the opening salvo of a lengthy, and often unresolved battle. Not being able to agree on a choice of Guardian should not discourage you from appointing the person of your choice either as part of your Will or in a separate writing. The thing to keep in mind is that the Guardian of your choice will take over only if the other parent is deceased or incapacitated. Even if you both die simultaneously, and you each name someone different to serve as Guardian, your choice of Guardian will at least be brought to the attention of the Court.

It is important that the person you choose to serve as Guardian be compatible with the child. If your choice of Guardian is not that of the child's, the child can object to the appointment. If the child is at least 12, the Court will listen carefully to the child's objection, and then appoint a Guardian based on the what the Court determines to be in the child's best interest (Probate 680).

LEAVING PROPERTY FOR THE CHILD

As any parent is well aware, it is expensive to raise a child. The person you consider to be the best choice to serve as Guardian might not be able to do so unless you leave sufficient monies to pay for the care of the child. If you have limited finances, consider purchasing term insurance on your life and/or on the life of the other parent of the child.

A *term life insurance policy* insures your life for a certain period of time. You can limit the term until the child is grown. The cost of the policy is relatively inexpensive because it has no cash surrender value and no money is paid unless the insured person dies during the term of the policy. If you can only afford one policy, insure the life of the parent who contributes most to the support of the child. Some companies offer a combination of term life and disability insurance, in the event that the bread-winner becomes disabled and unable to work. As with any other purchase, it is important to comparison shop to obtain the best price for the coverage.

If you are married, you may want to name your spouse as the beneficiary of the term insurance policy with your child as an alternate beneficiary. Married or single, you can name your minor child as the primary beneficiary of the policy. Under Texas law, the insurance company may give amounts up to $10,000 to the child by transferring the funds to an adult member of the minor's family. The company is required to seek Court permission before transferring funds that exceed that amount (Property 141.008).

If the proceeds do not exceed $100,000, the Court may allow the funds to be placed with the County Clerk to be held, invested, and managed until the child is 18. During that time, the child's parent can ask the Court to allow some or all of the monies to be used for the child's benefit (Probate 887).

If the proceeds are greater than $100,000, the Court will probably require that a Guardian of the property be appointed. You may think it best that the child inherits more than $100,000, this way a Court will see to it that the funds are held safely till the child is an adult. But as we will see, that only presents a new set of problems.

AVOIDING AN UNNECESSARY GUARDIANSHIP

We discussed the ways parents can control who is appointed to serve as the Guardian of their minor child should both parents be incapacitated or deceased. Guardianship is a necessity in such cases. But if at least one of the parents is able to care for the person of the child, it may be wise to avoid the need for the Court to appoint a Guardian of the property. If you leave the child a significant amount of money, the Court will appoint a Guardian of that property. Even if the surviving parent is appointed to serve as Guardian, the amount you leave to the child will be reduced by the cost of establishing and maintaining the guardianship.

An attorney must be employed to establish the guardianship. Once appointed, the Guardian must prepare an inventory and file an annual accounting with the Court. He may need to employ an accountant to assist with the preparation of the inventory and the annual accounting. If the Estate is sizeable, he may need to employ a financial advisor to manage the property. The Guardian and the people he employs to help him are entitled to be paid for their services. Their fees are proper charges to the child's guardianship property (Probate 665).

Monies left for the care of the child may be significantly reduced by the cost of caring for the property. This can be avoided by leaving property to the child in such a manner, that will make it unnecessary for the Court to appoint a Guardian of the property of the child. One way to do so is to set up a Revocable Living Trust that includes provisions for the care of the child. If you have limited finances, a good alternative is to appoint someone to serve as Custodian of the gift under the TEXAS UNIFORM TRANSFERS TO MINORS ACT.

THE UNIFORM TRANSFERS TO MINORS ACT

The **Texas Uniform Transfers to Minors Act** is designed to protect gifts made to a minor by appointing someone to be the **Custodian** of a gift until the child is an adult. For example, you can make a minor child the beneficiary of your life insurance policy, and name a trusted relative or friend or even a financial institution to be the Custodian of the gift. Should you die while the child is a minor, the insurance company will give the proceeds of the policy to the person you named as Custodian to hold until the child is an adult.

You can make a gift to a minor in your Will. You can appoint your Personal Representative (or anyone else) as Custodian of the gift. For example:

I give the sum of $100,000 to _____(name) as custodian for _____ (name of minor) under the Texas Uniform Transfers to Minors Act (Property 141.004, 141.006).

THE LIFETIME GIFT

You can even use the Texas Uniform Transfers to Minors Law to make a gifts during your lifetime of items such as shares in a corporation or a limited partnership interest (Property 141.005, 141.010). You can nominate yourself as Custodian of the gift, or you can name another person to serve as Custodian. Once the lifetime gift is made it becomes irrevocable, so this method is not appropriate unless you are sure that you want the child to have the gift once he/she is an adult.

In general, the Custodian must distribute the gift when the child reaches 18; however, if you make a lifetime gift, or include a gift as part of your Will or Trust, the Custodian will distribute the gift no later than the minor's 21st birthday (Property 141.021).

MANAGING THE PROPERTY

Under Texas law, while the Custodian is in possession of the gift, he can use as much of the gift as he thinks advisable for the benefit of the child. He can pay monies directly to the child, or use the funds for the child's benefit. In making the distribution he is not obliged to take into account that someone else has a duty to support the child — even if the Custodian is the child's parent and it is his own responsibility to support the child (Property 141.015).

The Custodian can do the opposite and distribute nothing. He can refuse to use any of the monies for the child and just keep the funds invested until the funds are distributed when the child is an adult. In such case, the child's parent or Guardian — or even the child once he is 14, can ask a Court to order that the monies be used for the care of the child. The judge will determine what is in the child's best interest and then rule on the matter.

Hopefully, the Custodian will give a regular accounting to the child's parent or Guardian. If not, any member of the child's family, or the child once he/she reaches 14, can ask the Court to order a full accounting of the custodial property (Property 141.013, 141.020).

As with any type of Estate Plan, you need to examine all aspects of the transfer to see if there is anything that may be objectionable to you.

THE CUSTODIAN'S FEE

The law requires the Custodian to invest and manage the property in a responsible, prudent manner. The Custodian is entitled to be paid for his effort (Property 1451.016). If the gift is sizeable, his fee can be sizeable. Before appointing a person or a financial institution as Custodian, it is best to come to a written agreement about how the property will be managed and the charge for doing so.

NO GROUP GIFT

You cannot make a single gift to more than one child under the Uniform Transfers To Minors Act. For example, if you want to make a single gift of real property to two or more minor children, you need to do so by another method, such as creating a Trust for the children (Property 141.011).

THE COST OF PROBATE

As discussed, you can include a gift to a minor in your Will by naming a Custodian for the gift. As with any gift made under a Will, a Probate procedure will be necessary to distribute the gift to the Custodian (or to the child if he is 21). If you are trying to avoid Probate, this may not be the best way to go. If your gift is significant, the better route is to set up a Revocable Living Trust. You can manage the Trust while you are able. Should you become incapacitated or die before the child is grown your Successor Trustee will take over. Unlike the Uniform Gift to Minors, you can direct the Trustee to give the gift to the child at any age you think proper.

Which brings us to another problem, namely, that there is no flexibility as to the final distribution of a gift made under the Uniform Transfers to Minors Act.

MANDATORY DISTRIBUTION

A Custodian appointed under the Uniform Transfers To Minors Act must distribute the gift by the child's 18th birthday (21st if your Will directs) (Property 141.021).

The gift must be made regardless of whether the child is mature enough to handle the money in a responsible manner. A sizeable gift to an immature beneficiary is not the best Estate Plan.

PROVIDING FOR THE STEPCHILD

Perhaps the reason that the story of Cinderella has such universal appeal is that many stepchildren, at one point or another, feel left out. The law seems to reinforce that perception. Unless a married person makes provision otherwise, a spouse has priority over the child in health matters both before and after death. If a married person is too ill to make medical decisions, the doctors will turn to the spouse for directions. Should a married person die, the decedent's spouse and not the child, has the authority to agree to an autopsy or anatomical gift (Crim. Proc. 49.13, Health & Safety 692.004).

If a married couple hold all of their property jointly, that property will go to the surviving spouse and not to the child of the deceased parent. This might not be a problem if the surviving spouse is the natural parent of the child. It could be a major problem if the natural parent dies first. The stepchild of the surviving parent may be left with nothing.

In such situations, the stepparent comes across as villain, but it is the parent, and not the stepparent, who decides whether the child will inherit property belonging to the natural parent. Too often the stepchild is left out by default, i.e., the natural parent doesn't give the matter any thought, or perhaps the natural parent is confident that the stepparent will do "what's right."

That was the case with Walter. He always wanted to be a father, so he was pleased when Todd was born just before the first anniversary of Walter's marriage to Nancy. Twin girls were born just 15 months later. Unfortunately the twins' birth was premature, causing them to have medical and developmental problems. Nancy had her hands full just caring for the three children, so it was up to Walter to support the family.

Walter was up to the job. He was both conscientious and ambitious. He started his own interior decorating business, complete with a retail sales storefront to sell fabrics, and an upholstery shop in the rear of the store. With hard work and long hours, he was able to make a comfortable living. But the strain of raising a family and running a business took its toll, both on him and the marriage. At 40, he felt like an old man.

All that changed when he hired Annie to manage the retail part of his business. Her energy and sunny disposition were just what the business (and Walter) needed.

Walter's divorce from Nancy was amicable. Walter was a loving father who took his responsibilities seriously. He was generous when it came to supporting the children. Walter had only finished high school, and he wanted more for his son. He encouraged Todd to do well in school so that he could go on to college, and maybe become a doctor or lawyer. The twins had developmental problems; but Walter encouraged them to reach their maximum potential. It was his goal to help them become self sufficient.

Annie got along very well with her stepchildren. She had no trouble with Walter's desire to support the children and give them a good start in life. Even though they held all of their money in a joint account, she never questioned any expense made on behalf of the children.

Walter never gave much thought to an Estate Plan. After all, he was healthy, and in the prime of his earning capacity. He often said that he was fortunate to have married two wonderful women. If he had a dark thought, it soon passed, rationalizing that if something happened to him, Annie would take care of the children.

But she didn't.

Walter died in one of those freak accidents. He was trimming the branches from his tree with an electric saw and accidentally touched an overhead wire. All he owned was tied up in the business that he held jointly with Annie. Annie felt that she was a major factor in the success of that business. Why should she share any of her hard earned money with Nancy? As for the children, it was Nancy's job to raise them. After all they were Nancy's children, and not Annie's children. If it was a struggle to support the children, that was Nancy's problem!

A better argument (but one she didn't raise) was that Walter really wanted Annie to inherit everything. If he wanted to provide for his children, he could have done so in any number of different ways, beginning with his marriage to Annie:

✍   He could have insisted on a premarital agreement that would have provided for certain funds to be kept separate for the benefit of his children.

✍   He could have signed a partnership agreement with Annie that would have given his share of the business to his children, in the event of his death.

✍   If he didn't want to negotiate with Annie about a premarital or partnership agreement, he could have had his attorney prepare a Trust that would have cared for the children until they were old enough to be on their own.

✍   If nothing else, he could have purchased a life insurance policy with the children as beneficiaries of the policy.

THE SECOND MARRIAGE TRUST

Walter's situation is not unique. Second marriages are commonplace in America. Many who are widowed or divorced, remarry. If children are involved, the parent may have divided loyalties. The parent may want to provide income to the child until the child completes his education, and then leave whatever is left of his Estate to his surviving spouse. More often it is the other way around. The parent wants to be sure that the surviving spouse has sufficient income to support his/her current life-style, but once the surviving spouse dies, the parent wants all that remains to go to his children. A properly drafted Trust can provide for the care of a spouse and child in whatever way the Settlor of the Trust thinks best.

That was the case with an elderly widower who married a pretty girl less than half his age. Their Premarital Agreement made it clear that all his property would go to his son from his first marriage. Surprisingly, the marriage turned out well. So well that the couple had two daughters. The husband decided to divide his Estate equally between his three children and to provide for the care of his wife until the youngest child was grown.

His attorney suggested a Trust. "You can be Trustee during your lifetime. Once you die, your Successor Trustee can immediately distribute one-third of the Trust to your son who is now 55. No sense to keep him waiting. The rest of your money can remain in your Trust. Income from the Trust can be used to support your wife and children until the youngest is 25. Then, whatever remains in the Trust can be distributed equally to your daughters."

"Good idea" said the elderly gentlemen, with a smile "Just make sure it is revocable during my lifetime. Who knows what adventures I might be up to in the future?"

It isn't just stepchildren who can be left out if no provision is made. Even children from a long-standing marriage can be cut off against the wishes of a parent. A parent may assume that all of their children will be treated equally when both parents are gone, but if all your children are those of your spouse and neither of you have a Will, all of the property will go to the surviving spouse. The last parent to die is the one who gets to decide "who gets what." Too often, the wishes of the deceased parent are ignored, for example:

THE STRAINED RELATIONSHIP

A child may have a close relationship with one parent, and a strained, but tolerable, relationship with the other. Peace in the family is achieved because the parent who is close to the child acts as a buffer. Should the buffer parent die first, the relationship between the surviving parent and the child may fall apart altogether and the child's inheritance be cut off.

THE PARENT WITH DIMINISHED CAPACITY

The more common scenario, is that the surviving parent becomes increasingly dependent on one child — either for emotional support, or for physical assistance as the parent ages. The other children may live at a distance, or perhaps they are too involved with their own family to assist. The supporting child may end up with most, if not all, of what was intended for all of the children.

These problems can be avoided by having your attorney prepare a Will or Trust. He can suggest any number of ways to achieve your goals, such as giving your surviving spouse a Life Estate in your Separate Property and/or in your half of the Community Property, with the remainder going to your children.

The caregiver of someone who is incapacitated, or developmentally disabled needs to, as part of his Estate Plan, provide for the care of the incapacitated person as well as himself. Should the caregiver become disabled or die, someone will need to take over and make medical decisions for the incapacitated person and see to it that he/she is properly housed and fed.

An aging parent of a developmentally disabled child may worry about how the child will manage without the parent to oversee his care. An aged spouse caring for his incapacitated spouse, may be concerned about who will care for the ill spouse should he die first. Often a family member will agree to take responsibility for the care of an incapacitated person; but perhaps no one wants the job.

If there are large sums of money involved it may be the opposite case, too many people may want to be in control. One family member may want the incapacitated child or spouse to remain at home with the assistance of a home health care worker. Another may think the best place is an assisted living facility with 24 hour care. The caregiver may be concerned that a tug-of-war will erupt once he dies.

There several solutions to the problem, depending on the circumstances.

DECLARATION OF APPOINTMENT OF GUARDIAN
The parent of an adult incapacitated person may, by Will or by written Declaration, appoint an eligible person to be the Guardian of the person of the adult individual once the parent is deceased (Probate 677).

This is a relatively inexpensive way to ensure that the parent's choice of Guardian will be honored once he is deceased. However, as with the Declaration of Appointment of Guardian of a minor, the appointment does not become effective until the person presents the Declaration to the Court and asks to be appointed Guardian. Before making the appointment the Court will need to establish that the adult child is incapacitated and in need of a Guardian. The guardianship procedure make take a few weeks. If the parent is concerned about the care of the adult child during that time, he might consider having a Guardian appointed during his lifetime.

APPOINT A SUCCESSOR GUARDIAN
The parent of an incapacitated adult child, or the spouse of an incapacitated person, can petition (ask) the Court to be appointed as the Guardian of the person or property of the incapacitated person. Once appointed, the Guardian caregiver can file a Declaration with the Court appointing someone to serve as Successor Guardian (Probate 677 (b)).

The only problem with setting up a guardianship while the caregiver is able to care for the disabled spouse or child is the cost of the procedure. It may cost hundreds, if not thousands, of dollars to set up and maintain the guardianship. If the incapacitated person is without funds, the caregiver can ask the Legal Services for assistance. See page xii for information about finding the nearest Legal Services office.

Even those who have adequate funds may hesitate to go through the effort and expense to set up a guardianship if it may not be needed for years to come — if ever.

ESTABLISH A TRUST

If the primary concern of the caregiver is to see that the incapacitated person has sufficient funds for his care, his attorney may suggest that a Trust be established to provide funds to care for the incapacitated person. The only problem with establishing a Trust is the possible loss of government benefits. To avoid that problem the attorney can draft a SPECIAL NEEDS TRUST.

A TRUST FOR THE DISABLED

Government assistance is available to provide medical and custodial care for those who are disabled and without the means to care for themselves. Both state and federal government provide such assistance with programs such as Social Security disability benefits and Medicaid. The family often supplements the government program by providing for the incapacitated person's *special needs* or *supplemental needs* such as hobbies, special education, outings to a movie or a sports event — things that give the incapacitated person some quality of life. This is not a problem while family members are alive and able to provide for the incapacitated person. The worry is how to continue that care should the provider die.

To be eligible for government assistance programs the incapacitated person must essentially be without funds. Family members fear that leaving money to the incapacitated person in a Will or Trust will disqualify him from receiving government assistance. Parents of a disabled child may decide to solve the problem by leaving the money to a sibling or other family member with verbal instructions to take care of the child once the parent is deceased. The problem with that approach is that once the funds are left to the family member, they become his property, and as such are available to his creditors.

The funds could be lost in a divorce, or the family member could die and the funds inherited by someone who is not willing to care for the disabled child. A better solution is to have an Elder Law attorney set up a *Special Needs* or *Supplemental Needs Trust.* The Trust can be funded by the parent during his lifetime, or after his death by making the Trust the beneficiary of his Will or Trust. It can also be funded by a life insurance policy on the life of the parent. The parent can purchase the policy and name the Supplemental Needs Trust as the beneficiary of the insurance funds.

The Trustee of the Supplemental Needs Trust can use the monies in the Trust to provide for the child's supplemental or special needs during his lifetime. The Trust Agreement can provide that upon the death of the incapacitated person, whatever remains in the Trust be distributed to whoever the parent names as the remainder beneficiary of the Trust.

CAUTION NOT RECOMMENDED FOR DISABLED SPOUSE

The Trust we have just described is appropriate for a disabled child, who has no funds of his own. The Trust is funded with monies owned by a parent and not the child. This Trust may not be the way to go if the disabled person is married and the Trust is funded by monies owned by the well spouse. When determining Medicaid eligibility, the government considers monies owned by both the husband and wife. If a Trust is set up using money owned by either of them, the government will consider the Trust funds to be available to pay for the care of the disabled spouse (42 U.S.C.1382c(a)(3), 1396p(d)(4)(A)). In Chapters 9 and 10 we discuss different ways a married couple can arrange their finances to provide for their health care without jeopardizing their right to qualify for medical assistance.

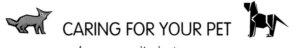

CARING FOR YOUR PET

A woman died at peace,
leaving her fortune
and care of her cat to her niece.
Alas, the fortune and the cat
disappeared soon after that.

You could leave money to someone with the understanding that the person will take care of your pet, but the moral of the above limerick, is that just leaving money will not guarantee care for your pet. The better route is to have your attorney prepare a Will that includes specific instructions and funds to provide for the care of your pet during its lifetime.

A TRUST TO CARE FOR YOUR PET

If you are financially able and have several pets, you may want to set up a special Trust for the care of your pets upon your death or incapacity. The person you name as Trustee will be charged with the duty to use Trust funds to pay for the care of those animals who survive you. You also need to name a residuary beneficiary (a person or perhaps a charitable organization) to receive whatever remains in the Trust once all of the animals are deceased. If you do not name a residuary beneficiary, what ever remains in the Trust will be distributed in the same manner as your Probate Estate, i.e., to the residuary beneficiaries of your Will, or if no Will to your next of kin as determined by the Texas Laws of Descent (Property 112.037).

Animal support groups, such as the Humane Society, have people who will care for the pet of a deceased owner. You might consider appointing such group as the remainder beneficiary of the Trust in exchange for the lifetime care of your pet(s).

An alternative to setting up a Trust for your pet is to ask your pet's veterinarian to consider starting an "Orphaned Pet Service" to assist in finding new homes for pets who lose their owners. It is good public relations and a potential source of income. If this is agreeable to the Veterinarian, you can make arrangements in your Will to pay the Vet to care for the pet until a suitable family can be found. This is a more humane approach than the, all too common practice of putting a pet "to sleep" rather than have the pet suffer the loss of its master. And in at least one case, that reasoning backfired.

Eleanor always had a pet in the house. After her husband died, her two poodles were her constant companions. When Eleanor became ill with cancer, she worried about what would happen to her "buddies" without her to care for them. She finally decided it best to have her family put them to sleep when she died.

Eleanor endured surgery, chemotherapy, radiation therapy, and even some holistic remedies, but she continued to go downhill. Eleanor's family came in to visit her at the hospital to say their last good-byes. She was so ill, she didn't even recognize them. No one thought she could last the day. Because the family was from out of state, and time short, they decided to put the pets to sleep so that when she died, they need only take care of the funeral arrangements.

To everyone's surprise, Eleanor rallied. She lived two more long, lonely years.

She often said she wished they had put her to sleep instead of her buddies.

THE CHARITABLE TRUST

We explained how a Trust can be set up to care for a pet and whatever is left over (the remainder) given to a charitable organization. There are other kinds of charitable trusts that can be set up to benefit the giver as well as the receiver. For example, suppose you own stock which has appreciated substantially over the years, but pays few dividends. This hasn't been a problem in the past because you earned a good income. But now you wish to retire, and will need additional income. You would like to cash in the stock and invest the funds in something that can supplement your retirement income, but your accountant says that a significant portion of the value of the stock will go to Uncle Sam as payment for the Capital Gains Tax.

By now you know that a clever Estate Planning attorney will have any number of ways to solve the problem. The dialogue with your attorney might go something like this:

ATTORNEY: "Do you have a favorite charity?"

"Yes, why do you ask?"

ATTORNEY: "You can set up a Charitable Remainder Trust and donate the stock to that charity by depositing the stock in the Trust. Charities don't pay taxes, so the stock can be sold and the proceeds invested in property that produces a good income. In return for the donation, you can receive an income for the next 20 years or you can receive a monthly annuity based on your life expectancy."

"What's in it for the charity?"

ATTORNEY: "The charity gets whatever is left after paying you the annuity."

"Yes, but suppose I die next year, and my wife is left without the securities and no income."

ATTORNEY: "No problem. If you decide on a 20 year annuity, you can name your wife or any other beneficiary to receive the balance of the annuity. If you wish, you can have an annuity based on your life expectancy and that of your spouse. If you predecease your spouse, then the income continues until she dies."

"It seems to me that if the annuity is based on my life expectancy AND my wife's life expectancy, there won't be much left for the charity."

ATTORNEY: "How much is left for the charity depends on the value of the gift and the cost of the annuity. The cost of the annuity depends on the combined life expectancy of you and your wife. I think the best way to understand this plan is for you to look at actual numbers. There are any number of ways to set up a Charitable Remainder Trust. I can explain each option to you. For each option, I will give you the cost of setting up the program; the amount of money you will get; and how much money will actually go to your favorite charity. Of course it must be an IRS approved charity. Once you see the numbers you can make an informed decision as to whether you want to sell the stock and pay the Capital Gains Tax, or set up a Charitable Trust and receive an income."

"Good idea."

THE FUTURE OF ESTATE PLANNING

Historically, Estate Planning for the wealthy was all about the Estate Tax. Estate Planning attorneys would spend their time dreaming up different ways to reduce Estate Taxes for their wealthy clients. The IRS would spend their time examining and challenging any Estate plan that appeared too innovative. It seems likely that by 2010 the federal Estate Tax will be a memory. Is the game over?

Hardly. As explained in Chapter 3, instead of paying an Estate Tax, the child who inherits property that has appreciated more than 1.3 million dollars will pay a Capital Gains Tax on the excess when he sells the property. In a way, that makes sense. A major criticism of the Estate Tax was that it had to be paid within nine months of the date of death. That created a hardship for those inheriting property with a high market value but with no cash to pay taxes on that value.

Critics of the Estate Tax often cited the example of the cash poor farm located on valuable land. Once the owner of the farm died, the family would be forced to sell the farm just to pay Estate Taxes. By substituting the Capital Gains Tax for the Estate Tax, that problem is eliminated. No tax is due until the beneficiary sells the property. Theoretically, the family farm can now be inherited generation to generation without a tax consequence.

But there are few family farms in today's economy. Future heirs are more likely to inherit highly appreciated real property or securities that they will want to sell. And when they do, they may need to pay a significant Capital Gains Tax.

The new game for Estate Planning attorneys will be to devise an Estate Plan that will reduce the Capital Gains Tax. The IRS will, no doubt, enjoy challenging those plans.

One tried (and legal) method of reducing the Capital Gains Tax is the Charitable Remainder Trust as was just discussed. It doesn't take a crystal ball to see that this could well be the basis of future Estate Plans, so we will take a few more pages to describe the pros and cons of the Trust.

THE CHARITABLE REMAINDER ANNUITY TRUST

A **Charitable Remainder Annuity Trust** is a Trust that is established according to the Internal Revenue Code (26 U.S.C. 664). Charities do not pay taxes, so property donated to the Trust can be sold by the Trustee free of the Capital Gains Tax. Money from the sale is invested so that it provides an income (an *annuity*) to the beneficiary (the *annuitant*) for a fixed period of time, say 20 years, or for the annuitant's lifetime as computed by actuarial tables (i.e., life expectancy tables). The charity receives whatever is left (the *remainder*) after payment of the annuity. How much income the donor will receive and how much the charity will receive, is agreed upon at the time the Trust is set up.

The Trust can be set up in any number of ways depending on the goal of the **donor** (the person making the gift). In the example just given, the goal of the donor was to convert non-income producing property to income producing property without paying a high Capital Gains Tax. A wealthy donor may be more concerned about his child paying a high Capital Gains Tax should the child inherit highly appreciated property.

For example, suppose you bought acreage in a rural area in northern Texas that appreciated significantly over the years and it is now worth 1 million dollars. You have been putting off selling the property because of the Capital Gains Tax. But it has been a burden to you. It produces no income and because the property continues to appreciate, each year you are paying more and more in property taxes. You did not mind the sacrifice because you figured that your son would inherit the property at a step-up in basis. But now with the new tax law, by the time you die, the property may be worth three million dollars. He is only allowed a 1.3 million dollar step up in basis, so your son may need to pay a significant Capital Gains Tax when he sells the property.

Setting up a Charitable Remainder Annuity Trust solves the problem of the Capital Gains Tax. The land is transferred to the Charitable Trust. Charities pay no tax, so the Trustee can sell the land and the full market value of the property will be available for investment.

The Trust could be set up with you receiving an income for life, and your son receiving the annuity after your death. The only problem with this arrangement is that your son is significantly younger than you are. There may not be much left to benefit the charity if they must wait for both of you to die. The solution is to have the annuity based on your life only and then use part of the income that you receive to purchase a three million dollar insurance policy on your life with your son as beneficiary. The three million dollars is the estimated value of the land that your son would have inherited at your death. But with this arrangement he will inherit the insurance proceeds free of any Capital Gains Tax.

The astute reader (and probably one with an accounting background) will say "Aha, you may have avoided the Capital Gains Tax, but the Estate Tax Exclusion value does not increase to 3.5 million dollars until the year 2009. The three million dollar life insurance policy counts as part of your taxable Estate, so if you die before 2009, your son will pay an Estate Tax! "

And of course our clever imaginary attorney has a solution in the form of an Irrevocable Insurance Trust. You can set up an Irrevocable Trust so that the Trust owns the insurance policy and not you. The insurance policy is not included in your taxable Estate, so your son pays no Estate Tax. See the end of Chapter 6 for an explanation of how the Irrevocable Insurance Trust works.

As with any Estate Plan you need to consider the downside, and the Charitable Remainder Annuity Trust is no exception.

⊠   ATTORNEY FEES
It may cost significant attorney fees to set up the Trust. Some charities may offer to have their attorney prepare the Trust at no cost to you, or perhaps they offer a "standard" Trust document that their attorney prepared. But using the charity's Trust document represents a conflict of interest. Their Trust was prepared by an attorney for the greatest benefit to his client (that's the charity, not you).

It is important that you employ your own attorney to represent you. He knows the extent of your Estate and he understands what you wish to accomplish.

⊠ THE COMPLEXITY OF THE PLAN

A Charitable Remainder Annuity Trust is a sophisticated Estate Planning tool designed to benefit the well-to-do donor and an IRS approved charity. There are any number of ways to set up the plan. It is important to have an attorney who will take the time to explore different plans until you determine the best plan for you.

⊠ THE TRUST IS IRREVOCABLE

Once established, the Trust is not revocable, so it is important to understand all of the aspects of the Trust. In particular, you need to know how much it will cost in attorney's fees to set up the Trust, how much income you will receive, and over what period of time. The income you receive as an annuitant is taxable to you. You need to consider that while taxes may change over the years, the terms of the Trust cannot be changed. Have your attorney, accountant or financial planner give you an educated guess as to what you might expect in terms of future income tax liability.

Although future income tax payments may be uncertain, the power of the Charitable Remainder Trust is the tax benefit to the donor at the time the Trust is set up.

☑ NO CAPITAL GAINS TAX

Had you sold the property and invested the money yourself, you would have paid a Capital Gains Tax. That tax could have been substantial, depending on the tax rate in effect at the time of the transfer. By gifting the property, the full value of the land can be used to produce investment income.

☑ NO PROPERTY TAX

Once your property is transferred into the Trust, you will no longer need to pay annual property taxes.

☑ NO GIFT TAX

The property you transfer into the Trust is a gift to a charity and as such is not included in the sum total of taxable gifts that you give during your lifetime.

☑ INCOME TAX DEDUCTION

Because you are making a charitable donation, you should be able to take a charitable deduction on your income tax return in the year of the donation.

There are other "perks" in addition to the tax benefits:

☑ NO PROBATE EXPENSE

It might take an expensive and time consuming Probate procedure to transfer the property to a beneficiary upon your death. By transferring the property to the Trust during your lifetime, you avoid the need for a Probate procedure to transfer the property after your death.

☑ GIVE WHEN NEEDED INSTEAD OF LATER

A Charitable Remainder Annuity Trust can be set up in any number of different ways to accommodate your Estate Plan. For example, if you are not in need of a present income, but expect that you will spend significant sums on your child's education, you can set up a 20 year annuity with your child as the annuitant. This will get the child through college and probably be a great help should the child decide to start a family.

Why have the child inherit property in later, high earning years rather than in the early, high expense/low income years?

☑ CREDITOR PROTECTION

If you keep the land and are sued, you could lose it to pay your creditors. If a beneficiary inherits the land, it could be lost to his/her creditors. But once the property is transferred to the Trust, the gift is made. Neither your creditors nor your beneficiary's creditors can gain access to the Trust funds. The most a creditor can do is seek payment from the money that is received as an income.

☑ GOOD DEED

If you are concerned that your son will be tagged with a Capital Gains Tax once you die, it means that your property has appreciated more than 1.3 million dollars, and you are fortunate indeed. By setting up a Charitable Trust, you are making a donation to the charity of your choice. You are sharing your good fortune with others. You can consider this as "giving back" to the community, or just plain doing a good deed.

BECOME A PHILANTHROPIST

Instead of giving the property to an established charity, you can become a philanthropist and set up your own Charitable foundation. The foundation can be in the form of an IRS approved Charitable Trust. You can be the Trustee of the Charitable Trust and your child the Successor Trustee. The Trust can be set up according to your specific charitable purposes. You can use the Trust to benefit a single cause or several worthy projects. This can be an exciting adventure for those with ample resources and a community spirit.

An Estate Plan For Your Person

The law makes a distinction between your property (what you own) and your person (your body). We have been discussing how to set up an Estate Plan for your property with the goal of maximum control over your Estate during your lifetime, and minimum cost and hassle to your heirs once you die. An Estate Plan for your body is just as important as an Estate Plan for your property. The goals are much the same. Maximum control over your body during your lifetime. Minimum cost and hassle to your family for your final disposition.

You may think it strange to speak of planning for maximum control of your body during your lifetime. After all, it's your body. Who else but you has any right to control what you do with your body? That may be true so long as you have capacity, but should you become seriously ill, you may be unable to express your wishes about the care you wish to receive. If you do not have an Estate Plan in place for your person, your next of kin, or maybe the state of Texas, may make health decisions for you.

The same applies to the final disposition of your body. If you don't make arrangements for your funeral and burial, someone will need to make these decisions for you.

As this chapter will show, it is relatively simple and inexpensive to set up an Estate Plan for your Person.

MAKING BURIAL ARRANGEMENTS

People with a large family often arrange for a family burial site. Over the years deceased family members come to occupy a space in that site, but others may have been buried elsewhere. Surviving family members often lose track of the number of spaces left. If this is the case with your family, you need to take inventory of the number of spaces available and who in the family expects to use those spaces. It is important to keep in touch with the cemetery and let them know if there is a change in the expected occupant of the burial site.

OUT OF STATE BURIAL SITE

It may be that the family burial site is not in the state of Texas. In such case, it is important to consider the cost of transporting the body from Texas to the out-of-state cemetery. That cost can be substantial, in some cases doubling the cost of the burial. If there is no emotional attachment to the out-of-state burial site, you may want to consider assigning the burial site to a family member who lives closer to the site and making your own burial arrangements here in Texas.

It is important to make your own burial arrangements. Even if it is not important to you where you are buried, it may be very important to your family. That is often the case in second marriages. If you have children from a first marriage, they may want their parents to be "reunited in death." Your current spouse may not take kindly to having you buried with your former spouse. This might result in hard feelings, if not an out-and-out battle.

The same problem can arise with those in a gay relationship. The decedent's family might not have acknowledged the relationship. The family might decide to have the decedent buried in the family plot and exclude the gay partner from participating in the burial arrangements.

You can head off disputes about your final resting place, by making your own burial arrangements. If you do not do so, any relative who takes responsibility for the burial will make the decision. If no relative takes responsibility, any of your friends can do so (Health & Safety 691.024).

The Texas statute does not state who has priority in deciding how to dispose of the body, so if two people decide to take responsibility for your final disposition, there could be a battle over who should make the decision.

ARRANGING FOR CREMATION

Increasingly people are opting for cremation. The reasons for choosing cremation are varied, but for many, it is a matter of finances. The cost of cremation is approximately one-sixth that of an ordinary funeral and burial. A major saving is the cost of the casket. A casket is not necessary for the cremation. An alternate container of fiberboard or similar materials, can be used to transport the body. Embalming is not necessary either, unless there is to be a funeral with a viewing. Federal law prohibits a funeral director from saying that a casket or embalming is necessary for a direct (immediate) cremation (16 Code of Federal Regulations ("CFR") 453.3 (b)(1)(ii)).

For those who are considering cremation, there are a few things to consider.

THE PACEMAKER

Cremating a body with a pacemaker or any radiation producing device can cause damage to the cremation chamber and/or to the person performing the cremation. If you have such an electronic aid, it will need to be removed prior to the cremation. You might check with the cremation service to determine the cost of having the pacemaker removed.

A pacemaker can be donated for use in animals with a medical need for the device. If you are interested in making such donation, you can ask your local veterinarian to refer you to an animal clinic that performs the procedure, and then arrange to have it removed prior to your burial or cremation.

THE OVERWEIGHT

Cremation technology has kept up with the expanding waist line of our population. Most Cremation Services can accommodate a body weighing up to 400 pounds. But if you are extremely obese, you need to ask the cremation service whether their facility is large enough. If you cannot locate a crematory that can accommodate your weight, you will need to make burial arrangements.

WHAT TO DO WITH THE ASHES

In addition to planning for the procedure, you need to give your family some guidance as to where to place the ashes. Some cemeteries allow an urn containing the cremated remains of a family member to be placed in an occupied family plot. Similarly, some cemeteries will allow the cremated remains to be placed in the space in a mausoleum currently occupied by a member of the decedent's family.

If you intend to be cremated and all your family spaces are occupied you may want to call the cemetery and ask them to explain their policy as it relates to the burial of urns in occupied sites.

If burial in the family site is not an option, you will need to arrange for a separate burial space. Many cemeteries have a separate building called a *columbarium*, which is especially designed to store urns. You can purchase a storage place for the urn in the same manner as the purchase of a burial space in a cemetery.

If you wish to have your cremated remains scattered, you need to let your next of kin know where and how this is to be done. If you want your ashes spread out to sea, your family will need to arrange to have a boat go out at least three nautical miles, because federal law prohibits ashes from being scattered any closer than that distance from land (40 CFR 229.1).

If you are an honorably discharged veteran or the spouse of such veteran, you have the right to be buried in a Veterans National Cemetery. If your Veteran spouse was buried in a Veterans National Cemetery, you have the right to be buried in that same grave site unless soil conditions require a separate burial site.

You can get information about burial at a Veterans National Cemetery by calling the Veteran's Administration at (800) 827-1000, or visiting their Web site.

 VA CEMETERY WEB SITE
http://www.cem.va.gov

The site has information on the following topics:

> National and Military Cemeteries
> Burial, Headstones and Markers
> State Cemetery Grants Program

You cannot reserve a grave site in advance, so your family will need to make arrangements and establish your eligibility to be buried in a Veterans National Cemetery. At that time, they will need to provide the following information:

> your rank, serial, social security and
  VA claim numbers
> the branch of service in which you served,
  the date and place of your entry into and
  separation from the service
> a copy of your official military discharge
  document bearing an official seal or a
  DD 214 form.

If you wish to be buried in a national cemetery, you need to make your military records readily accessible to your family.

THE PREPAID FUNERAL PLAN

In addition to making arrangements for a burial space or for a cremation, consider purchasing a funeral plan. It will be easier on your family emotionally and financially if you make your own funeral arrangements.

Federal law requires that you receive a general price list at the beginning of any discussion for the purchase of funeral services (16 CFR 453.2). Once you decide upon a plan, the seller should give you a contract that states the prices charged for *services* (embalming, viewing, transportation, etc.) and *merchandise purchased* (casket, urn, acknowledgment cards, register books, clothing, etc.) and *cash advance items*, i.e., things paid for by the funeral director and then reimbursed back to him. This includes paying for death certificates, arranging to have the obituary printed, payment for religious services, etc. (16 CFR 453.5).

Once you decide on a plan, the funeral director will present you with a *Prepaid Funeral Benefits Contract*. Texas law requires that the seller use a form approved by the TEXAS DEPARTMENT OF BANKING (Finance 154.002, 154.151). Even though the seller gives you a contract that says that it has been approved by the Department it does not mean that it cannot be changed. If you are not satisfied with the way a certain section of the contract reads, attach an addendum to the contract that explains, in plain English, your understanding of that passage. If you are concerned about something that is not mentioned in the contract, insist that the contract be amended to include that item.

In particular, check to see whether the contract answers the following questions:

Does the contract cover all costs?
The contract should contain an itemized list stating exactly what goods and services are included in the sales price (Finance 154.151(b)(3)). Your contract may include an allowance towards cash advance items such as the printing of the obituary or payment to the clergy, or your contract may provide that payment be made at the time of the funeral. Your contract should state that the funeral director will not charge more for the cash advance than he actually pays for the goods or services.

Is the price guaranteed?
Some Prepaid Funeral Benefits Contracts have a fixed price for the goods and services you choose, meaning that the funeral director will provide the goods and services at the same price as agreed at the time of the contract. It is important that your contract state that the person or company who is selling you the Prepaid Contract is the same person or company who will actually provide those goods and services. If not, Texas law requires the provider of the goods and services sign the contract saying that he agrees to be bound by the terms of your agreement. If the seller says that it is not necessary for the provider to sign your contract because he and the provider have a separate written agreement, have that agreement attached to your contract (Finance 154.151).

You might opt for a Prepaid Funeral Benefits Contract that is not a fixed price. Upon your death, the company can charge additional money for the plan that you chose. In these days of inflation and increasing life expectancy, it is important that such contract clearly state how the price will be determined when the contract is finally put into effect.

How are your contract funds protected?

Texas laws are designed to protect the purchaser of a Prepaid Funeral Benefits Contract. Funeral firms are required to protect funds paid by the consumer by placing the monies into a Trust account, or by having the funeral firm purchase a life insurance policy to cover the funds paid by the buyer.

TRUST ACCOUNT

You may decide to have your funds protected by having them placed in a Trust account. Texas law requires that the funds be placed in a Trust account in a bank within the state within 30 days of receipt (Finance 154.253). Have the funeral firm agree to furnish you with proof of deposit, and promise, in writing, to notify you should they decide to change banks. Ask the funeral firm whether there will be any service charge on the account, and if so to give you a written statement of those charges.

The monies in the account belong to you during your lifetime, and will be paid to the funeral firm upon your death. Because you own the account, interest on that account will be included as taxable income to you.

INSURANCE

If the funds are to be paid by insurance, the funeral firm must submit the premium you paid to the insurance company within 30 days (Finance 154.203). Have the company furnish you with proof of payment of the premium.

Can you cancel the contract?

Texas law gives you the right to cancel the contract and receive your money back. The only question is how much the funeral firm is required to return to you. A buyer of a Trust funded contract who cancels the contract during the first year of the contract is entitled to receive all of the monies deposited into the Trust account or 90% of the amount paid by the buyer, whichever is the larger value (Finance 154.254). If you are paying on an installment plan the seller is entitled to keep up to half of all of the monies you paid until the seller receives 10% of the contract price (Finance 154.252). If your Prepaid Funeral Contract is funded by an insurance policy and you cancel the contract within the first year, you are entitled to the cash surrender value of the policy (Finance 154.205).

It is important that your contract state how much money you will receive should you cancel the contract after the first year. Your contract should also state how to cancel the contract. Texas law requires that you give written notice of the cancellation to the seller on a form approved by the Texas Department of Banking (Finance 154.002, 154.155). You may want to have that form attached to your contract, so that it is available to you in the event that you decided to cancel the contract. One you send the notice of cancellation to the seller, he has 30 days to return your money.

FUNERAL PLANS FOR THOSE ON PUBLIC ASSISTANCE

People who are applying for, or receiving, Medicaid, Supplemental Security Income ("SSI") or other public assistance program have limits on the amount of assets that they may own. If someone purchases Prepaid Funeral Benefits, the monies paid into the plan count as an asset because the purchaser of the plan can revoke the contract and get his money back.

Understanding the problem, the Texas legislature included a provision in the law allowing the buyer to sign a waiver giving up his right to cancel the contract (Finance 154.156). If you purchase a contract and later need to apply for a public assistance program, you can have the funeral firm change the contract to one that is irrevocable by signing the waiver.

Even if you are in good health at this time, it is a good idea to have your contract provide that you can change your plan to conform to state and federal law, without charge to you, if at any time you need to apply for a public assistance program.

Is the funeral firm reputable?

All these protections don't do much good if you are not dealing with a reputable company. It is important to take the time to check up on whoever is selling you the contract. In Texas, anyone who offers Prepaid Funeral Services to the public must be licensed with the TEXAS FUNERAL SERVICE COMMISSION. Before signing the contract, it is prudent to call the Commission and ask them if the funeral firm is licensed, how long they have been in business and whether any complaints have been filed against them.

The toll free number of the Texas Funeral Service Commission is (888) 667-4881.

Suppose you die in another state or country?

Your contract should spell out what provision will be made in the event that you move to another state or die in another state or country. Many funeral firms are part of a national funeral service corporation with funeral firms located throughout the United States. You may be able to have the contract provide that there will be no additional charge if the contract is performed by one of the funeral firms owned by the parent company.

Can the plan be changed after your death?

It may happen that your heirs need to cancel the plan after your death because:

➢ your body is missing or cannot be recovered, or

➢ you were buried by another facility because no one knew that you had a Prearrangement contract, or

➢ you died in another country and were buried there.

Your contract should address these potential problems, and spell out how much money will be refunded and who is to receive the refund.

You may also want to specify whether your heirs have the right to alter your funeral plans. In the absence of such a provision in the contract, funeral firms usually allow the family to arrange for a more expensive plan, provided they agree to pay the difference.

You may wonder why anyone would think of changing the decedent's funeral plan, but consider that in today's market, it is not uncommon for a top end prepaid funeral plan complete with solid bronze casket to cost upwards of $30,000. Some heirs might be motivated to save money by changing the plan to one of a lesser value.

That was the case with Lester. His mother, Mona, was a difficult woman with a personality that can only be described as "sour." Her husband deserted her after four years of marriage leaving her to raise Lester by herself. Once Lester was grown, Mona made it clear to him that she had done her job and now he was on his own. Lester could have used some help. He married and had three children. One of his children suffered with asthma and it was a constant struggle to keep up with the medical bills.

Mona believed in being good to herself. She did not intend to, nor did she, leave much money when she died. She knew that Lester would not be able to afford a "proper" burial for her, so she purchased a funeral plan and paid close to $20,000 for it. She was pleased when the funeral director told her that the monies would be kept safely in a Trust account until the time they were needed.

Lester was not familiar with Texas law, so when Mona died he asked an attorney at the Legal Services office to determine whether the prepaid contract was revocable.

It was.

You know the ending to this story.

The reader might be thinking "Revocable. Irrevocable. All this contract stuff is giving me a headache. Why can't I just set aside some money and let my kids figure it out?"

The problem with that approach is that the cost of your final illness may leave you with little or no funds for your burial. To avoid the problem, you could purchase a life insurance policy to fund your funeral and burial, naming one or two trusted family members as the beneficiary of the policy.

It is important that the beneficiary agree to use the money for the intended purpose. It isn't so much that a family member is not trustworthy as it is that they may not understand what you intended — especially in those cases where other funds are available to pay for the funeral. Too often insurance funds are left to a child who refuses to contribute to the cost of the funeral saying "Dad wanted me to have this money. That's why he left it to me."

To avoid a misunderstanding, put it in writing. It need not be a formal contract. It could be something as simple as a letter to the insurance beneficiary, with copies to your next of kin:

Dear Paul,

I purchased a $20,000 insurance policy today naming you as beneficiary of the policy. As we discussed this money is to be used to pay for the following:
- *my funeral, grave site and headstone*
- *perpetual care for my grave*
- *airfare for each of my grandchildren to attend the funeral*
- *dinner for the family after the wake*
- *lunch for the family after the funeral*

If there is any money left over, please accept it as my thanks for all the effort spent on my behalf. Love, Dad

P.S. I am sending a copy of this letter to your sister so that she will know that all arrangements have been made.

If you wish to make an anatomical gift, you can include it as part of your Will; but it may be some time before your Will is located (Health & Safety 692.003). The better route is to make the donation by a separate writing. You can complete an *Organ Donor Card* when you apply for your Texas driver's license or Texas Identification Card (Transp. 521.401). If you wish to make a donation but do not want to advertise that fact on your driver's license or photo identification card, you can have your attorney prepare an Organ Donor Card to meet your special needs, or you can download a form to complete from the Internet.

 ORGAN DONOR PROGRAM
http://www.ordonorprogram.org

You can keep your Organ Donor Card at home with your important papers.

FACE TRANSPLANT

The Organ Donor Card allows you to give specific instructions about parts of the body that you do (or do not) wish to donate. In 2005, the first partial face transplant was performed in France. It was accompanied by a flurry of controversy regarding the use of the face of a donor without her prior written permission. It is important that you indicate on your Organ Donor Card whether you do, or do not, wish to make a donation of all, or part, of your face.

Regardless of whether you have an Organ Donor Card filed with the Texas Department of Transportation or whether you keep it at home, let your next of kin know that you wish to make a donation, if medically acceptable. Tell them that you have signed an Organ Donor Card and where it is located in the event it is ever needed.

GIFT FOR EDUCATION AND RESEARCH

Doctors will probably not consider your body suitable for transplantation if you are of advanced age, but you can still donate your body to a medical school for education and research. The ANATOMICAL BOARD OF THE STATE OF TEXAS is a state agency composed of one representative from each school of chiropractic, osteopathy, medicine or dentistry in the state of Texas. Their job is to distribute donations to schools throughout the state and to provide information about donations to the public (Health & Safety 691.030).

Schools will not accept a donation if the person died from a contagious disease, or crushing injury, or if the decedent was obese, so you need to have alternate disposition plans in place to provide for such condition.

Schools generally pay for local transportation of the body to the school. There could be a substantial transportation cost should you die far from the school, so you need to give your family instructions about what to do in such event.

You can get information about making an anatomical gift donation by calling the TEXAS DEPARTMENT OF STATE HEALTH SERVICES at (800) 222-3986 or visit the TEXAS DEPART-MENT OF HEALTH Web site.

 TEXAS DEPARTMENT OF HEALTH
http://www.tdh.state.tx.us/

If you do not wish to make an anatomical gift, let your family know how you feel. If you do not make provision for a gift, and do not tell anyone how you feel about donating any or all of your body, the decision will be up to your family.

Texas statute (Health & Safety 692.004) gives an order of priority for those who can make an anatomical gift on your behalf:

1st   your spouse
2nd   your adult son or daughter
3rd   either parent
4th   an adult brother or sister
5th   the person who was your court appointed Guardian, if any
6th   anyone else authorized to dispose of the body

Texas law requires that every effort be made to contact those people with highest priority. No gift can be made, of someone agrees to the donation and someone with the same or a higher priority objects. And Texas law prohibits the gift if the decedent, prior to death, refused to make a gift, or ever expressed an objection to someone with authority to make the gift.

AUTOPSIES

An autopsy is one of those things that most of us do not think about; reasoning that if it is needed, it will be carried out and, being dead, you will have no choice in the matter. But there are many times when an autopsy is optional. Sometimes a doctor is not sure of the cause of death, and asks the family to allow an autopsy. It may be in the family's best interest to consent to the procedure. The examination might reveal a genetic disorder, that could be treated if it later appears in another family member. An examination might reveal that death from a car "accident" could have been caused by a stroke or heart attack at the wheel. Perhaps the patient who died suddenly in a hospital was misdiagnosed. The nursing home resident could have died from negligence and not old age.

Texas statute (Crim. Proc. 49.13) gives an order of priority for the person who can authorize the procedure:

1st   the spouse   2nd   an adult child of the decedent
3rd   the legal guardian of the decedent's child
4th   a parent   5th   the decedent's guardian
6th   a next of kin

If none of these are available, a friend or whoever is responsible to arrange the burial may authorize the autopsy.

The person giving authorization for an optional autopsy must agree to pay for the autopsy because the cost is not covered under most health insurance plans. An autopsy can cost anywhere from several hundred to several thousand dollars. Still another reason family members hesitate to allow the procedure is that they do not know how the decedent would have felt about the examination. If you have strong feelings one way or another, it is important to let your family know whether you would want an optional autopsy.

Of course, there are problems with just telling someone how you feel about your burial arrangements, autopsies, and anatomical gifts:

YOU TELL THE WRONG PERSON

You may tell someone who does not have authority to carry out your wishes. That was the case with James. When his wife died, he moved to a retirement community where he lived for several years until his death. James had two sons who lived in different states. Although he loved his sons, he had difficulty talking to either of them about serious matters. It was easier for him to talk with his friends in the retirement community. They often spoke about dying and how they felt about different burial arrangements.

James would reminisce about his youth and growing up in a farming community in the plains state of Kansas. "I was happy and free. Out there I had room to breathe. It would be nice to be buried there — peaceful and spacious."

When he died, his friends told his sons about their father's desire to be buried in Kansas. They met the suggestion with scepticism and pragmatism:

"Dad didn't say anything like that to me."

"It would cost us double, if we had to arrange for burial in another state. I'm sure he didn't have that kind of expense in mind."

THE PERSON DOES NOT CARRY OUT YOUR WISHES

Sometimes the person you tell about the disposition of your body may not understand what you said or perhaps they hear only what they want to hear. Whether they follow your burial instructions or authorize an anatomical gift or an autopsy may depend more about what costs are involved, and their own feelings, rather than what you may have wanted.

Even if you tell someone and trust that person to carry out your wishes, it could be that the person you confide in cannot carry out your instructions. For example, if you tell your spouse what arrangements to make, he/she may become incapacitated or die before you do; or perhaps you both die together in a natural disaster or in a plane crash.

WHO WANTS TO TALK ABOUT IT?

For many people the main problem with telling someone what to do when you die is talking about your death. It may be an uncomfortable, if not unpleasant, subject for you to bring up, and for your family to discuss. If this is the case, then consider putting the information in writing and give the instructions to the person who will have the job of carrying out your wishes.

Making provision for the disposition of your body is important, but it is more important to make sure that you are in control of the health care you receive should you become seriously ill. This is not a problem when you are well enough to make your own medical decisions; however, it could happen that you are too ill to let people know what you want.

The solution to the problem is appoint someone to serve as your **HEALTH CARE AGENT**. You can give your family and physicians instructions about medical treatment that you do, or do not, want to receive. You can give your Health Care Agent authority to see that your instructions are followed.

You can legally appoint someone to carry out your wishes relating to the care of your person, by signing a document called a **Medical Power of Attorney.** You can have your attorney prepare a Medical Power of Attorney or you can prepare your own Power of Attorney by using the form provided in Texas statute Health & Safety 166.164 The person you appoint as your Health Care Agent under this Medical Power of Attorney will be able to make your medical decisions in the event that you are too ill to do so yourself.

You can express your wishes about whether you do (or do not) want life support systems to be used in the event that you are dying and there is no hope for your recovery by signing a document known as a *Directive To Physicians and Family or Surrogate.* The document is also referred to as a **Living Will.** Texas Statute (Health & Safety 166.033) contains statutory a form of Living Will. You can complete the form and attach it to your Medical Power of Attorney. Once attached, your Health Care Agent will see to it that the wishes you expressed in your Living Will are respected.

You can copy the statutory form of Medical Power of Attorney and Directive To Physician by looking up statutes Health and Safety 166.033 and 166.164 at your nearest law library. You can also download the statutes from the Texas statute Web site.

http://www.capital.state.tx.us/statutes

The statutory forms are basic forms. If you have special needs, you can have your attorney prepare a Medical Power of Attorney designed especially for you.

You can instruct your attorney to authorize the following as part of your Medical Power of Attorney:

ANATOMICAL GIFTS
If you want to make an anatomical gift, you can include an organ donor card in your Medical Power of Attorney and give your Health Care Agent authority to carry out your wishes. If you do not wish to make an anatomical gift, you can direct your Health Care Agent not to allow the procedure.

AUTOPSY
You can use your Medical Power of Attorney to authorize an autopsy, or you can withhold your consent for the performance of an optional autopsy, or you can leave the decision in the hands of your Health Care Agent.

ACCESS MEDICAL RECORDS
In 1996, the federal government passed the Health Insurance Portability and Accountability Act ("HIPAA"). The U.S. Department of Health and Human Service issued the Privacy Rule to implement HIPAA. The Privacy Rule restricts access to your medical records (45 CFR 164.524). The rule allows your Health Care Agent to access your medical records, however, it is a good idea to include a paragraph in your Medical Power of Attorney referring to HIPAA and giving your Health Care Agent specific authority to access health information that may be protected under HIPAA.

MEDICAL DECISIONS IF NO HEALTH CARE AGENT

If you do not appoint someone to act as your Health Care Agent and you are too sick to make your own medical decisions, then the person with priority to make medical decisions is established by Texas statute:

> 1st   your spouse
> 2nd   your adult children
> 3rd   your parents
> 4th   your nearest living relative.

A person with priority must be reasonably available, willing and competent to act. If not, the next one with priority will make the decision. Whoever makes the decision must base the decision on their knowledge of what you want and of course you can make your wishes known to them by signing a Directive as described on the prior page (Health & Safety 166.039).

If this order of priority is not as you wish, or if there is someone you wish to exclude altogether from making your health care decisions, it is important to sign a Medical Care Power of Attorney and appoint the person of your choice to act as your Health Care Agent. If not, life decisions made for you, may not be as you would have wished.

Some readers may be thinking "My family will surely respect my wishes as to my final disposition. Why bother with a Medical Power of Attorney? I probably will never need anyone to assist me. And even if I did, my family will tell the doctor what I want."

Those were George's thoughts exactly.

George was a devoted husband and father. His wife came down with Alzheimer's disease. George cared for her at home, but finally it was too much for him and he had to place her in a nursing home. He and his daughters often visited, although she scarcely recognized them.

George met Emily during one of his visits. Her husband also suffered from Alzheimer's and was a resident of the nursing home. George and Emily had much in common. After visiting with their respective spouses, they would go to the local coffee shop. One thing led to another and soon they were fast friends.

George's daughters were not happy with his "lady friend." They criticized everything about her. From the way she dressed, to her table manners. Emily did not take it personally. She believed the girls were more interested in their expected inheritance, than George's happiness. A second marriage might cut into what they considered to be rightfully theirs.

Not that George and Emily planned to wed. They both loved their respective spouses and had no intention of trying to obtain a divorce. They just enjoyed each other's company. Caring for their respective spouses , they learned to take it one day at a time. That philosophy carried over into their relationship. They were both content to enjoy social outings with each other — dinner, movies, playing golf, and so on.

Both were happier than they had been in years. But that happiness was short-lived. George suffered a stroke while driving a car. He was seriously injured and lapsed into a coma. The prognosis was not encouraging.

Doctors said George would die unless they put him on a ventilator and inserted a feeding tube. Even with these life support systems, they were not promising that he would survive.

Emily pleaded to keep him alive. "Let's try everything. If he doesn't improve, we can always discontinue the life support systems later."

George's daughters did not see it that way. "Why torture him with needles and tubes. Let him pass on peacefully."

George never signed a Living Will, so no one knew how he felt about life support systems. He never appointed anyone to be his Health Care Agent to make his medical decisions now that he was unable to do so himself. In the absence of written authorization, the doctors followed Texas law. George's spouse had priority to direct his treatment however because she was unable to do so, his daughters had the right to make medical decisions for their father.

Emily being just a friend, had no legal authority to direct his treatment.

George died.

A Health Care Estate Plan

We discussed an Estate Plan as it relates to the distribution or management of your Estate once you are deceased. In this age of extended life expectancy, a more pressing concern is how to manage and preserve your Estate in the event of a debilitating illness. As life expectancy increases, so does the percentage of the population who suffer incapacitating strokes, Alzheimer's disease or Parkinson's disease. It is estimated that more than half of the population who are 85 or older, have some degree of dementia. Your best Estate Plan could be sabotaged by a lengthy illness. In this chapter we will explore ways to pay for the health care that you may require as you age.

In addition to paying for your health care, you need to consider who will care for your finances and everyday physical needs in the event that you are too ill to do so yourself. A *Health Care Estate Plan* is a plan designed to care for your person and property in the event of an incapacitating illness. In the last chapter, we discussed how you can appoint a Health Care Agent to care for your person in the event of your incapacity. But there is still the problem of who will care for your property. In this chapter we discuss how you can appoint someone to care for your property and manage your finances in the event of your incapacity.

The optimum way to provide for the care of your property in the event of your incapacity is to set up a Trust and appoint a Successor Trustee to care for your property in accordance with the directions you give in the Trust.

The optimum way to provide for the care of your property in the event of your incapacity is to set up a Trust appointing a Successor Trustee to care for your property according to the directions given in your Trust. You can be Trustee of the funds while you have capacity. Should you become incapacitated, then the person you name as Successor Trustee will take over. But if you do not have sufficient assets to justify the cost of employing an attorney to draft a Trust, then there are other strategies that you can use to solve the problem.

THE JOINT ACCOUNT

You can set up a joint checking account so that a trusted family member can write checks on the account. Of course there are all the inherent problems of a joint account that we discussed in Chapter 2. You can avoid many of those problems by limiting the amount of money that can be accessed by the family member. For example, you can arrange your finances so that all of your bills are paid from a single checking account and your family member can access that account, only.

THE CONVENIENCE ACCOUNT

If you set up a joint account, your family member will own whatever is in the account should your die. If this is not as you wish, you can instruct the bank that this is a **Convenience Account** and that in the event of your death the family member may no longer access your account (Probate 439A). But ultimately the family member must be trustworthy because the bank is under no duty to stop your family member from writing checks on your account until the bank learns of your death (Probate 438A).

The joint or convenience account solves the problem of how to pay your bills in the event you are temporarily ill. It does not solve the problem of how to manage your business affairs in the event of an extended illness. For example, suppose you have a stroke and can no longer be cared for at home. Should it be necessary for you to sell your home and move to an assisted living facility, no one will have the authority to sell the house for you. In such case, your friends or family members may be forced to ask the Court to appoint a Guardian to manage your finances, and if you did not appoint a Health Care Agent, to make your medical decisions and care for your person.

Before doing so, the Court will need to be convinced that you are unable to do so yourself. The judge will set a time for a hearing on the matter. He will send a notice of the hearing to you and your next of kin as determined by the Texas Laws of Descent (Probate 633). You will need to be examined by a physician who will submit his report to the Court (Probate 687). Determining whether you have capacity to take care of yourself can be an embarrassing, and demeaning experience, if you are sufficiently aware of the proceedings. You may even want to employ an attorney to fight the matter (Probate 694K).

If the judge determines that you are incapacitated, he will appoint a Guardian of your person or property, or both (Probate 693). If a Guardian of your property is appointed he will take possession of your assets and file an inventory with the Court within 30 days of his appointment (Probate 729).

The Court may order your Guardian to employ someone to appraise your property (Probate 727). If you have significant assets he may require the Guardian to obtain a bond for the protection of your assets (Probate 702).

Each year the Guardian of your property must account to the Court for money spent (Probate 741). Your Guardian may need to employ an accountant to help prepare the inventory and annual accounting. If a Guardian of your person is appointed, he will see to your health care. He will need to prepare and file a report each year regarding your place of residence and mental health (Probate 743). The Guardian will need to employ an attorney to establish the Guardianship and to see that reports are properly and timely filed.

The Guardian is entitled to be paid for his services. The Court will need to approve the Guardian's application for compensation. Under Texas law, total compensation paid to the Guardian of your person and the Guardian of your property each year may not exceed 5% of the gross income of your Estate, plus 5% of all money paid out of your Estate (Probate 665).

Court filing fees, the examination fee, the cost of a bond, accounting fees, the Guardian's fee, your attorney's fee and the Guardian's attorney fees, are all charged to you! (Probate 665A, 669).

Guardianship procedures are expensive to set up and maintain. Curious that so many people worry about how to avoid Probate, when the larger concern should be how to avoid guardianship. Consider that it is not all that hard to arrange your finances so that Probate is not necessary. The cost to administer your estate should be minimal.

Even with a full Probate procedure, whatever it costs to Probate your Estate is a one-time expense. And Probate is a one-time procedure. Once monies are distributed to your beneficiaries, it is over. Not so if you become incapacitated. It can cost thousands of dollars to set up the Guardianship; and more money to care for you and your property each year. And this expense goes on, year after year, until you are returned to capacity, or die (Probate 694).

As with Probate it is not all that hard to avoid these unnecessary charges to your Estate. To avoid the need for a Guardian of your person, you can appoint a Health Care Agent to make your medical decisions should you be too ill to do so yourself (see Chapter 8).

To avoid the need for a Guardian of your property, you can set up a Trust and appoint a Successor Trustee to care for your property in the event of your incapacity. For those of limited means, the **DURABLE POWER OF ATTORNEY** is the next best Estate plan.

A POWER OF ATTORNEY FOR FINANCES

A ***Power of Attorney*** is a legal document by which someone (the *Principal*) gives another (his *Agent* or *Attorney In Fact*) authority to do certain acts on behalf of the Principal. If you wish to have someone to be able to conduct business on your behalf in the event of your incapacity, you can make the Power of Attorney ***durable*** by including the phrase:

> This power of attorney is not affected by the subsequent disability or incapacity of the Principal (Probate 482, 483).

Texas statute (Probate 490) contains a STATUTORY DURABLE POWER OF ATTORNEY. You can copy the statute at your local library or you can download it from the Internet.
http://www.capital.state.tx.us/statutes

With this document you can give your Attorney In Fact power to manage your finances and do much the same with your property as you can do yourself, such as:

⇨ buy or sell real property on your behalf

⇨ buy or sell personal property for you

⇨ trade in securities (stocks, bonds, etc.)

⇨ do your banking (pay your bills, taxes)

⇨ have access to your safe deposit box

⇨ operate your business

⇨ borrow money on your behalf

⇨ purchase insurance policies and name beneficiaries

⇨ sue or defend a law suit on your behalf

⇨ apply for government benefits on your behalf

⇨ have access to your business and personal records.

Notice that there are many things that your Agent can do for you personally, such as defending a law suit or suing on your behalf or applying for government benefits. Even if you have a Trust, it is important to appoint an Agent under a Durable Power of Attorney to do these important, personal, things for you, in the event you can't. Your Trust can only authorize your Successor Trustee to manage property that is placed in your Trust. Your Successor Trustee has no authority over you, personally. But you can give him (or anyone else) that authority by making him your Agent under a Power of Attorney.

 **STATUTORY FORM MAY GIVE MORE POWER THAN YOU WISH**

The statutory Power of Attorney is easy to complete, however, if you sign the document without deleting any of the powers granted in that document, you are, in fact, giving far more power to your Attorney In Fact than appears on the face of the document. The powers that appear in the document are short-hand for broad powers that are identified in later statutes. For example, by giving your Attorney In Fact the power to make "real property transactions" you are actually giving him all of the powers stated in Probate statutes 491 and 492. That includes giving him the right to sell, transfer or mortgage any real property that you now own (including your home) and to buy real property with your money. Statute 492 also gives your Attorney In Fact the right to insure your property, pay your real estate taxes, make repairs or additions to your property; employ people to do these things, and pay the workers with your money.

If you are going to sign the Statutory Power of Attorney, it is important that you read the entire Durable Power of Attorney Act; i.e., Probate statute 481 through 500.

GENERAL VS. LIMITED POWER OF ATTORNEY

You can sign a Power of Attorney giving your Attorney In Fact broad general powers. With these powers your Attorney In Fact can do much the same with your property as you can. If this is of concern to you, instead of giving a General Power of Attorney, you can give a **Limited Power of Attorney** and restrict the things your Attorney In Fact can do to just those things authorized in the document.

One power that should be specifically granted in your Power of Attorney, is the power to apply for medical assistance benefits in the event of your incapacity. In the next chapter we will be discussing the many things you can do to qualify for Medicaid. You need to give someone authority to take the necessary steps for you to become eligible for government benefits, in the event you are too ill to do so yourself. Even if you do not wish to give someone control over your finances at this time, you should give someone a Limited Power of Attorney for the purpose of qualifying for Medicaid.

Limited or General, the operative word in any Power of Attorney is POWER. Once your Attorney In Fact has authority to act, he essentially steps into your shoes and can do whatever you gave him authority to do. Your primary consideration in choosing an Agent is trustworthiness. You need to choose someone who will follow your instructions and put the Power of Attorney to the use you intended. You need to choose someone, who, when using your Power of Attorney, will always put your interests ahead of his.

You may be less concerned with trustworthiness than the loss of independence. But the thing to keep in mind is that you still have the power to do all of the things you gave your Attorney In Fact authority to do. The only difference is that now, you both have the power to conduct your business transactions.

Of course, shared authority is still less independent than sole authority; so you may hesitate to give someone a Power of Attorney until it is needed. But if you wait until it is needed, you may be too sick to sign the document. There are two simple solutions to this dilemma — keep it in your possession, or make it effective only upon your incapacity:

USING THE POWER OF ATTORNEY

An Agent under a Power of Attorney cannot operate on behalf of the Principal, unless the Agent has possession of the original Power of Attorney and presents it to whomever he wants to rely on that document. For example, if your Agent wants to use the Power of Attorney to sell one of your securities, he will need to produce the original document and perhaps sign an *Affidavit* (a written statement sworn to before a Notary Public) saying that the Power of Attorney is still in effect and that you did not revoke that Power of Attorney.

KEEP THE DOCUMENT IN YOUR POSSESSION

Before anyone (a bank, stockbroker, closing agent, etc.) will accept the Power of Attorney they will want to see the original document so that they are assured that your Attorney In Fact has authority to transact business on your behalf. If you keep the original document in your possession and do not give anyone a copy, your Attorney In Fact will not be able to act for you.

The only problem with this arrangement is that you need to arrange to make the document accessible to your Attorney In Fact in the event of your incapacity. If he is a trusted family member, you can give him the location of the document with instructions to take possession of the Durable Power of Attorney in the event of your incapacity.

THE SPRINGING POWER OF ATTORNEY

A better solution may be to have your sttorney draft a "springing" Durable Power of Attorney that is not operational until your family doctor and/or independent physician says that you are incapacitated and unable to manage your financial affairs.

Your Attorney In Fact can hold the original document, but cannot use it until it "springs to life" when a doctor determines that you are too ill to care for your property. You can create a Springing Durable Power of Attorney by adding the following provision to the document

> This Durable Power of Attorney becomes operational only when my regularly attending physician and _____ (name of family member) sign an Affidavit stating that I am disabled or incapacitated.

Your attorney can design a Durable Power of Attorney, to meet your special needs. He can even include powers that relate to your health care. But as a practical matter, it may be better to have a separate Medical Power of Attorney. As explained in the last chapter, you can use a Medical Power of Attorney to appoint a Health Care Agent. You can also sign a Living Will giving your Health Care Agent directions about the care you wish to receive in the event you are too ill to direct your own medical treatment.

There are at least two reasons to have a separate Medical Power of Attorney:

APPOINT DIFFERENT PEOPLE TO SERVE

You may want one person to serve as your Health Care Agent and another to serve as your Attorney In Fact. One family member may be an excellent choice to make your health care decisions, yet that person may not be the best person to make financial decisions on your behalf.

PRIVACY

Even if you want the same person to serve as your Health Care Agent and Attorney In Fact, there is still the matter of privacy. Your Health Care Agent will give a copy of your Health Care Advance Directive to your physician to be placed in your medical file. Your doctors have no need to know of your business dealings; and vice versa. To conduct business on your behalf your Attorney In Fact will need to give a copy of the Power of Attorney to your business associates (banks, stockbrokers, etc.). Your business associates have no need to know of your medical decisions.

A Will Is Not Enough In Texas

ACCESS MEDICAL INFORMATION

As explained in the last chapter, under the Privacy Rule of Health Insurance Portability and Accountability Act ("HIPAA"), the person you appoint as your Health Care Agent under a Health Care Power of Attorney may access your medical records. However, in general, a Power of Attorney for finances is not sufficient to access your medical records under HIPAA. You can read the summary of the HIPAA Privacy Rule for more information about who can access your medical records. The summary appears on the U.S. Department of Health and Human Services Web site.

 U.S. DEPT. OF HEALTH & HUMAN SERVICES
http://www.hhs.gov/hipaa

For privacy, and perhaps security reasons, consider having a separate Medical Power of Attorney and a separate Financial Power of Attorney rather than try to get it all into a single multipurpose document.

CARING FOR YOU WHEN YOU CAN'T

It is relatively simple and inexpensive to head off guardianship. All you need do is appoint an Attorney In Fact under a Durable Power of Attorney to manage your finances, and a Health Care Agent under a Medical Power of Attorney to make your medical care decisions. These documents authorize people of your choice to care for your person and your property in the event of your incapacity. But, despite your best plans, something unusual could happen causing a Court to decide that you or your property need protection. For example, suppose you disappear and cannot be found after a diligent search. It might be necessary to have a Court appoint a *Receiver* to manage your property in your absence (Civ. Prac. & Rem. 64.102).

Or perhaps you develop an addiction or a mental illness causing self-destructive behavior. Your friends or family might decide that you are in need of protection and ask a Court to appoint a Guardian to care for you.

Although it may not be possible to avoid all guardianship procedures, you can have a measure of control over your fate. Texas statute gives you the right to name the person of your choice to serve as your Guardian. You can name someone to be the Guardian of your person and/or the Guardian of your property by signing a document entitled:
DECLARATION OF GUARDIAN IN THE EVENT OF LATER INCAPACITY OR NEED OF A GUARDIAN

The Declaration form is given in Texas statute (Probate 679). You can copy the statute at your nearest law library, or download the statute from the Internet.
http://www.capital.state.tx.us/statutes

The form for the Declaration allows you to name your choice of Guardian, and three alternates. The form also enables you to disqualify someone from serving as Guardian (Probate 679). The judge will honor your wishes and appoint your choice of Guardian, but if that person is unable or unwilling to serve, the judge will appoint your first alternate, and so on (Probate 689).

Even though a statutory form is available, it is best to have the document drafted by your attorney because the judge may want evidence that at the time you signed the document you were at least 18 years old and that you had sufficient mental capacity to make an intelligent choice of guardian. Your attorney can have you sign the document in the presence of two credible witnesses (usually himself and a member of his office staff) who can testify that you knew exactly what you were doing when you signed the document.

If you do not express your choice of Guardian, the Court will appoint your spouse to serve as Guardian. If your spouse is unwilling or unable to serve, or if you are single, the Court will appoint your next of kin as Guardian. Usually family members decide among themselves who should serve as Guardian, but if two family members with equal priority want the job (say two of your adult children), the judge will make the decision, choosing the person he thinks will do the best job in caring for you (Probate 677).

But the problem with having the judge make the selection is that he knows little about those who come before his Court. Some people may look good on paper, but in fact may be a poor choice. That was the case with a woman who the Court determined was not capable of handling her finances. She had a stroke and was unable to speak. The Court ruled that she was in need of a Guardian of her property. Her son and daughter both wanted the job.

The Court considered their backgrounds and current commitments. The son was a college graduate with a degree in business administration. The daughter was a homemaker with three small children. The judge thought the son the better choice because of his educational background and the fact that he was single and would have more time to devote to the care of his mother. The mother was too ill to express her choice of Guardian, but she never would have chosen her son to handle her finances because of the many times she had to bail him out of debt.

Again, it is a matter of planning ahead, and being in charge of your own destiny, rather than leaving the choice up to a judge to decide.

The good news: You are going to live longer.

The bad news: It's going to cost you.

Scientists are doing a great job of prolonging life, but unless they find Ponce De Leon's fountain, the general population will continue to age. Along with age comes infirmities. Eyes fail. Hearing diminishes. Mobility declines. Digestive systems either speed up or slow down, all to the discomfort of the unhappy occupant of the body. It's all part of the "golden" years.

The pharmacology industry is well motivated to produce drugs that manage the ills associated with aging. Their research has led to a wealth of pharmaceutical products that do not cure, but do allow people to live in relative comfort into advanced age. The only problem is the cost of these drugs. Medicare covers the treatment of life-threatening brushes with heart disease, stroke, cancer and diabetes, but paying for maintenance medication is up to you. Even if you belong to a Medicare Prescription Drug Plan or have some other prescription insurance, you will need to contribute to the payment of your medication.

Medicare is also limited in long term nursing care coverage. The structure of Medicare has changed giving people the option of staying with the *Original Medicare Plan* or choosing a *Medicare Advantage Plan* such as a Medicare Health Maintenance Organization ("HMO"), or other Medicare Health Plans. Coverage depends on which plan is chosen. If you remain with the Original Medicare Plan you do not pay for the first 20 days of a stay in a skilled nursing facility (i.e., a nursing home). You pay up to $124** per day for days 21 through 100.

**This is the value for the year 2007. The federal government adjusts the amount each year.

Unless you have Medicare Supplemental Insurance coverage, it will cost you up to $9,920 for the next 80 days. After 100 days, you are on your own. A nursing home stay of one or two years can wipe out the life savings of most working people. Once savings are gone, the government provides care in the form of Medicaid coverage. If you have no assets to speak of, and a relatively low income, the cost of long-term nursing care is the least of your worries. Medicaid is available to take care of your medical and nursing care needs. And no need to worry if you are wealthy. You have enough money to pay for the care you might need. The rest of us need to think about ways to provide for long-term health care.

For those concerned about the loss of life savings because of illness, there is supplemental and/or long-term health care insurance. There are many different insurance plans available. You can call the National Association of Insurance Commissioners at (816) 783-8300 for information about long-term health care insurance.

Texas has a HEALTH INFORMATION COUNSELING AND ADVO-CACY PROGRAM ("HICAP"). If you have a specific question, a counselor with HICAP can help you. You can reach a HICAP counselor at any local AREA AGENCY ON AGING. Call (800) 252-9240 for the telephone number of the Area Agency On Aging office nearest you.

LONG TERM INSURANCE FOR FEDERAL EMPLOYEES

The Long Term Care Security Act is designed to make long term care insurance available to federal employees, including postal workers, members of the uniformed services, civilian and military retirees, and their qualified relatives. You can call the Office of Personnel Management at (800) 582-3337 for information about the federal long term care insurance program or you can visit their Web site.

OFFICE OF PERSONNEL MANAGEMENT
http://www.opm.gov/insure/ltc

The National Association Of Retired Federal Employees ("NARFE") was actively involved in developing the federal long term care insurance program. You can get information about the program by calling the NARFE Legislative Hotline toll-free (877) 217-8234 or by visiting their Web site.

NATIONAL ASSOC. OF RETIRED FEDERAL EMPLOYEES
http://www.narfe.org

THE PROBLEM OF COST AND ELIGIBILITY

Long Term Care Insurance sounds like the perfect solution, until you start examining the cost. The cost isn't too bad if you are comparatively young, say in your 50s. But can you imagine paying that premium each month until you are in your 80s and never needing nursing care?

Many decide to wait till they are old and going downhill. But that just brings other problems. The older you are, the greater the cost of insurance. And there is the risk that you will be refused coverage because of a "pre-existing" condition, i.e., the insurance company may consider you to be too great a risk for them to insure.

Different insurance companies have come up with insurance plans that may provide a solution for the person who is relatively young and in good health. Some companies offer long-term care insurance that is paid-up within a fixed period of time. Once payments are made for a certain number of years, the person is insured for long-term care without further payment.

Other companies combine long-term care insurance with a life insurance policy. They offer long-term care insurance that converts to a life insurance policy, if it happens that the insured person dies before needing long-term care. When shopping for a long-term care policy, consider including different insurance alternatives in your investigation.

Purchasing Long Term Care Insurance represents a significant investment. Before signing a contract, it is important to check with the Texas Department of Insurance to determine whether they have a good record of paying claims. This is no small problem. A newspaper article reported that in the year 2007, almost a quarter of insurance claims for long term care were denied in the state of California. No doubt there are similar statistics in other states.

Before purchasing Long Term Care Insurance, call the Texas Department of Insurance, Consumer Help Line at (800) 252-3439 and ask about the number of complaints that have been filed against the company for non-payment of claims.

For some people long term care insurance is not an option. An elderly person living on a low fixed income may not have enough money to pay the monthly premium for a long term care insurance policy. And long term care insurance is not an option for the person who has been diagnosed with a chronic, debilitating disease.

People in such a position worry that they may need to deplete their life savings, just to pay for a year or two of nursing care.

Both of these problems can be solved by using current law to become qualified for Medicaid. Medicaid is a public assistance program that is funded jointly by the federal and state government. There are state and federal laws governing who may become eligible for the program.

A *Medicaid Qualifying Plan* is a plan that takes both state and federal laws into consideration. Operating within the boundaries of these laws, those who are concerned about becoming impoverished in order to pay for long-term care, seek to preserve and protect their Estate by implementing a Medicaid Qualifying Plan.

There has been controversy about plans designed to qualify a person for Medicaid. Some think that to intentionally arrange finances to qualify for Medicaid is immoral — a legal method of working the system.

Those people may argue: "Why are such things allowed? After all, wasn't Medicaid designed to help poor people? Why should people be allowed to make themselves poor to get on the public dole??

Those who feel they need to qualify for Medicaid have a different point of view. They may argue:

"I worked all my life and hoped to leave a few pennies for the kids. Why did I work so hard? To give it all to a nursing home? I paid my taxes just like everyone else. The government pays hundreds of thousands of dollars for people on Medicare to have open heart surgery, and they pay for lengthy and expensive cancer treatments. Why should those who have Alzheimer's or Parkinson's or those who suffer a debilitating stroke, not be entitled to receive equal benefits?"

Although we can understand and appreciate both points of view, our job, as we see it, is to just explain the law as it is at the time of publication. We think it is important to do so because many people take a position (pro or con) based on what they perceive the law to be, and not based upon the law as it actually is.

Once the reader understands what it takes to qualify for Medicaid in the state of Texas, he can decide for himself whether the law is basically fair to the people who need to qualify, or whether it is flawed (either too restrictive or too liberal) and needs to be changed.

Hopefully, those with a strong opinion will share those views with their legislators.

A Medicaid Qualifying Plan 10

A better name for this chapter might be "A Health Care Contingency Plan." A lengthy stay in a nursing home is something most of us do not want to even think about, much less prepare for. Why prepare for something that may never happen? Yet as we age, there is that nagging "What if?" "What if I need long term nursing care? How will I pay for it?"

An effective way to put this anxiety at rest is to have a contingency plan. To form a contingency plan, you need to know your options. In this case, your options are directly related to your ability to pay for that care. But it is hard to predict future fortunes. People win the lottery. Those with a large portfolio may have their fortunes disappear in a market melt-down. There is no need for concern if it turns out that you can afford to pay for your own nursing care; and there is no concern should you become impoverished because there are government programs that provide for your health care. The worst case scenario is that you will be able to afford long-term care, but at the cost of your life savings.

In this chapter, we will discuss options available to you under that worst case scenario. We will explain current state and federal law as it relates to qualifying for medical assistance programs.

WHO IS ENTITLED TO MEDICAID?

Medicaid is a program that provides medical and long term nursing care for people with low income and limited resources. The program is funded and regulated by both federal and state government. The governing agency for the federal government is the Centers for Medicare and Medicaid Services. The TEXAS HEALTH AND HUMAN SERVICES COMMISSION is the state governing agency for all of the Texas Medical Assistance programs (Hum. Res. 32.003, 32.021, 32.026). Applications are taken and the program administered at the local level by the DEPARTMENT OF AGING AND DISABILITY SERVICES.

Medicaid is an entitlement program, meaning that whoever meets the financial standards for the program is entitled to receive benefits under that program. Those who do not qualify are not entitled to any Medicaid benefits.

There are many benefits offered under Medicaid, from health care for mothers and children; to community based services for those who need some assistance with their health care; to full nursing care for those who need assistance with dressing, bathing, eating, walking and toileting. We will limit our discussion of Medicaid to aged persons in need of long term institutional nursing care. You can get information about other Medicaid programs by calling the Area Agencies On Aging at (800) 252-9240.

You can also get information about Medicaid from the Department of Aging and Disability Services Web site.

 THE DEPARTMENT OF AGING AND DISABILITY SERVICES
http://www.dads.state.tx.us

Persons who are receiving Supplemental Security Income ("SSI") may be eligible to receive Medicaid benefits in Texas because the requirements for these programs are much the same. If a person is not receiving SSI, he may be eligible for Medicaid if he is 65 or older, or blind, or disabled.

When a person applies for Medicaid (the "Applicant"**) the Texas Health and Human Services Commission Health Services ("HHSC") *Eligibility Specialist* will investigate his citizenship, medical condition, income, and assets. If the Applicant is too ill to apply for himself, his spouse, or a family member or friend, may apply for him (42 US Code of Federal Regulations ("CFR") 435.908, Medicaid Eligibility Handbook ("MEH") 4111, 4112).

**For simplicity, we will use the male gender for the Applicant and the female gender for his spouse.

CITIZENSHIP ELIGIBILITY
To be eligible for Medicaid in Texas, the Applicant must be a resident of the state, and either a U.S. citizen or a *Qualified Alien*, i.e., an alien who is lawfully admitted for permanent residence (42 U.S. 1396a(10), 1382c(a)(1)(B)). You can find the definition of a Texas Resident in section 2221 of the MEDICAID ELIGIBILITY HANDBOOK (MEH 2221) and the definition of Qualified Alien in section 2220 (MEH 2220).

The Handbook is available at Forms & Handbook section of the Department of Aging and Disability Services Web site. http://www.dads.state.tx.us

MEDICAL ELIGIBILITY

Generally an Applicant who is currently receiving institutional care is medically eligible for Medicaid. However, if there is any question regarding his Health, a Disability Review Team will review the Applicant's medical report to determine whether he requires institutional care. The Disability Review Team is composed of a psychological or medical consultant and another person qualified to interpret and evaluate medical reports and other evidence relating to the Applicant's medical eligibility (42 CFR 435.541).

INCOME ELIGIBILITY

In Texas, there is a limit on the amount of income earned by the Applicant each month. For the year 2007, the Applicant may have a monthly income of no more than $1,869. If the Applicant is over this *Income Cap* by even one penny, he will be disqualified. However, this problem is easily solved, because the state of Texas allows the Applicant's excess income to be place in a *Qualified Income Trust* (MEH 2310).

A Qualified Income Trust is a Trust drafted in conformity with state and federal law. Each month the Applicant's excess income is added to the Trust. The Trust must be irrevocable with the state of Texas as the beneficiary of the Trust, i.e., once the Applicant dies all the Trust property goes to the state of Texas as reimbursement for monies spent on his behalf. An experienced Elder Law attorney will be able to draft the Trust so that it meets HHSC specifications. Once drafted, the Applicant can immediately qualify for Medicaid — provided he meets all other medical and Resource criteria.

The reader may be wondering why the state of Texas has an Income Cap when it is so easily overcome. Money placed in Qualified Income Trust eventually go to the state. Why not (as many other states do) simply require the Applicant to contribute all of his income towards the cost of his nursing care?

This is one of those questions to ask your legislator.

PERSONAL NEEDS ALLOWANCE

Once he qualifies, the *Medicaid Recipient* is allowed to keep $60 a month for his personal needs, such as clothing or hair cuts. The rest of his income will go towards the payment of his nursing care; and/or to the Qualified Income Trust if his income is over the Cap.

RESOURCE ELIGIBILITY

In addition to the Income Cap, there is a limit on the amount of **Resources** owned by the Applicant. Resources are cash and other real or personal property, owned solely or in part by the Applicant, that can be converted to cash and that are countable for purposes of qualifying for Medicaid (MEH 2310, 2313). The Applicant's Resource limit is $2,000 (MEH 2311)

An Applicant who is over the Resource limit on the first day of the month that he applies for Medicaid needs to "spend down" his assets to $2,000. If he becomes eligible at any time during the month that he applies, his Medicaid benefits will begin on the first day of the next month. If he is not over the Resource limit when he applies, he will be eligible for benefits any day during the month of application that he meets all other eligibility requirements (i.e. income and medical need).

The spouse of an Applicant who lives in their home or elsewhere in the community (i.e., not in a nursing home) is called the **Community Spouse**. Prior to 1988, the Community Spouse was required to use whatever assets she had to pay for the nursing care of her spouse. The Applicant could not qualify for Medicaid until they both were virtually impoverished. In addition to being unfair to the Community Spouse, this was not good government policy because it often resulted in the Community Spouse turning to local government social service programs for support. The Medicaid provisions of the Medicare Catastrophic Coverage Act of 1988 remedied the situation by considering the assets of the couple as being part of a common pot and allowing the Community Spouse to keep a portion of their combined income and assets.

The amount allowed has been increased over the years. In 2007, the federal government allows the Community Spouse to keep up to $101,640 of their combined Resources. The federal government also considers that the Community Spouse needs money each month for her maintenance. If her income is not sufficient to support her, the income of the Medicaid Recipient can be used to supplement the income of the Community Spouse up to a maximum of $2,541 per month.

NOTE ⇨ The figures used in this Chapter are for the year 2007. The federal and state government adjust these values on an annual basis. Check the UPDATE section of the EAGLE PUBLISHING COMPANY Web site for later values. http://www.eaglepublishing.com

The federal government sets these maximum value (namely $101,640 for Resources and $2,541 for maintenance). States have the right to administer the Medicaid program according to their state law, provided their state law is within federal guidelines and does not exceed maximum and minium values set by the federal government ($101,640 and $20,328, respectively for the year 2007). This being the case, the actual amount allowed to the Community spouse can vary significantly state to state.

THE SPOUSE'S INCOME

The state of Texas uses the maximum federal guideline as the *Monthly Maintenance Needs Allowance* for Community Spouse's monthly income. The Community Spouse is not required to contribute her income to the cost of the nursing care of her spouse, even if her income is greater than the maximum federal guideline (currently $2,541). Income attributed to the Community Spouse is determined by the "name on the check" rule, without considering the state's marital property rules. If her name is on the check, it's her money. If an income check is paid jointly to the husband and wife, each is entitled to half of the value of the check (42 U.S.C. 1396r-5(b), MEH 2410).

If for some reason (high medical bills, the need for special care, etc.), the Community spouse needs more than the maximum federal guideline, she can appeal to have that value increased. See the next chapter for a discussion of the appeal process.

If, the Community Spouse's monthly income from employment, Social Security, pension, etc. is less than $2,541, she is entitled to keep as much of the combined income of her income and her spouse's income each month as necessary to get her to that value (1 TAC 358.503 (a)).

For example, suppose the Community Spouse has a monthly income of $2,000, The HHSC will combine the income of the Recipient and his Spouse and allocates $2,541 of that combined income to the Spouse (1 TAC 358.503 (a)).

THE SPOUSE'S RESOURCE ALLOWANCE

Assets owned by the Applicant or his spouse, are considered to be available to the Applicant for purposes of Medicaid eligibility. Under federal law, the Community Spouse is entitled to keep a share of the couple's assets up to the current maximum of $101,640. That share is called the *Community Spouse Resource Allowance* (42 U.S.C. 1396r-5(c)(2), 1396r-5f). The Community Spouse to allowed to keep half of their common pot of assets with a minimum value of $20,328 up to the federal maximum value of $101,640.

For example, suppose the couple own $22,000 between them. The Community Spouse is allowed to keep $20,238 as her Resource Allowance. The Applicant is allowed to keep the remainder (22,000- 20,238 = $1,762) as part of his $2,000 Resource Allowance. All other things being equal, the Applicant should qualify for Medicaid.

Suppose instead that the couple have $200,000 between them. The Community spouse can keep her half ($100,000) as a Resource Allowance. The Applicant can keep his $2,000, but that leaves him with $98,000 above the Resource limit. The first question to ask in such a situation is whether all of their assets count as a Resource.

WHAT COUNTS AS A RESOURCE?

Real or personal property, owned by the Applicant, or his spouse, that can be converted to cash and used for their support, are considered to be a Resource. This includes bank accounts, certificates of deposit, property in a Revocable Living Trust, stocks and bonds.

Some things owned by the Applicant, or his spouse, can be converted to cash, but are not counted as a Resource. Such items are called "Exempt Assets" or "Non-Countable Assets." We will refer to them as *Excluded Resources* (42 U.S.C. 1382b).

EXCLUDED RESOURCES

The following items are Excluded and are not counted as a Resource for purposes of determining Medicaid Eligibility.

AUTOMOBILE

A car that is in use is an Excluded Resource. In general, an Applicant who is in a nursing home, cannot use his car. In that case the HHSC will determine the fair market value of his car and count anything over $4,500 as a Resource (MEH 2342.1). If the Applicant is married and his Community Spouse is using the car as transportation, the entire value of the car is Excluded. The full value of a second automobile counts as a Resource with the exception of an automobile that is specially equipped to permit a member of the family to drive it (Title 1, Chapter 358.442(a) of the Texas Administrative Code ("TAC")).

HOUSEHOLD GOODS AND PERSONAL EFFECTS

⇨ Household goods being used by the Community Spouse do not count as a Resource.

⇨ An engagement ring and/or a wedding ring do not count as a Resource, regardless of its value.

In general, household items owned by a single Applicant do not count as a Resource, however if the Applicant lists an item worth more than $500 on his application form, the HHSC caseworker will investigate further to determine the value of his personal property. If the equity in the household goods and personal effects exceeds, $5,000, the caseworker will count the excess as a Resource. For example, if the caseworker determines the value of all of the single Applicant's personal property is $6,000, the caseworker will count $1,000 of that property as a Resource (MEH 2342.2).

BURIAL ARRANGEMENTS

⇨ Burial spaces for the Applicant and/or his immediate family (spouse, parent, children, siblings, and spouses of those family members) are Exempt Resources. This includes pre-paid grave sites, mausoleums, urns, niches, etc. (MEH 2341.5).

⇨ An Irrevocable Prepaid Funeral Benefits Contract as described in Chapter 8 is an Excluded Resource.

⇨ A burial fund of up to $1,500 is Excluded provided the fund is in a separate bank account and clearly identified as being set aside for the burial of the Applicant. The Spouse may also set up her own burial fund of up to $1,500 (1 TAC 358.442(e)). The burial fund is not available as an Excluded Resource if other burial arrangements have been made such a life insurance policy of $1,500, or a Prepaid Funeral Benefits Contract (1 TAC 358.503 (i), MEH 2331.9)

The value of a <u>revocable</u> Prepaid Funeral Benefits contract can be used in place of a burial fund; however if the value of the contract exceeds $1,500 the excess counts as a Resource because it can be converted to cash at any time (1 TAC 358.442(e)((2)(A), MEH 2331.9). As explained in Chapter 8, the purchaser of a Prepaid Funeral Benefits contract can make his contract irrevocable by signing a waiver (Finance 154.156). Texas law allows an Applicant to do this without affecting his right to qualify for Medicaid.

LIFE INSURANCE

An insurance policy owned by the Applicant or his spouse, is an Excluded Resource if the *Face Value* (the amount paid at death) is $1,500 or less per insured person. For example, if the Applicant owns a $1,000 life insurance policy on each of his three children, then none of these policies count as a Resource. But if the Applicant owns a policy whose face value is more than $1,500, then the Cash Surrender Value (the amount paid if the policy is cancelled) counts as a Resource (MEH 2331.91). The Cash Surrender Value can be obtained from the insurance company.

A term life insurance policy is a life insurance policy covering the life of the insured party for a given period of time. No monies are paid unless the insured person dies during that time period. A term insurance policy has no cash value, so it does not count as a Resource regardless of the Face Value of the policy.

PROPERTY ESSENTIAL TO SELF-SUPPORT

Property that is essential for the support of the Applicant or his spouse does not count as a Resource (MEH 2343.1). This includes real property, equipment, supplies, safety equipment, tools, uniforms. For example, if the Applicant owns a restaurant that produces an income that he uses to support himself and his family, the restaurant and all of the equipment within it does not count as a Resource — however, income from the property still counts.

LIVESTOCK

Livestock used in a trade or business, or kept for the family's consumption are Excluded Resources (1 TAC 358.442(f)), MEH 2343.3).

INCOME PRODUCING PROPERTY

Up to $6,000 of the value of non-business income producing property maybe excluded if it produces a rate of return of at least 6% (MEH 2343.2). The return on investment is equal to the Applicant's equity (market value less loans) divided by the annual income from the property. For example, if the Applicant owns stock worth $5,000 and it pays dividends of at least 6% a year, the stock does not count as a Resource, however, the dividends count as income. If his equity in the stock is greater than $6,000, or he is earning less than 6% per year, the stock counts as a Resource (MEH 2341.4)

PENSION PLAN

The cash value of the Applicant's pension plan counts as a Resource, however, his spouse's pension plan (including IRA's and Keogh accounts) is an Excluded Resource.

JOINTLY OWNED ACCOUNT

A joint account that is freely accessible to the Applicant or his spouse counts as a Resource unless it can be proven that the other joint owner contributed money to the account. For example, if the Applicant owns a joint account with his son, the entire balance counts as a Resource unless it can be proven that the money in the account really belongs to the son. In such case, HHSC will allow the son to withdraw his share of the account. The funds that remain in the account will be included as part of the Applicant's Resources (MEH 2331.3).

THE HOMESTEAD — EXEMPT (MAYBE)

Home property (house, condominium, cooperative apartment, or mobile home) is counted as a Resource if the client is not living in the home, and he does not intend to return home, and no dependent relative lives there. A *dependent relative* is a child, grandchild, sibling, parent, grandparent who was living in the home before the Applicant left and who is unable to support himself due to medical, social or other reasons (MEH 2341.13, 2341.14).

It used to be that the primary residence owned by the Applicant and/or his Community Spouse was an Excluded Resource for purposes of qualifying for Medicaid. The Applicant could not be denied Medical Assistance because he or his spouse owned a home — regardless of his *equity* in the home (the current market value less mortgages and liens on the property). However, that changed in 2006. The early 21st century spiral of residential property values did not go unnoticed by the federal government. A home purchased years earlier was now worth a substantial amount of money, so in 2006, THE DEFICIT REDUCTION ACT was signed into law.

In addition to reducing federal spending on Medicare, Medicaid and other domestic programs, the Deficit Reduction Act placed a limit on the amount of equity that a person could have in his home and still qualify for Medicaid. In Texas, that limit is $500,000 (MEH 2341.18). A person whose equity in his home is greater than $500,000 cannot qualify for Medicaid. Beginning in 2011, the law requires that the above dollar amount be increased by the cost of living rounded to the nearest $1,000 (42 U.S.C. 1396p(f)).

EXCEPTIONS TO THE RULE

This equity limit does not apply in any of the following cases:

☑ the Applicant's spouse and/or dependent relative are occupying the home.

☑ the Applicant's minor (under 21), blind or disabled child lives in the home.

☑ the Applicant is legally unable to convert the equity in his home to cash. For example, an Applicant may not be able to convert the equity in his home for cash if he owns the home jointly with his sister, and she refuses to sell her interest in the home.

☑ the home is farmland, or part of other excluded property essential to self support.

OTHER EXCLUDED RESOURCES

We have listed many of the more common items that HHSC considers to be Excluded Resources. You can find the complete list of Excluded Resources in the Medicaid Eligibility Handbook which is available at the Department of Aging and Disability Services Web site.

http://www.dads.state.tx.us

THE SPEND-DOWN OPTION

Now that we know what does (and does not) count as a Resource, the next question is what options are available to a couple whose Resources are over the limit. Those with no knowledge of the law, might think the only option available to the couple is to pay for his nursing care until the amount over the limit is spent. Those who carefully read the previous pages, might suggest that the couple check to see whether they can use the money to purchase items that do not count as a Resource.

Both state and federal law allow the Applicant and his spouse to use their excess Resources to purchase Excludable Resources, without losing the right to receive Medicaid benefits, provided they pay a fair market value for the item. This being the case, the couple can make funeral or burial arrangements, if they have not already done so. They can purchase household items such as furniture, a television set, a new refrigerator or stove, etc.

REPAIRING EXCLUDED ITEMS

Paying money to repair an Excluded Resource is a good spend-down strategy. Perhaps the Exempt family car needs new brakes, or tires. The Community Spouse may decide to replace the Excluded car with a new model (MEH 2315).

If the house is in need of repair or improvement, this is the time to fix it up. A new heating, plumbing, electric or security system can use up funds quickly.

If the couple do not own their own home, the Community Spouse might consider using the excess cash as a down-payment on a home.

SPEND-DOWN BY TRANSFER TO DISABLED PERSON

As explained earlier in Chapter 7, if a child is receiving Social Security disability benefits, the parent can transfer money to a Special Needs Trust for the child. This transfer will not disqualify the child, or the parent, from receiving government benefits, provided the Trust is drafted according to state and federal law (MEH 2320).

SPEND-DOWN BY PAYING DEBTS

Some sceptics might think $98,000 is a lot of money for the couple in the given example to spend down. Maybe the couple previously made all funeral arrangements. Perhaps they really don't need (or want) new furniture or appliances. In such case, the solution may be to pay off all of their outstanding debts. If the couple have a credit card balance, they can reduce that balance to $0.

If their car is an Excluded Resource, they can pay off money they may owe on the car. Paying off a car loan is a good strategy provided the car is an Excluded Resource. But, if the Applicant is single and owns a car that he is too ill to drive, only $4,500 of the value of his car is Exempt. Paying off a car loan may not reduce his Resources. For example, suppose he owes $10,000 and the car is worth $15,000. Paying off the $10,000 will not reduce his Resources. Anything over $4,500 still counts as a Resource.

 TIMING IS IMPORTANT
WHEN SPENDING DOWN

The couple's Resources are counted as of the first day of the month in which the application is filed (MEH 2310). That date is called the *Snap Shot Date* because the HHSC takes a "picture" of their assets on that date.

If the couple have $150,000 and a mortgage of $75,000 on the Snap Shot Date, he can apply for Medicaid at that time. The Community Spouse is allowed to keep half as her Resource Allowance ($75,000). The Applicant is allowed $2,000, so he is over the Resource limit by $73,000. He can use that money to pay down mortgage, and be eligible for Medicaid the following month. This will leave the Community Spouse with $75,000 and an almost paid up mortgage.

Suppose instead that they pay the mortgage before the Snap Shot date. In that case, they will have $75,000 left. This leaves them in a worse position because HHSC will allow the Community Spouse to keep half of the $75,000 (only $37,500). The Applicant will be allowed to keep his $2,000, but he will be over the Resource limit by $35,500 and will need to spend down in some other manner. The same concerns arise when buying Exempt Resources or making repairs. If a married Applicant spends down before the Snap Shot Date, the Community Spouse may be left with less assets than if they had spent down after that date.

Before using any spend down strategy, you may want to consult with Elder Law attorney.

PROVING PAYMENT TO HHSC

Paying off loans is a valid spend-down strategy because it is just a return of monies given to the Applicant by the lender for the purchase of an Excluded Resource (car, house, clothing, household items). The Applicant will need to prove to his caseworker at HHSC, that the monies he spent were used to pay off a valid debt. If he paid off a credit card debt, the HHSC will want to see the original contract with the company and the monthly bill showing what items were purchased.

If a car loan was paid, HHSC will want to see the original promissory note (marked "PAID"), and the release of lien on the car. If the money was used to pay down a mortgage on his home, HHSC will want to see the original loan documents and an acknowledgment by the lender of the new balance; or if paid in full, a satisfaction of mortgage.

MAYBE SPEND-DOWN IS NOT NECESSARY

Suppose the couple with too much in Resources has too little income. For example, if the Community Spouse needs at least $2,541 per month, but the couple's combined income is only $2,000. In such case, she can ask the HHSC to allow her to keep as much of couple's excess assets as is necessary to give her this minimum income. In effect, she needs to ask "May I keep more than my Resource Allowance so that the income from this property will help to get me to that minimum income?"

It is the legal right of the Community Spouse to receive the minimum Needs Allowance allowed by both state and federal government. It is reasonable to ask the HHSC to allow her keep as much of their Resources as is necessary to achieve that income, even if it means keeping more than allowed. If HHSC agrees to allow additional Resources to generate more income, they will use the current interest rates for a one-year Certificate of Deposit (MEH 4133.8).

For example, if a one-year CD is paying 4% interest and the Community Spouse needs $541 more per month, i.e., $6,492 per year, she will be allowed to keep $162,300 above her Resource Allowance to generate that income:

$$\$162,300 \times 0.04 = \$6,492$$

Even though the Texas Administrative Code and the Medicaid Eligibility Handbook explain how to compute the additional Resource Allowance, the caseworker is not authorized to agree to the increased value. The Community Spouse will need to go through the appeals process and ask the Hearing Officer to approve the greater Resource Allowance.

But an appeal can drag on for months. Meanwhile, the status of the Applicant remains in limbo. Because of the legal cost of the appeal and the uncertainty of whether the Hearing Officer will agree that additional Resources are necessary for the support of the Community Spouse, it may be better to use a spend-down strategy that enables the spouse to obtain additional income.

One such strategy is the **MEDICAID ANNUITY**. The Community Spouse uses the excess resources to buy an Annuity that will give her additional income. This spend-down strategy is permissible provided it conforms to state and federal law.

USING THE ANNUITY TO SPEND-DOWN

A spend-down strategy that is currently allowed by both federal and state law is the purchase of an *Immediate Pay Annuity*; i.e., an annuity whose payments begin the month after the purchase and continues for a fixed period of time. For purposes of Medicaid eligibility, that fixed period of time must be less than, or equal to, the life expectancy of the Annuitant (in this case, the Community Spouse). She can name a Successor Annuitant to receive the payments in the event she dies earlier than her life expectancy.

The life expectancy of the Annuitant is determined by referring to the actuarial table as published in Appendix IX of the Texas Medicaid Eligibility Handbook (MEH 2342.8). You can find the table at the HHSC Web site.
http://www.dhs.state.tx.us

By purchasing an Immediate Pay Annuity, excess Resources are converted to a monthly income that continues for the term of the policy.

In order to qualify as a permissible spend-down strategy, the Annuity must meet both state and federal criteria; specifically:

NO CASH VALUE/EQUAL PAYMENTS
The Annuity contract must have no value other than the monthly payments to the Annuitant. The monthly payments must be of equal value, with no deferred payment and no balloon payment (42 U.S.C. 1396p(c)(1)(G)), 1 TAC 358.442(g)(1)(B), (C)).

ACTUARIALLY SOUND

The Annuity contract must be *actuarially sound,* meaning that the money invested in the Annuity (plus a reasonable rate of interest) must be returned to the Annuitant during his life expectancy as printed in the federal State Medicaid Manual (SM3 3258.9(B), 3259.1). There is no rounding "up." For example, according to the federal State Medicaid Manual a 65 year old man has a life expectancy of 14.96 years. An Annuity that makes regular payments to the Annuitant for 14 years is actuarially sound, but an Annuity that makes payments for 15 years is not.

UNASSIGNABLE AND IRREVOCABLE

The Annuity contract cannot be transferred, sold or assigned. It must be irrevocable (1 TAC 358.442(g)(1)(A)). In other words, nothing can be changed; not the monthly payment, nor the number of payments, nor the identity of the Annuitant.

THE STATE IS THE RESIDUARY BENEFICIARY

The Deficit Reduction Act requires that the state be the residuary beneficiary of the Annuity up to the amount paid by the state for his care (1 TAC 358.442 (g)(1)(D)). This requirement does apply to an Annuity purchased by the Community Spouse for her own benefit (1 TAC 358.442(g)(4)).

We will refer to an Annuity that meets all of these criteria (no cash value, unassignable, irrevocable, actuarially sound) as a *Medicaid Annuity*.

VERIFY THAT THE ANNUITY MEETS HHSC CRITERIA PRIOR TO PURCHASE

Once the annuity is purchased it is irrevocable, so before you buy it, have your Elder Law attorney, or the agent who is selling the annuity, check with HHSC to be sure the annuity meets state and federal requirements. If you purchase the annuity and for some reason the Department determines that the annuity does not meet current state and federal criteria, the entire value of the annuity might count as an impermissible transfer of assets and a **PENALTY PERIOD** of ineligibility will be imposed, i.e., a period of time that the Applicant is disqualified from receiving Medicaid benefits. The Penalty Period is discussed later in this Chapter.

USING THE ANNUITY TO GENERATE INCOME

Purchasing a Medicaid Annuity could solve the problem for the Community Spouse who has too little income and too much in Resources. She can use her excess Resources to buy the Annuity. She will keep the income from that investment, just as she would if she had invested in a stock, bond or Certificate of Deposit. Unlike these investments, part of the money she paid for the Annuity is returned to her each month along with interest. Most importantly, the Annuity does not count as a Resource.

This spend-down strategy can be used by the Community Spouse even when her income is not a problem. But it may not make economic sense if the sum of her monthly income, including the income from the Annuity, exceeds the current Monthly Maintenance Needs Allowance ($2,541). For example, suppose her income from pension and Social Security is $2,000.

The Spouse was short $541. If the Annuity pays $541 or more per month, she may keep none of her husband's income. All of his income will be used for his nursing care. In other words, purchasing the Medicaid Annuity may enable the Applicant to qualify for Medicaid, but it may not result in extra income for Community Spouse. And there are other things to consider.

⇨ THE COMMUNITY SPOUSE MAY DIE
OR NEED NURSING CARE

Buying a Medicaid Annuity for a Community Spouse who is herself aged or in frail health may not be the best option. It could happen that she needs long-term nursing care and will need to apply for Medicaid. If she purchases an Annuity and later becomes a Medicaid Recipient, that extra income will be used as her contribution to her nursing care.

⇨ LOSS OF LIQUIDITY

Should the Applicant die shortly after his Community Spouse buys the Annuity, she cannot cash it in. She must keep the investment for the full term.

⇨ RISK OF LOSS

By purchasing an Annuity, the Community Spouse is giving her money to a company in exchange for the company's promise to return part of the principal each month, together with interest. The company promises to make these payments every month for a certain number of years. Should the company become bankrupt during that period of time, the monies invested might be lost.

⇨ FIXED RETURN ON INVESTMENT

Annuities offer a fixed rate of return on the money invested. There is no way to adjust that rate for periods of inflation. The rate of return on the Annuity is set at the time of purchase. If you purchase an Annuity in a period of low single digit interest rates, it will remain at that same low rate even if the interest rate goes into the double digit range. You may find that you are able to earn more on your savings account than the rate of return that you are receiving from your Annuity.

All these concerns need to be addressed before investing in a Medicaid Annuity. Consultation with an Elder Law attorney prior to the purchase is a must.

NOT THE BEST OPTION FOR THE SINGLE APPLICANT

Although purchasing a Medicaid Annuity may work for the Community Spouse with a low fixed income, it may not be the best strategy for the single Applicant, because any income he receives from the Annuity will be used for his nursing care. One exception may be the single Applicant, with a low income, who intends to return home after a few months. For example, suppose an elderly unmarried father with $100,000 needs extensive nursing care because of a car accident. If doctors expect he will be able to return home after several months of therapy and nursing care, he might consider purchasing a Medicaid Annuity for $98,000, provided, of course, that the income from the Annuity does not put him over the Income Cap. Once he makes the purchase, he can immediately apply for Medicaid. He will of course report the purchase to the HHSC. The HHSC will examine the terms of the annuity to be sure they satisfy current regulations. If they do and he meets all other requirements, he should qualify for Medicaid.

He's happy because he did not need to spend down his $100,000 in nursing home bills. He's hoping that his condition improves enough so that he can return home. In such case, his nursing care will be paid by Medicaid, and he will continues to receive the income from the Annuity when he returns home.

The HHSC is happy because any income he receives while in the facility will go toward payment of his nursing home bill; leaving that much less for the HHSC to contribute to his care. By purchasing a Medicaid Annuity, he is betting that he will not need nursing care for the rest of his life expectancy. If he loses his bet, none of his assets are protected because the income from the Annuity will be used to pay for his nursing care. And the state is named as primary beneficiary, so if he dies before all of the funds are paid, the state will be reimbursed up to the amount it paid for his care (1 TAC 358.442(g)(1)(D)). In such case it may be better for him to use a strategy better designed for the single Applicant.

THE TRANSFER OPTION

If the Applicant has a medical condition, but he does not expect to need nursing care for several years, he may decide to simply transfer all of his money to his child with the hope that he will not need long term nursing care for at least five years. The five years is the **Look-back Period** that HHSC uses to investigate the finances of a person who applies for Medicaid. The Look-back Period starts on the date the Applicant enters the nursing home or applies for Medicaid (whichever is the later date) and goes back five years from that date (MEH 2323).

If the HHSC determines that the Applicant, or his spouse, made *uncompensated transfer* during the Look-back Period, the HHSC will impose a *Penalty Period*. An uncompensated transfer is one in which the Applicant gets nothing in return for the transfer (love and affection don't count).

COMPUTING THE PENALTY PERIOD

Rules relating to the Penalty Period for uncompensated transfers are fairly complex, but in general, the Penalty Period is computed by dividing the amount transferred by the average daily cost of nursing home care in the state of Texas. The value for the average daily cost of nursing care currently being used by the HHSC is $117.08. Using a 30 day month this works out to be approximately $3,512 per month.

If the Applicant in the example just given, decided to transfer the $98,000 to his child he would be disqualified for 8,37.03 days: $98,000/$117.08 = 837.03 days
HHSC rounds down to the nearest whole day (MEH 2324).

Using a 30 day month, 837 days is approximately equal to 28 months: 837/30= 27.90 or 28

If the father made the transfer anytime within the five year period before he applied for Medicaid, the Penalty Period will start on the day he applies for Medicaid and is otherwise eligible for Medicaid. If the money is returned to the father, the Penalty Period is erased retroactive to the month of transfer (MEH 2324.4). But this is not a complete solution because the father still has too much to qualify for Medicaid. He will need to spend-down his assets (probably on nursing home care) before he can qualify for Medicaid.

In 2006, profound changes were made to the Medicaid law:
** FIVE YEAR LOOK BACK INSTEAD OF THREE
** PENALTY PERIOD STARTS WHEN YOU APPLY
** DENIAL OF MEDICAID IF HOME HAS EQUITY OF $500,000
($750,000 IN SOME STATES)
AND NO DEPENDENT LIVES THERE.

The federal government recognized that the transition from the old law to the new could cause *undue hardship,* so they included the following provision to 42 U.S.C. 1396p:

> Each State shall provide for a hardship waiver process ... (1) under which an undue hardship exists when application of the transfer of asset provision would deprive the individual —
>
> (A) of medical care such that the individual's health or life would be endangered; or
>
> (B) of food, clothing, shelter, or other necessities of life; and
>
> (2) which provides for —
>
> (A) notice to recipients that an undue hardship exemption exists;
>
> (B) a timely process for determining whether an undue hardship waiver will be granted; and
>
> (C) a process under which an adverse determination can be appealed.

In other words, the state may not deny the Applicant Medical Assistance if to do so will be dangerous to his health, or deprive him of food, clothing, shelter and other necessities.

The criteria adopted by HHSC appears in section 2329 of the Medicaid Eligibility Handbook. According to the Handbook, undue hardship may exist when the Applicant has no place to return in the community and/or receive care required to meet his needs AND any one of the following conditions exists:

♦ location of the receiver of the asset is unknown to the client, or other family members

♦ physical harm may come as a result of pursuing the return of the asset

♦ the receiver of the asset is unwilling to cooperate such as an Adult Protective Services exploitation or potential fraud case.

Although the federal definition of undue hardship and the HHSC criteria seem clear enough, applying it is complicated. It may take the efforts of an experienced Elder Law attorney to convince the HHSC that a particular case meets the criteria. For example, suppose a father set up a Medicaid Qualifying Plan under the old law. He kept enough money to pay for his nursing care for three years, and transferred $98,000 to his son. When the father applies for Medicaid, the HHSC looks back five years and sees the transfer. They will deny him Medical Assistance for 837 days beginning on the day he applied for Medicaid. If the son refuses to return the money, and the father has no other way to pay for the care he needs, will the HHSC consider this a case of undue hardship?

A father, in another state, with a similar set of circumstances was denied Medicaid. The state determined that this was not a case of undue hardship because the father gave away the money of his own free will.

It could happen that a person is diagnosed in the early stages of a progressive disease that is expected to ultimately result in a lengthy stay in a nursing facility. A person in such a situation may decide to give his property away, with the hope that he will not need long term nursing care for at least five years. If he becomes incapacitated and someone applies for Medicaid for him during that period, they are required to report the transfer to HHSC.

And this is not a game of "Catch me if you can." Under both state and federal law, the Applicant or whoever applies for him, is required to make a full disclosure of transfers made during these periods. Anyone who knowingly and wilfully makes a false statement in an application for Medical Assistance Programs can be prosecuted for fraud. Depending on the amount of improper benefits received, whoever commits such fraud can be convicted of a Class C misdemeanor (for amounts less than $50) up to a 1st degree felony (for amounts $200,000 or more) (Penal Code 35A.02).

The reader may be thinking "Yes, but if I come down with an illness that I know will cause me to deteriorate over a period of time, all I need to do is give all my money to my child, be sure to wait five years. My child will keep my money safe. Should I need that money, my child will return as much as I need to me. Money that I don't use will be protected for my child."

The Medicaid Qualifying Plan of giving away all assets and waiting five years is allowed under current law, but this is a "brute force" approach to the problem. It is a drastic step to take and fraught with peril. Once the money is transferred, a completed gift is made.

The child becomes the legal owner of the money and with all of the obvious "what ifs."
- What if the child becomes bankrupt?

- What if he dies?

- What if the child is sued? Will a Court order the child to use the money you gave to pay the judgment?

- What if the child is divorced? Will a judge decide that your child's spouse is entitled to half of that money?

And what if you give the money away and never need long term nursing care?

The medical field is advancing with amazing speed. Although few cures have been found for mankind's ills, there have been many breakthroughs in treatment. With modern drugs, many patients are able to function on their own. Even those who have been diagnosed with a progressive disease may not need nursing care for several years — maybe not at all. Meanwhile, your money is gone, and your independence along with it.

Being impoverished at a time in your life when you are unable to supplement your income, and when your health is declining, can lead to much sadness. Imagine going to your child and asking for money. Imagine the child thinking, or worse yet, asking: "What's the money for?"

Many of these concerns can be remedied by a transfer into an Irrevocable Trust with the understanding that you will not be able to apply for Medicaid for at least five years. But even that has its risks. A lot can happen in five years. The federal law could change the Look-back period to six years — or more. You could require full nursing care the day after you transfer your assets into the Trust. The Trust assets could be depleted in less than five years, yet you will not be able to apply for Medicaid because of the transfer.

For those in good health, an alternative is to do nothing until you actually need nursing home care and then implement a Medicaid qualifying strategy at that time. Of course, there is the chance that you take suddenly ill, say with a stroke, and are unable to implement a Medicaid Qualifying plan. A Durable Power Of Attorney that is properly drafted and signed while you have capacity should solve the problem. You can appoint someone to be your Agent to implement a Medicaid Qualifying plan for you.

It is important that the Durable Power of Attorney be properly drafted. A New Jersey Court refused to allow a son to transfer property on behalf of his incapacitated mother for the purpose of qualifying for Medicaid. Although his mother gave him a Power of Attorney authorizing him to apply for Medicaid on her behalf, the Court refused to allow the transfer because the Power of Attorney ". . . did not provide for him to make gifts on her behalf to himself or anyone else, either to qualify her for Medicaid or for any other reason" (*In the Matter of Mildred Keri*, Superior Court of New Jersey, Appellate Division, A-5949-01T5).

This case was reversed by the New Jersey Supreme Court and eventually the son was able to transfer the assets on behalf of his mother. But a transfer of property under an improperly drafted Power of Attorney can still be challenged. HHSC may challenge transfers made under a Power of Attorney that does not give the Attorney In Fact specific authority to implement a Medicaid Qualifying plan.

It is important that your Power of Attorney be drafted by an Elder Law attorney who knows what provisions to include in the document so that it will stand up to HHSC scrutiny.

 THE ONLY THING CERTAIN IS CHANGE

Significant changes were made in 2006 to the Medicaid law. This is not the end of changes to the Medicaid law. There is a proposal in the federal government to give states new powers to reduce, eliminate or increase Medicaid benefits within the state. Under this proposal, benefits for welfare recipients, poor children and other groups who are automatically eligible for Medicaid would remain regulated by federal law. The state would be given autonomy to administer the Medicaid program for other groups; and in particular for the elderly in need of nursing care. Proponents of state autonomy explain that with autonomy, the state could increase benefits, but in these days of budget deficits, more likely the states will opt to decrease Medicaid benefits to the elderly.

If states are given autonomy in administering the long-term nursing care program, uniformity would no longer be imposed by the federal government. Medicaid benefits for the elderly could vary significantly state to state. Not only would there be variation state to state, there could be variation within the state. State programs could be administered with different eligibility criteria county to county. There could even be a difference in benefits county to county!

The point is that there is no certainty when it comes to future Medicaid qualifying options. But we did not write this chapter to give the reader a definitive Medicaid Qualifying strategy. Rather, it was to give the reader an understanding of the law as it relates to qualifying for Medicaid; and to let the reader know that under current law, options are available should the need for long-term nursing care arise.

We also wrote this chapter to let the general public understand how this federal program is administered here in the state of Texas. And, incidentally, we touched only on the basics. There are other, more sophisticated, Medicaid Qualifying options available that an experienced Elder Law attorney can explain to you. The prudent thing to do is to visit an Elder Law attorney if and when you become concerned about a long term care problem. He can explain current law to you as it relates to qualifying for Medicaid. He can suggest the best path for you to follow, given your set of circumstances.

It is also important to keep up with changes in policy both in the state and federal government; and to let your legislators know how you feel about such changes.

Protecting the Homestead 11

As explained in Chapter 10, whether a home in the name of the Applicant counts as a Resource for purposes of qualifying for Medicaid depends on his equity in the home, and if over $500,000 whether his spouse or a dependent family member is living there. Even if no family member is living in the home, the Applicant cannot be denied Medical Assistance provided his equity in the home is less than the state limit, and he says he intends to return home. Once on Medicaid, the state has the right to have a physician determine whether he can reasonably be expected to return home within a year. If not, the state has a right to place a TEFRA Lien on the property for monies spent on his behalf. TEFRA stands for TAX EQUITY AND FISCAL RESPONSI-BILITY ACT, a federal law. A home encumbered by a TEFRA lien cannot be sold or transferred until the monies spent by the state for the care of Recipient are paid.

Even if the state does not place a lien on his home during his lifetime, if the Medicaid Recipient received Medical Assistance after age 55, the state can place a TEFRA Lien on the property to seek recovery from the sale of his home once the home is sold or he dies. The state will not seek recovery from a home owned by a deceased Recipient while his spouse, or minor or disabled child are living there. However, once the child reaches 22, or the spouse and disabled child are deceased, whoever inherits the home will need to pay off the lien or the state can force the sale of the property and take the money from the proceeds of the sale (42 U.S.C. 1396p). In this chapter we discuss ways to protect the home from a *TEFRA Lien.*

TRANSFERRING THE HOME

Protecting the homestead is easy to do if the Medicaid Recipient is married. Under state and federal law, the Applicant can transfer his home to the Community Spouse without penalty. He can make the transfer either before or after he applies for Medicaid (42 U.S.C. 1396p (c) 2A)

If the home is in the name of the Medicaid Recipient only, he can sign a deed transferring the property to his spouse. If he and the Community Spouse own the property jointly, they can sign a deed transferring his interest to his Spouse. It is important to make the transfer of the Recipient's interest — otherwise the state can place a TEFRA lien on the property, and seek recovery for medical assistance given to the Recipient, once both husband and wife are deceased.

Protecting the home is more of a problem for the aged, single parent; and it is a problem for aging parents who both are not in the best of health. Who knows which of them will require long term nursing care? Maybe both will need such care. Maybe neither of them will require nursing care.

Many parents want to have their children inherit the one thing the parent has of value, namely his home. Parents fear that if they ever need Medicaid benefits, their home will be sold to reimburse the state. This idea is so distressing to some people that even though they are in relatively good health, they may decide to transfer their home to a child with the understanding that the parent will continue to live there for the rest of his life.

Those planning such a move need to understand that they are trading one risk (need to apply for Medicaid) for several other risks.

⊠ RISK OF LOSS

Once you transfer the property to your child it becomes his property and that property can be lost or used to pay for his debts just like anything else he owns. Your child could run into serious financial difficulties. Your child could be sued. This is especially a risk if your child is a professional (doctor, nurse, accountant, financial planner, attorney, etc.). If your child is found to be personally liable for damages, your home could become part of the settlement of that law suit.

If your child is (or gets) married, then this complicates matters even more. If the child divorces, the value of your home might be included as part of the property settlement agreement. This may be to your child's detriment because the child may need to share the value of the property with his/her former spouse. If you do not transfer the property, it cannot become part of his marital equation.

Even if your child is single there is a risk of loss. Your child may want to take out a business loan. If the loan is significant, the lender will want to include everything your child owns as collateral (security for the debt). If the lender learns that you are occupying the house, he will especially want to include your house as collateral because that will motivate your son to repay the loan.

The point is, transferring the house to your child could be bad for both of you. And that is not the only downside.

⊠ LOSS OF HOMESTEAD TAX EXEMPTION

In Texas, a person who owns and occupies real property as his principal residence is entitled to a Homestead Tax Exemption. In addition, he can receive Homestead Tax Credits if he is disabled or over 65 (Tax 11.13, 11.26). A disabled veteran is entitled to an exemption from taxation of a portion of the assessed value of his homestead (Tax 11.22). If you transfer your homestead, you lose your right to receive these tax breaks.

⊠ LOSS OF HOMESTEAD CREDITOR PROTECTION

The entire value of your homestead is protected from creditors during your lifetime. With the exception of property taxes and the loan on your homestead, none of your creditors can force the sale of your property (Property 41.001, 41.002). By transferring your home to a child, you lose your homestead protection against creditors. If you are married, it is a double loss of creditor protection. Not only do you lose creditor protection for yourself, you lose it for your spouse as well (see Chapter 5).

If the child does not occupy that property as his homestead, there is no homestead creditor protection whatsoever. The child's creditors can force the sale of the property (that's your home) for a relatively small amount of money owed.

⊠ POSSIBLE GIFT TAX

A federal Gift Tax needs to be paid if the value of the equity in your home (plus the value of all the gifts you gave over your lifetime in excess of the Annual Gift Tax Exclusion) exceeds the lifetime Gift Tax Exclusion. The current lifetime federal Gift Tax Exclusion is $1,000,000, so for most of us, this is not a problem. Yet there still is the hassle of filing a Gift Tax return.

☒ POSSIBLE CAPITAL GAINS TAX

Although Congress has expressed its intent to phase out the Estate Tax, there is no discussion to do away with the Capital Gains Tax. If you gift the property to the child during your lifetime, when he sells the property he will pay a Capital Gains Tax on the increase in value from the price you paid for your home to the selling price at the time your child sells the property.

If you do not make the gift during your lifetime, the child will inherit the property with a step-up in basis, i.e., he will inherit the property at its market value as of the date of your death. Under today's tax structure and continuing through 2009, that step-up in basis is unlimited. If your child sells the property when he inherits it, he will not pay a Capital Gains Tax, regardless of how large the step-up in basis. In 2010, there will be a limit on the amount that can be inherited free of the Capital Gains Tax but as explained on page 62, that limit is quite high so for most of us this is not a concern.

☒ POSSIBLE LOSS OF GOVERNMENT BENEFITS

If you are married and you make an uncompensated transfer of property to someone other than your spouse, both you and your spouse could be denied Medical Assistance if you apply within five years from the date of transfer of the property. It could happen that during that period of time, one of you takes suddenly ill and requires long-term nursing care. Why jeopardize your right to receive Medicaid for both of you?

Owning a home will not disqualify you from receiving Medicaid — unless the equity is greater than $500,000, so the next problem to consider is what to do if you own a home and the equity exceeds $500,000.

A stay in a nursing home of several years could easily cost more than $500,000. The elderly parent with equity in his home in excess of $500,000 may worry about being forced to sell his home to pay for his long-term nursing care. Not only will he lose the home for himself, his children will lose the legacy the parent had hoped to give them — namely his home.

As just explained, gifting the home to the child while the parent is well has major drawbacks, not the least of which is loss of creditor protection and loss of control over the homestead. If you wish to make any improvement to the home, such as adding a back porch or swimming pool, you will need your child's permission to do so.

To avoid some of the problems of an outright gift, you might consider gifting the home to your child and keeping a Life Estate for yourself. Upon your death, your child will own the property 100%, and without the need for Probate. The child will have no right to the home while you are alive so there is no fear that the property can be lost or taken during your lifetime.

By keeping a Life Estate for yourself, you not gifting the full value of the home but only of the *Remainder Interest.* i.e., what is left of the property after your death. The value of the Remainder Interest depends on your life expectancy. A gift of a Remainder Interest when you are 90 is worth more to your child than when you are 50.

DETERMINING THE VALUE OF THE REMAINDER INTEREST

The Centers for Medicare and Medicaid Services publishes a table of values for the Life Estate Interest and the Remainder Interest based on the age of the Grantor at the time of the transfer (State Medicaid Manual, Part 3 (SM3 3258.9) LIFE ESTATE AND REMAINDER INTEREST TABLE). The table is printed as Appendix X of the Medicaid Eligibility Handbook. You can download the table from the Internet. http://www.dads.state.tx.us

Fortunately, this table goes up to age 109, so the value they assign to the remainder interest is relatively low. For example, according to this table, if a 70 year old makes a transfer to his son and keeps a Life Estate for himself, his Life Estate is equal to 61% of the value of the property. The remainder interest is worth only 39%.

The actual percentage given in the table for the Remainder Interest is .39478. If the home is worth $600,000 it means the value of the gift of the Remainder Interest is $236,868.
$$\$600,000 \times .39478 = \$236,868$$

The value of the Life Estate Interest as of the date of transfer is $363,132: $600,000 - $236,868 = $363,132 — well under the $500,000 limit.

Remember the current average monthly nursing home cost in the state of Texas is $3,512. The Penalty Period for the transfer of the Remainder Interest is over 67 months:
$$\$236,868 / \$3,512 = 67.45 \text{ months}$$

This Penalty Period will be enforced if you apply for Medicaid at any time during the five years after the date of transfer. And that is not the only problem.

CONTROL

You will not be able to sell your home, or get a mortgage on the property, without permission from your child.

TAX ISSUES

As explained at the end of Chapter 2, if you sell the home, you (or your child) might need to pay a Capital Gains Tax.

RECOVERY BY THE STATE

The worse drawback is that the state has the right to recover monies spent on your behalf if you receive nursing care under Medicaid after the age of 55. Money can be recovered from property you own at the time of your death. This includes property you own jointly with another, and property in which you own a Life Estate interest (42 U.S.C. 1396p(b)(4)(B)). The state has the right to place a TEFRA lien on your Life Estate interest. Once you die, the state may demand that your child reimburse them for monies spent on your behalf, or they can force the sale of the house and collect the money from the proceeds of the sale.

Still, it could happen that you never need nursing care, or if you do, the state does not spend that much money on your care. In such case, your child will be able to inherit the bulk, if not all, of the value of your homestead.

THE REVERSE MORTGAGE

Another possible solution to the problem of owning a home whose equity exceeds the state limit is the REVERSE MORTGAGE (MEH 2341.18). A *Reverse Mortgage* is a mortgage such that the lender gives the borrower a certain amount of money, with the agreement that the loan does not need to be repaid until the house is sold or the borrower dies. The money may be given as a lump sum or the borrower may opt to receive a certain amount of money each month based on his life expectancy.

For example, suppose a couple with low monthly income own a home with equity that exceeds the state limit. If they have a child who earns a substantial income, the couple may take out a Reverse Mortgage with their son as lender. The son will pay his parents a certain amount of money each month. Because the parents are getting value from the transaction, no Penalty Period will be imposed should either parent need to apply for Medicaid at any time. Meanwhile they are receiving a regular income that will enable them to increase their standard of living, and pay for home health care, if it is needed.

The mortgage on the property reduces the equity in the home, so should one parent die, and the other parent need to apply for Medicaid, the $500,000 limit may not be a problem. Of course, should either parent become a Medicaid Recipient, the state can place a TEFRA lien on the property, but that lien cannot be paid until both parents are deceased, and their lender son is fully paid. This is one way to protect the equity in the home for their child.

If the child does not have sufficient income to become the lender of a Reverse Mortgage, the parent can take out a Reverse Mortgage with a lending institution. A single Applicant whose equity in his home is greater than $500,000 may be able to reduce his equity in the home by taking a Reverse Mortgage, but there are downsides for the single Applicant:

ABSENCE FROM HOME MAY RESULT IN FORECLOSURE

The lender may require the homestead to be occupied by the borrower. The mortgage agreement may allow the lender to foreclose in the event the borrower/Recipient does not occupy the home for 365 days or more.

STATE REIMBURSED FROM SALE PROCEEDS

The state has the right to place a TEFRA lien on the property. Once the property is sold, the Reverse Mortgage will be paid from the proceeds of the sale. The state will be reimbursed from whatever remains of the net proceeds of the sale. It could happen that there will be nothing left for the child to inherit.

TRANSFERS THAT PROTECT

As explained, you can own a home and still qualify for Medicaid, but there still is the concern that once you become a Medicaid Recipient, the state may place a TEFRA Lien on your homestead for monies spent on your behalf. Under current law, there are several ways to protect your home from such lien. For a married person, the home can be protected by transferring it to the Community Spouse.

TRANSFERRING THE HOME TO THE SPOUSE

The Applicant is free to transfer his home to his spouse without penalty, either before or after he qualifies for Medicaid (42 U.S.C. 1396p(C)(2)(A)(i), MEH 2320, 2325). Once the house is in the name of the Community Spouse, she can arrange to have it inherited by a family member and not the Medicaid Recipient.

Should the Applicant be too ill to make the transfer himself, the deed can be signed by his Agent under a properly drafted Durable Power of Attorney. If he did not give an Agent authority to make the transfer, and he is too ill to sign his name, it may be necessary to have a Guardian appointed who can ask the Court for permission to make the transfer.

Establishing a guardianship may be expensive and time consuming, but as explained earlier in this Chapter, it is important that the homestead be transferred to the Community Spouse. The downside is that there is no guarantee that the judge will allow the transfer of the homestead to the Community Spouse. Before you apply for a guardianship it is important to ask your attorney whether such transfers have been allowed in the past.

TRANSFERRING THE HOME TO A SIBLING

Under state and federal law, if an Applicant owns his home together with a sibling and the sibling lived with the Applicant for at least one year before entering the nursing facility, the Applicant can transfer the home to the sibling without a Medicaid transfer penalty (42 U.S.C. 1396p, MEH 2320). This law presents an opportunity for an unmarried Applicant who has a brother or sister to protect the homestead. The only question is how the sibling becomes co-owner. If the Applicant and his sibling purchased the property together, and the sibling lived in the home for a year prior to the Applicant entering the nursing home, then the sibling's interest in the property is protected. The Applicant can transfer his share of the homestead to his sibling without penalty, and that will protect all of the homestead.

If the house is in the Applicant's name only, it is important to consult with an Elder Law attorney to determine the best way for the sibling to become part owner of the home. Federal law only requires that the sibling have an *equity interest* in the property. An equity interest could be joint ownership or a Tenancy In Common or a Remainder Interest in the homestead. An Elder Law attorney will be able to suggest a method of transferring an equity interest to the sibling that will result in a short Penalty Period. Remember, the Penalty Period does not begin until the homeowner applies for Medicaid.

The attorney will also assist with preparing documentation to present to the Texas Health and Human Services Commission ("HHSC") to verify that:
- ⇨ the sibling owns an equity interest in the home
- ⇨ the sibling occupied the home for a year prior to the Applicant entering the nursing home.

TRANSFER TO A CAREGIVER CHILD

A law similar to a transfer to a sibling applies to the Medicaid recipient who owns his home and wants to transfer it to his child. The federal law allows a transfer of the homestead to the child without penalty, provided the child lived with and took care of his parent for at least two years before the parent entered the nursing home.

There is no requirement that the child own an equity interest in the property; but the federal statute does require that the state verify that the child lived in the home and provided care to the parent for the two years; and that this care enabled the parent to remain at home rather than be placed in a nursing home (42 U.S.C. 1396p(c)(2)(A)(iv)), MEH 2322).

It is important to consult with an Elder Law attorney, preferably prior to the two year period. He may suggest that parent and child sign a Caregiver's Agreement that sets out the terms and conditions of the transfer; i.e., what care the child promises to give to the parent over the next two years in exchange for the transfer of the homestead to the child.

The attorney will explain how to document that care over the two year period so that the information can be presented to HHSC when the parent applies for Medicaid. Some of the things HHSC will want to know are:

⇨ the Applicant's medical condition during the 2 years
⇨ whether the child lived in the home during that time

And especially, that the child provided most of the following services without receiving compensation from the HHSC to do so:

prepare meals; shop for food and clothing
help maintain the home; assist with financial affairs
run errands; provide transportation
provide personal services
arrange for medical appointments.

The HHSC may want someone (friend, family member, physician) to verify that the child did provide the necessary care during the two years. Once it is established by HHSC that federal requirements are satisfied, the property can be transferred to the child without affecting the right of the Applicant to receive Medicaid benefits (MEH 2322).

TRANSFER TO A DISABLED CHILD

In Texas, the Applicant or his spouse may transfer their home or any other of their Resources to a child (minor or adult) who is blind, or disabled without penalty (42 U.S.C. 1396p(c)(2A). In the event the child does not have a determination of blindness or disability from the Social Security Administration, the HHSC will review the child's medical records to determine whether the child is blind or disabled.

If the child is receiving Social Security disability benefits, the parent can transfer their home or other assets to a Special Needs Trust for the child (see Chapter 7). This transfer will not disqualify the child (or the parent) from receiving government benefits, provided the Trust is drafted according to state and federal law.

IMPACT OF DEFICIT REDUCTION ACT

Laws relating to the transfers of the home to the spouse, sibling and child were enacted prior to the Deficit Reduction Act. Whether these laws will still apply if the home is worth more than $500,000 is unknown as of the time we went to print in 2007.

 DON'T TRY THIS ON YOUR OWN

A Medicaid Qualifying Plan is not something to attempt on your own. The Medicaid program is complex and volatile. There are many levels of law that govern Medicaid. There are the federal statutes (Social Security Act Title XIX/P.L. 89-97); the U.S. Code of Federal Regulations (42 CFR 430-435) and the Centers for Medicare and Medicaid Services State Medicaid Manual, Part 3 explaining how federal statutes are to be administered in the United States.

There are the Texas Medicaid statutes (Chapter 32: Medical Assistance Programs) and the Texas Administrative Code (Title 1 Administration, Part 15 Texas Health and Human Services Commission, Chapter 358 Medicaid Eligibility) that state how the Medicaid program is to be administered in Texas. That's five levels of law that are constantly changing — often with little or no notice to the general public.

And the laws are not well written. Judges in the federal District Court observed: "The Social Security Act is among the most intricate ever drafted by Congress. Its Byzantine construction ... makes the Act 'almost unintelligible to the uninitiated.' ... The District Court . . . described the Medicaid statute as 'an aggravated assault on the English language, resistant to attempts to understand it'." (*Schweiker v. Gray Panthers*, 453 U.S. 34(1981)).

In *Rehabilitation Association of Virginia v. Kozlowski*, 42 F.3d 1444, 1450 (4th Cir 1994), the Court had nothing but sympathy for officials who must interpret or administer these laws. "There can be no doubting that the statutes and provisions in question, involving the financing of Medicare and Medicaid, are among the most completely impenetrable texts within human experience. Indeed, one approaches them . . . with dread, for not only are they dense reading of the most tortuous kind, but Congress also revisits the area frequently, generously cutting and pruning in the process and making any solid grasp of the matters addressed merely a passing phase."

Most states have a manual that they provide to workers who are in charge of implementing the Medicaid Program. In Texas, that manual is the TEXAS MEDICAID ELIGIBILITY HANDBOOK. Even with the Handbook available to the workers, because of the complexity of the law, there is variation in the way the law is applied. A Medicaid qualifying option may be accepted in one county and challenged in another. If HHSC decides to challenge a particular strategy, even though that strategy is based on federal or state law, you will have no choice but to appeal the ruling.

THE MEDICAID APPEAL

An Applicant who is denied Medicaid benefits will receive notice from HHSC that he has the right to appeal (MEH 1341). The first step in the appeal process is for the Applicant, or someone acting on his behalf, to request a "Fair Hearing." This must be done within 90 days from the date the decision goes into effect, or from the date of the notice — whichever is later (MEH 1342).

Once requested, HHSC will appoint a Hearing Officer to conduct the hearing and decide the matter. The person appointed as Hearing Officer must be someone who has not been directly involved in denying the application. A Department Representative will appear on behalf of HHSC. It will be up to the Department Representative to prove that their denial of benefits was proper (MEH 1641.1).

The appeals process is explained in the *Fair Hearings and Fraud Handbook*. The Handbook is available at local Department of Aging and Disability Services offices (MEH 1310). It is also available at the Forms & Handbook section of the Department of Aging and Disability Services Web site. http://www.dads.state.tx.us

If you read the handbook you will see that even though a Fair Hearing is informal, it is none-the-less a complex legal proceeding. To win you need to have a complete understanding of all applicable law. You will need to know how to discover and present evidence to prove your case. It is important that you have an attorney present at the hearing to represent you. If you cannot afford to employ an attorney, ask Legal Services for assistance. See Page xii for the Legal Services office nearest you.

You can also get assistance from the TEXAS HEALTH AND HUMAN SERVICES COMMISSION, OFFICE OF THE OMBUDSMAN by calling (877) 787-8999.

If the Hearing Officer does not rule in your favor, you may, within 30 days of the decision, ask for an administrative review by the regional attorney of the Office of the General Counsel. The Hearing Officer can provide you with the correct address (1 TAC 357.11(b)(1)).

As you can see, appealing the HHSC decision is complicated, and time consuming. It is important to employ an attorney to help with the appeal and that can be expensive.

In Chapter 10, we presented many different options that are legally available to the Applicant at this time. The goal is to get the Applicant qualified for Medicaid as quickly as possible, and with the least amount of hassle. It is better to choose a strategy that has been allowed in the past, rather than chance a denial of the application and be forced to appeal the decision.

An experienced Elder Law attorney can explain what strategies have been allowed in the past in your county and which strategies are likely to be challenged. The key word is "experienced." Before employing an attorney, determine what percentage of his practice is devoted to Medicaid eligibility; how long he has practiced Elder Law in that county; and whether he is familiar with the appeals process, should the need arise.

Guiding Those You Love 12

Once you are satisfied with your Estate Plan, the final thing to consider is whether your heirs will be able to locate your assets after you're gone.

Most people have their business records in one place, their Will in another place, car titles and deeds in still another place. When someone dies, their beneficiaries may feel as if they are playing a game of "hide and seek" with the decedent. The game might be fun were it not for the fact that unlocated items may be forever lost. For example, suppose you die in an accident and no one knows you are insured by your credit card company for accidental death in the amount of $25,000. The only one to profit is the insurance company, which is just that much richer because no one told them that you died as a result of an accident.

And how about a key to a safe deposit box? Will anyone find it? Even if they find the key, how will they locate the box?

It is not difficult to arrange things so that your affairs are always in order. It amounts to being aware of what you own (and owe) and keeping a record of your possessions. A side benefit is that by doing so, you will always know where all your business records are. If you ever spent time trying to collect information to file your taxes or trying to find a lost stock or bond certificate, you will appreciate the value of organizing your records.

Heirs need all the help they can get. It is difficult enough dealing with the loss, without the frustration of trying to locate important documents. Your heirs will have no problem locating your assets if you keep all of your records in a single place. It can be a desk drawer or a file cabinet or even a file storage box that you purchase from the stationary store. It is helpful if you keep a separate file or folder for each type of investment. You might consider setting up the following folders:

📁 THE BANK & SECURITIES FOLDER

📁 THE INSURANCE FOLDER

📁 THE PENSION AND ANNUITY FOLDER

📁 THE DEED FOLDER

📁 THE TAX RECORD FOLDER

📁 THE LIABILITY (DEBT) FOLDER

📁 THE PERSONAL PROPERTY FOLDER
(title and appraisal of motor vehicles, jewelry, etc.)

📁 THE PERSONAL RECORDS FOLDER
(birth certificate, military, social security records, etc.)

📁 THE ESTATE PLANNING DOCUMENT FOLDER
(Will, Trust, Medical Power of attorney, etc.)

If you do not feel like doing a complete job of organizing your records at this time, consider an abridged version. You can set up a single folder and place all of your important papers in that folder. You need to make the folder easily accessible to whomever you wish to manage your affairs in the event of your incapacity or death. You can do this by letting that person know of the existence of the folder and how to get it in an emergency.

WHEN TO UPDATE YOUR ESTATE PLAN

We discussed people's natural disinclination to make an Estate Plan until they are faced with their own mortality. Many believe that they will make just one Will and then die (maybe that's why they put off making a Will). The reality is, most people who make a Will, change it at least once before they die. If you have an Estate Plan, it is important to update it when any of the following events take place:

✍ **CHANGE IN MARITAL STATUS**

GETTING MARRIED

Unless you enter a marriage with no property and no children, it is fool-hardy to marry without signing a Premarital Agreement. The example given in the stepchild section of Chapter 7 shows how the lack of planning on the part of a parent who remarries can be to the detriment of his children. A Premarital Agreement could have provided for a fair distribution of his property.

Hopefully, your marriage will prosper and you along with it. You should review your Premarital Agreement on a regular basis as your finances change or as you have children. With the consent of your spouse, you can amend your Premarital Agreement. If it needs a complete revision, you can revoke the agreement, and replace it with a Post-marital (i.e., Marital) Agreement (Family 4.005).

Changes to the Premarital Agreement need to be prepared and signed in the same manner as your original agreement. Texas Courts will not uphold a Premarital or Marital Agreement unless, the document was signed voluntarily after full disclosure of the finances of each party (Family 4.006). A document that is too one-sided can be challenged in Court, so it is important that both parties be represented by their own attorney.

GETTING A DIVORCE

If you get divorced, there are certain changes that take place by law. For example, if you divorce and then die before you get around to changing your Will or Trust, any provision that you made for your former spouse in the document will be read as if your former spouse died before you (Probate 69, 485A).

SEPARATION HAS NO LEGAL EFFECT

You are free to live separately from your spouse, but until and unless you divorce, the law considers you to be married. None of the legal changes described above, apply to couples who separate. If you expect your separation will be permanent, you need to change your Will, Trust, insurance policies, etc. on your own. However, you will not be able to change title to real property that you own together with your spouse, unless your spouse agrees to the change.

NOTIFY EMPLOYER OF CHANGE

If you change your marital status (either marry or divorce), you need to tell your employer of the change so that the employer can change your status for purposes of paycheck tax deductions. If you have a health insurance plan or a pension plan, that provides benefits to your spouse, then these need to be changed as well.

✍ A CHANGE IN RELATIONSHIP

Getting married, separated or divorced; having a child; having a beneficiary of your Estate die, are all profound changes in one's life. When the dust settles, it is important to examine your Estate Plan to see if it needs revision. If you have a Trust, you can change it by having your attorney prepare an *amendment* to the Trust. If you have a Will, your attorney can prepare a *codicil* (a supplement) to the Will.

It is important to have changes made by a properly drafted and signed document. If you make changes by crossing things out or writing over your Will, or Trust, the validity of the document can be challenged once you die.

If you simply rip up the old Will, that will effectively revoke the Will (Probate 63). But it could happen that someone (perhaps your attorney) has a copy of the Will. If no one knows that you revoked the Will, they may think the Will is lost and then offer the copy of the Will for Probate. If you draft a new Will, the first paragraph should say, "I revoke all prior Wills ..." This makes it clear that you want the new Will to replace all other Wills.

 NEW SPOUSE OR CHILD CAN
CHALLENGE OLD WILL

CHALLENGE BY SURVIVING SPOUSE
Texas is a Community Property state. As soon as you say "I do" your spouse has Community Property rights. If you marry and "forget" to change the Will you prepared prior to your marriage, unless you have a Community Property Agreement that provides differently, your spouse can challenge any part of your Will that affects his/her half of your Community Property.

CHALLENGE BY AFTERBORN CHILD
A child born or adopted after you prepared your Will is entitled to receive as much as any of your other children provided for in your Will. If you did not have any other child, or if you had other children but make provision for any of them, the *afterborn* child is entitled to as much of your property as (s)he would have inherited had you died without a Will, but not including property you gave to the other parent of your afterborn child (Probate 67).

EXCEPTIONS

There are exceptions to the rule. The afterborn child may not challenge the Will if:

⇨ you left all your property to your surviving spouse who is the parent of the omitted child

- or -

⇨ you made other provisions for your child outside the Will (i.e., Trust, POD accounts, joint property, insurance, etc.) (Probate 67).

If you had one or more children when you signed your Will, and none of the above exceptions apply, gifts given to your children under the Will must be shared equally with the afterborn child. This could lead to disagreements and hard feelings for those forced to contribute to the afterborn child's share.

It is better to change your Will when a child is born so that your child receives no more and no less than you intended.

✍ **BENEFICIARY MOVES OR DIES**

Most people remember to name an alternate beneficiary should one of their beneficiaries die. But how many of us remember to notify the pension plan or insurance company when a beneficiary moves?

It is important that your beneficiary's address be available to those in charge of distributing funds upon your death. Many life insurance proceeds are never paid because the company cannot locate the beneficiary.

The Actuarial Office of the Federal Employees' Group Life Insurance Program reported that as of September, 2003, they had over 55.8 million dollars in unpaid benefits, mostly because they could not locate the beneficiary at the last given address.

✍ RELOCATION TO A NEW STATE OR COUNTRY

There is no need to change your Estate Plan for a move within the state of Texas. However, if you deposited your Will with the Probate Court and you move to a different county, you need to retrieve your Will and deposit it with the Probate Court in the county of your new residence (Probate 71). If you move out of state, you need to take your Will with you. Not all states allow a Will to be deposited prior to death, so you may need to make other arrangements for the storage of your Will..

If your attorney has your original Will or any other original of your Estate Planning documents, then unless you plan to continue to employ him, you need to retrieve these documents and take them with you when you move.

HOLOGRAPHIC WILL MAY NOT BE ACCEPTED

You need to determine whether your Will conforms to the laws of the state of your new residence. A Will that is signed and witnessed according the laws of the state, is generally accepted into Probate regardless of where it is drafted. However, many states will not accept an unwitnessed Holographic Will into Probate. If you have a Holographic Will, it is best to draft a new Will that conforms to the laws of the state of your new residence.

If you do not have a Will, it is important to check out the Laws of Descent for that state. In some states they are referred to as the *Laws of Intestate Succession*. Each state has its own laws of inheritance of property and those laws are very different from each other. Who has the right to inherit your property in the state of Texas may be different from who can inherit your property in another state. If you do not have a Will, this is the time to think about who will inherit your property should you die in the state of your new residence. This is especially important for those who are married. The right of a spouse to inherit property varies significantly from state to state. The rights of a spouse in other Community Property states (Arizona, California, Idaho, Louisiana, Nevada, New Mexico, Washington and Wisconsin) may differ significantly from the rights of a spouse in Texas.

OTHER ESTATE PLANNING DOCUMENTS

A *Medical* or *Health Care Directive* is a document that gives instructions about the health care a person does (or does not) want to receive in the event there is no hope for his recovery and he is too ill to make his own health care decisions. As explained in Chapter 8, in Texas, that document is called a *Directive To Physicians and Family or Surrogate.* You can also sign a Medical Power of Attorney appointing someone (your Health Care Agent) to carry out the directions given in your Directive (Health & Safety 166.164). Other states have laws that enable you to appoint someone with powers similar to a Health Care Agent, but the laws of the state may refer to such person as a *Patient Advocate* or a *Health Care Surrogate* or a *Health Care Representative.* It is best to have a Health Care Directive using the forms and terms that are recognized in that state, rather than chance any confusion should you become ill and find yourself in an emergency situation.

Similarly, if you appointed someone to handle your finances under a Durable Power of Attorney, you may want to have another prepared in conformity with the laws of the new state, so there will be no question of the right of your Attorney In Fact to conduct business on your behalf.

CREDITOR PROTECTION
Creditor protection is another item that is significantly different state to state. As explained in Chapter 5, there are many items that are creditor proof in the state of Texas. This is not the case in most other states. If you have much debt, you need to determine what items are available to your creditors in that state, and what items can be inherited by your family free of your debts.

TAX CONSIDERATIONS
You need to check out the taxes of the new state. Each state has its own tax structure. Some states have an inheritance tax, or a transfer tax on all inherited property. If state taxes are high, you may need an Estate Plan that will minimize the impact of those taxes.

RELOCATING THE MEDICAID RECIPIENT
If your family member is a Medicaid Recipient, and you want to take him with you to another state, you need to check out whether he will continue to be eligible for Medicaid in that state. As explained in Chapter 10, Medicaid is both a state and federal program. Once a person qualifies for Medicaid in one state, he can be transferred to another state, provided he qualifies under that state's Medical Assistance Program. Before moving a Medicaid Recipient to another state, it is important to check with an Elder Law attorney in that state. He can explain the laws relating to Medicaid eligibility.

As you can see, state law has an important impact on your Estate Plan. When moving to another state, you need to educate yourself about the laws of that state, or consult with an attorney who can assist you in reviewing your Estate Plan to see if that plan will accomplish your goals in that state.

✍ A SIGNIFICANT CHANGE IN THE LAW

We pay our legislators (state and federal) to make laws and, if necessary, change those in effect. We pay judges to interpret the law and that interpretation may change the way the law operates. The legislature and the judiciary do their job and so laws change frequently. Tax laws are particularly volatile. The 2001 change in the federal Estate Tax law gradually increases the Exclusion amount so that by 2010 no federal Estate Tax will be due regardless of the value of your Estate. You may be thinking that there is no need for an Estate Tax plan because you don't intend to die prior to 2010. But any certainty relating to death and taxes is false security (especially taxes, in this case). As explained in Chapter 3, the law as passed in 2001, is effective only until December 31, 2010. If lawmakers do nothing, then on January 1, 2011, the federal Estate Tax goes back into effect, and perhaps the Texas Estate Tax along with it. If so, Estates that exceed one million dollars will once again be subject to federal and state Estate Taxes.

You need to keep up with the news to learn about changes in the law that affect your Estate Plan. It is a good idea to check with your attorney on a regular basis to see if any change in the state or federal law affects your current Estate plan. And also check out the Eagle Publishing Company Web site for changes we will post to keep this book fresh.   http://www.eaglepublishing.com

SPRING CLEAN YOUR RECORDS

Used to be, that housewives did a once a year, floor to ceiling, "spring housecleaning." We know of no survey telling whether today's houseperson conducts an annual purge of dirt and clutter. We suspect it went by the wayside when housewives entered the work force as full time employees. But it was a good practice. In many cases, it was the only time of the year when the house was truly clean and tidy.

It is a good idea to apply that old-fashioned housecleaning practice to your financial records and clean them up on a regular basis. There is no need to keep the deed to real property that you have long since sold; a lease agreement to an apartment you no longer rent; a credit card to a closed account, etc.

Many hesitate to toss out some scrap of paper for fear it will not be available for future reference. There are documents you may need to keep for a lengthy period of time to establish a basis for tax purposes. You can avoid the problem of keeping too much, or not enough, by taking your box (or folder) of records with you the next time you visit your accountant or attorney. You can ask your advisor to help you organize your records and assist with your "housecleaning."

Keys are another item to keep up to date. You may have a sentimental reason to keep old keys, but there is no business reason to keep a key to a car you no longer own, a safe deposit box you no longer lease, etc. Keeping such keys can only cause confusion should you become disabled or die. Whoever takes possession of your property will be left with mysterious keys. He will probably think the keys are protecting something of value.

Unless you enjoy picturing an heir's frustration as he seeks an imaginary treasure, pitch the key.

ABSTRACT OF TITLE An *Abstract of Title* is a condensed history of the title to the land. It consists of a summary of recorded documents that affect the land, including mortgages.

ACTUARIAL TABLE An *actuarial table* is a table organized according to statistical data that indicates the life expectancy of a person.

ADDENDUM An *addendum* to a contract is an addition to the contract.

ADMINISTRATION The *administration* of a Probate Estate is the management and settlement of the decedent's affairs. There are different types of Probate Administration. See ANCILLARY AND SUMMARY ADMINISTRATION.

ADMINISTRATIVE LAW JUDGE An *Administrative Law Judge* is someone who is appointed to conduct an administrative hearing. He has the power to administer oaths, take testimony, and then decide the facts of the case. Although he can decide the facts of the case, the final outcome of the hearing is decided by the government agency that appointed the Administrative Law Judge.

ADMINISTRATIVE CODE OF REGULATIONS The *Administrative Code of Regulations* is the set of rules used by governmental agencies to apply laws enacted by the legislature. The Administrative Code of Regulations interprets the law and describes the agency's requirements to implement that law. See *CFR.*

AFFIANT An *Affiant* is someone who signs an affidavit and swears or acknowledges that it is true in the presence of a notary public or other person with authority to administer an oath or take acknowledgments.

AFFIDAVIT An *Affidavit* is a written statement of fact made by someone voluntarily, under oath, or acknowledged as being true, in the presence of a notary public or someone else who has authority to administer an oath or take acknowledgments.

AGENT An *Agent* is someone who is authorized by another (the principal) to act for or in place of the principal.

AMENDMENT An *amendment* to a Trust is an addition to the Trust that changes the provisions of the Trust.

ANATOMICAL GIFT An *anatomical gift* is the donation of all or part of the body of the decedent for a specified purpose, such as transplantation or research.

ANCILLARY ADMINISTRATION An *Ancillary Administration* is a Probate procedure that aids or assists the original (primary) Probate proceeding. Ancillary administration is conducted to determine the beneficiary of the decedent's property located within that state, and to determine whether the property is taxable in that state.

ANNOTATED STATUTE A statute that is *annotated* is a statement of the law followed by cases which illustrate or explain the statute.

ANNUAL GIFT TAX EXCLUSION The *Annual Gift Tax Exclusion* is the amount a person can gift to another each year without being required to file a federal Gift Tax Return. The Exclusion amount is $12,000 for the year 2007.

ANNUITANT   An *Annuitant* is someone who is entitled to receive payments under an annuity contract.

ANNUITY CONTRACT An *annuity contract* is a contract that gives someone (the annuitant) the right to receive periodic payments (monthly, quarterly) for the life of the annuitant or for a given number of years.

ASSET   An *asset* is anything owned by someone that has a value, including personal property (jewelry, paintings, securities, cash, motor vehicles, etc.) and real property (condominiums, vacant lots, acreage, residences, etc.).

ASSIGN To *assign* is to transfer one's rights in or to something to another. For example, a person who has the right to receive income from a partnership may assign that right to another person.

ATTORNEY or ATTORNEY AT LAW   An *attorney*, also known as an *Attorney at law*, or a *lawyer*, is someone who is licensed by the state to practice law in that state.

ATTORNEY IN FACT An *Attorney In Fact* is someone appointed to act as an Agent for another (the *Principal*) under a Power of Attorney.

BASIS   The *basis* is a value that is assigned to an asset for the purpose of determining the gain (or loss) on the sale of the item or in determining the value of the item in the hands of someone who has received it as a gift.

BENEFICIARY A *beneficiary* is one who benefits from the act of another or from the transfer of property. In this book we refer to a beneficiary as someone named in a Will, Trust, or deed to receive property, or someone who inherits property under the Laws of Intestate Succession.

BENEFICIARY ACCOUNT A *beneficiary account* is a bank account with a named beneficiary. The owner of the funds in the account directs the bank to give the funds remaining in the account to the named beneficiary upon the death of all of the owners of the bank account. *Pay On Death* and *In Trust For* accounts are beneficiary accounts.

BONA FIDE A *bona fide* act is something that is done in good faith; honestly, openly and without deceit or fraud.

BURDEN OF PROOF The *burden of proof* is the duty of one of the parties in a dispute to establish the facts in the case. Who has the burden of proof is established by law.

CAPITAL GAINS TAX A *Capital Gains Tax* is a tax on the amount the net sales proceeds exceeds the basis of a capital asset sold by a taxpayer.

CASH SURRENDER VALUE The *Cash Surrender Value* of a life insurance policy is the amount of money the insurance company will pay to the owner of an insurance policy in the event the owner cancels the policy before the death of the person who is insured under the policy.

CERTIFICATE OF TRUST A *Certificate of Trust* is a document that contains basic information about the Trust such as the date of execution of the Trust; the Trust tax identification number; the identity of the Grantor, the current Trustee, the identity of Successor Trustee and the beneficiaries of the Trust, etc. Attorneys usually prepare a Certificate of Trust to give to the bank as identification instead of giving them the entire Trust document.

CFR **CFR** is the abbreviation for the ***Code of Federal Regulations***. The Code of Federal Regulations is the annual cumulation of regulations set by federal executive agencies combined with previous regulations that are still in effect. The CFR contains the general body of laws that govern the practices and procedures of federal administrative agencies.

CHARITABLE REMAINDER ANNUITY TRUST A ***Charitable Remainder Annuity Trust*** is a Trust that pays an annuity to a beneficiary (the *Annuitant*) for a certain period of time or until his death. Once the annuity is paid, whatever remains in the Trust is donated to a tax exempt charity.

CLAIM A *claim* against the decedent's Estate is a demand for payment. To be effective, the claim must be filed with the Probate court within the time limits set by law.

CLOSE CORPORATION A ***Close Corporation*** is a corporation whose voting shares are held by a single shareholder or a small, closely-knit, group of shareholders.

CODE A *Code* is a body of laws arranged systematically for easy reference e.g. the Internal Revenue Code.

CODICIL A *codicil* to a Will is an addition to the Will that changes or replaces certain parts of the Will.

COLUMBARIUM A *columbarium* is a vault with niches (spaces) for urns that contain the ashes of cremated bodies.

COMMON LAW MARRIAGE A *Common Law marriage* is one that is entered into without a state marriage license or any kind of official marriage ceremony. A Common Law marriage is created by an agreement to marry, followed by the two living together, and telling everyone they know that they are husband and wife. See INFORMAL MARRIAGE.

COMMUNITY PROPERTY Certain states (Arizona, California, Idaho, Louisiana, Nevada, New Mexico, Texas, Washington, and Wisconsin) have laws stating that property acquired by husband or wife, or both, during their marriage is *Community Property* and is owned equally by both of them.

COMMUNITY PROPERTY ACCOUNT A *Community Property Account* is an account owned by a married couple. Should one of them die, half of the account becomes the property of the surviving spouse. The other half is distributed according the decedent's Will or Trust; or if neither of these, according to the Texas Laws of Descent and Distribution.

COMMUNITY PROPERTY WITH RIGHT OF SURVIVORSHIP *Community Property With Right of Survivorship* is property owned by a married couple such that if one of them dies, the other owns all of the property without going through a Probate procedure.

CONFLICT OF INTEREST A *conflict of interest* is a conflict between the official duties of a fiduciary (guardian, Trustee, attorney, etc.) and his own private interest. For example, it is a conflict of interest for a Successor Trustee to use Trust property for his own personal profit.

CONVENIENCE ACCOUNT A *Convenience Account* is a bank account in which the owner of the funds in the account authorizes another to make bank transactions as his Agent under a Power of Attorney. The Agent has no ownership interest in the account.

CORPORATION   A *Corporation* is a company created by one or more persons according to the laws of the state. The company is owned by the *shareholders* or *stockholders*. Each owner has limited liability (see Limited Liability).

COURT The *Court* as used in this book is the Court that handles Probate matters. The term is synonymous with "judge," i.e., an "order of the Court" is an order made by the judge of the Probate Court.

CREDITOR A *creditor* is someone to whom a debt is owed by another person (the *debtor*).

CUSTODIAN A *Custodian* under the *Texas Uniform Transfers to Minors Act* is a financial institution or person who accepts responsibility for the care and management of property given to a minor child pursuant to the Act.

DAMAGES *Damages* is money that is awarded by a Court as compensation to someone who has been injured by the action of another.

DADS *DADS* is the abbreviation for the Texas Department of Aging and Disability Services.

DEBTOR A *debtor* is someone who owes payment of money or services to another person (the *creditor*).

DECEDENT The *decedent* is the person who died.

DESCENDANT A *descendant* is someone who descends from a common ancestor. There are two kinds of descendants: a *lineal descendant* and a *collateral descendant*. The lineal descendant is one who descends in a straight line such as father to son to grandson. The collateral descendant is one who descends in a parallel line, such as a cousin. In this book, unless otherwise stated, the term *descendant* refers to a *lineal descendant*. The word **issue** has the same meaning as the word descendant.

DIRECTIVE TO PHYSICIANS *Directive to Physicians and Family or Surrogates* is a document that gives specific instructions regarding the health care that the person wants to receive in the event he is too ill to speak for himself. See LIVING WILL.

DISSENT A *dissent* is a refusal to agree with something stated or ruled upon. A dissent by a judge sitting on the Supreme Court is often in the form of a written opinion that opposes a ruling made by the Court. The dissent does not change the ruling of the Court.

DISTRIBUTION The *distribution* of a Trust or Probate Estate is the giving to the beneficiary that part of the Estate to which the beneficiary is entitled.

DURABLE As used in the Power of Attorney, the word *durable* means that the Power of Attorney will remain in effect in the event that the principal (the person giving the Power of Attorney) becomes incapacitated.

DURESS *Duress* is the use of force or threats to get someone to do something.

ELIGIBILITY SPECIALIST An *Eligibility Specialist* is someone employed by the Texas Health and Human Services Commission Health Services to investigate Medicaid Applicants to determine whether they qualify for Medical Assistance in the state of Texas.

ENTITLEMENT An *entitlement* is a legal right to receive a benefit of income, property or services.

EQUITY The *equity* in a home is the market value of the home less monies owed on the property (mortgages, tax liens, etc.)

EQUITY INTEREST An *equity interest* is an ownership interest. It is the value of the ownership interest over and above monies owed on the property.

ESTATE A person's *Estate* is all of the property (both real and personal property) owned by that person. The decedent's Estate may also be referred to as his *Taxable Estate* because all of the decedent's assets must be included when determining whether Estate Taxes are due. Compare to PROBATE ESTATE.

EXECUTOR An *Executor* (feminine *Executrix*) is a legal term found in many Wills. The term refers to the person named by the Will maker to carry out directions given in the Will. In modern Wills, that person is referred to as the *Personal Representative*.

FACE VALUE The *face value* of a life insurance policy is the value stated on the insurance certificate or policy. It is the amount to be paid upon the death of the insured person.

FAIR HEARING A *Fair Hearing* is an administrative procedure. It is the first step in the appeals process for someone who has been denied Medicaid benefits.

FIDUCIARY A *Fiduciary* is one who takes on the duty of holding property in Trust for another or acting for the benefit of another, such as a Personal Representative, Trustee, Guardian etc.. A fiduciary relationship is also one that is developed out of trust and confidence. For example, an attorney has a fiduciary relationship with his client.

FORECLOSURE *Foreclosure* is a court proceeding in which a creditor either takes title to, or forces the sale of, property owned by the borrower, in order to satisfy the debt.

GRANTEE The *Grantee* of a deed is the person who receives title to real property from the *Grantor*.

GRANTOR A *Grantor* is someone who transfers property. The Grantor of a deed, is the person who transfers real property to a new owner (the *Grantee*). The Grantor of a Trust is someone who creates the Trust and then transfers property into the Trust. Also see SETTLOR

GUARANTOR A *Guarantor* is someone who promises to pay a debt or perform a contract for another in the event that person does not fulfill his obligation.

GUARDIAN A *Guardian* is someone who has legal authority to care for the person or property of a minor or for someone who has been found by the court to be incapacitated.

HEALTH CARE AGENT A *Health Care Agent* is someone who is appointed by another (the *Principal)* to authorize medical treatment for the Principal, in the event the Principal is to too ill to do so himself.

HEALTH CARE POWER OF ATTORNEY A *Health Care Power of Attorney* is a document in which someone (the *Principal*) gives another (his *Health Care Agent*) authority to make medical decisions on behalf of the Principal.

HEARING OFFICER A *Hearing Officer* is someone who is appointed to conduct an administrative hearing. He has the power to administer oaths, take testimony, and then decide the facts of the case. Although he can decide the facts of the case, the final outcome of the hearing is decided by the government agency that appointed the Hearing Officer.

HEIR An *Heir* is anyone entitled to inherit the decedent's property under the Laws of Descent in the event that the decedent dies without a valid Will.

HHSC *HHSC* is the abbreviation for the *Health and Human Services Commission.* It is the agency that administers the Medicaid program in the state of Texas.

HIPAA *HIPAA* is the abbreviation for the *Health Information Private Access Act*, a federal law.

HOLOGRAPHIC WILL A *Holographic Will* is a Will written, dated and signed by the hand of the Will maker himself. Many states refuse to admit a Holographic Will into Probate unless it is witnessed according to the laws of the state. Texas Courts allow a Holographic Will to be probated, provided the material parts of the Will are written in the Will maker's hand.

HOMESTEAD The *homestead* is the dwelling that is owned, and occupied, within the state of Texas, as the owner's principal residence.

INCAPACITATED   The term *incapacitated* is used in two ways. A person is *physically incapacitated* if he lacks the ability to perform certain tasks. A person is *legally incapacitated* if a Court finds that he is unable to care for his person or property.

INFORMAL MARRIAGE An *Informal Marriage* is similar to a Common Law marriage in that the couple never applied for a marriage license, nor had their marriage solemnized by a ceremony. An Informal Marriage is valid in the state of Texas provided a man and woman agreed to be married, then live together in the state of Texas as husband and wife, and hold themselves out as being married.

INTER VIVOS TRUST   An *Inter Vivos Trust* (also known as a *Living Trust*) is a Trust that is created and becomes effective during the lifetime of the Grantor (or Settlor) as opposed to a Trust that he includes as part of his Will to take effect upon his death.

INTESTATE   *Intestate* means not having a Will or dying without a Will. *Testate* is to have a Will or dying with a Will.

IRA ACCOUNT An *Individual Retirement Account ("IRA")* is a retirement savings account created in conformity with the federal Internal Revenue Code. Income taxes on certain deposits and interest to the account are deferred until the monies are withdrawn.

IRREVOCABLE CONTRACT An *irrevocable contract* is a contract that cannot be revoked, withdrawn, or cancelled by any of the parties to that contract.

IRREVOCABLE TRUST An *Irrevocable Trust* is a Trust that cannot be changed, cancelled or terminated until its purpose is accomplished.

IRREVOCABLE INSURANCE TRUST   An *Irrevocable Insurance Trust* is a Trust that is set up to purchase life insurance. The proceeds of the life insurance policy can be used to pay taxes that may be due upon the death of the insured person.

JOINT AND SEVERAL LIABILITY   If two or more people agree to be *jointly and severally liable* to pay a debt, then each individually agrees to be responsible to pay the debt, and together they all agree to pay the debt.

JOINT TENANCY In Texas, a *Joint Tenancy* means that each tenant owns an equal share of the property. There are no rights of survivorship unless the deed specifically says so.

KEOGH PLAN A *Keogh Plan* is a retirement plan available to self-employed taxpayers. Certain tax benefits are available such as tax deductions for annual contributions to the plan. The plan is named for its author, Eugene James Keogh.

KEY MAN INSURANCE *Key man insurance* is a disability and life insurance policy designed to protect a company from economic loss in the event that an important employee of the company becomes disabled or dies.

LAWS OF DESCENT AND DISTRIBUTION   *The Laws of Descent and Distribution* are the laws of the state relating to who is entitled to inherit the decedent's Probate Estate when he dies without a valid Will. In some states these laws are referred to as the *Laws of Intestate Succession.*

LEGALESE *Legalese* refers to the use of legal terms and confusing text used by some attorneys when drafting legal documents.

LETTERS *Letters* is a document, issued by the Probate court, giving the Personal Representative authority to take possession of and to administer the Estate of the decedent.

LIEN A *lien* is a charge against a person's property as security for a debt. The lien is evidence of the creditor's right to take the property as full or partial payment, in the event that the debtor defaults in paying the monies owed.

LIFE ESTATE A *Life Estate* interest in real property is the right to possess and receive the income from that property for so long as the holder of the Life Estate lives. A one-third Life Estate interest means the person can occupy one-third of the property or receive one-third of the income generated by that property.

LIMITED LIABILITY *Limited Liability,* as related to a corporation or other company created according to state law, means that a shareholder of the company generally is not responsible to pay the debts of the company beyond the amount that he/she invested in the company.

LIMITED LIABILITY COMPANY A *Limited Liability Company* is a company created according to the laws of the state. In Texas, it can be organized to conduct any lawful business. All of the members of the company have limited liability.

LIMITED PARTNERSHIP A *Limited Partnership* is a partnership created according to the laws of the state. Each *Limited Partner* has limited liability. Each *General Partner* has control of the business and is personally liable for all of the debts of the company. (See Limited Liability).

LINEAL DESCENDANT   See *descendant.*

LITIGATION   *Litigation* is the process of carrying on a lawsuit, i.e., to sue for some right or remedy in a court of law. A Litigation Attorney is one who is experienced in conducting the law suit and in particular, going to trial.

LIVING WILL   A *Living Will,* also referred to a *Directive To Physicians and Family or Surrogate,* is a Health Care Directive that gives instructions to the physician about whether life support systems should be withheld or withdrawn in the event the *Declarant* (the person who made the Living Will) is terminally ill, or in a persistent vegetative state, and unable to speak for himself.

LOOK-BACK PERIOD   The *Look-back Period* is a period of consecutive months that can be reviewed for transfers of Resources to determine whether a period of ineligibility should be imposed for the Medicaid Applicant.

MEDICAID *Medicaid* is a medical assistance program sponsored jointly by the federal and state government to provide health care for people with low income and limited resources. In Texas, the program is also referred to as *Medical Assistance.*

MEDICAL POWER OF ATTORNEY A *Medical Power of Attorney* is a document in which someone (the *Principal*) gives another (his *Health Care Agent*) authority to make medical decisions on behalf of the Principal in the event that the Principal is too ill to do so himself.

MEH *MEH* is the abbreviation for the Texas Medicaid Eligibility Handbook.

NET WORTH A person's *net worth* is the fair market value of all of the property that he owns less the sum of his liabilities, i.e., what he owes.

NEXT OF KIN *Next of kin* has two meanings in law: *next of kin* refers to a person's nearest blood relation or it can refer to those people (not necessarily blood relations) who are entitled to inherit the property of a person under the Laws of Intestate Succession.

NON-PROBATE TRANSFER A *non-Probate Transfer* is a transfer made to a beneficiary of the decedent without going through a Probate procedure. This includes transfers from a joint account, a Trust, a Pay On Death account, a Transfer On Death security, etc.

PARTNERSHIP A business *partnership* is an agreement between two or more persons to use their assets, expertise and/or labor to carry on a business for profit as co-owners.

PERJURY *Perjury* is lying under oath. The false statement can be made as a witness in court or by signing an Affidavit. Perjury is a criminal offense.

PERSONAL EFFECTS *Personal effects* is personal property that is kept for one's personal use such as clothing, jewelry, books, and other items generally found in the home.

PERSONAL PROPERTY *Personal property* is all property owned by a person that is not real property (real estate). It includes personal effects, cars, securities, bank accounts, insurance policies, etc.

PERSONAL REPRESENTATIVE The *Personal Representative* is someone appointed by the Probate Court to settle the decedent's Estate and to distribute whatever is left to the proper beneficiary.

PER STIRPES *Per Stirpes* is a method of distributing property to a group of beneficiaries in the event that one of them dies before the gift is made. The deceased person's share goes to his descendants. If he has no descendants, the surviving beneficiaries share equally in the gift.

PETITION A *Petition* is a formal written request to a Court asking the Court to take action or issue an order on a given matter; e.g. a request to appoint a Guardian.

POSTMARITAL AGREEMENT A *Postmarital* or *Marital Agreement* is an Agreement made by a couple after marriage to decide their respective rights and responsibilities in case of a divorce or the death of a spouse.

POWER OF ATTORNEY A *Power of Attorney* is a document in which someone (the *Principal*) gives another person (his *Agent* or *Attorney-In-Fact*) authority to do certain things on behalf of the Principal.

PREMARITAL AGREEMENT A *Premarital Agreement* (also known as a *Prenuptial Agreement*) is an Agreement made prior to marriage to take effect once a couple marry. The Agreement states how the couple's property is to be managed during their marriage and how their property is to be divided should either die, or they later divorce.

PRINCIPAL OF A POWER OF ATTORNEY The *Principal* of a Power of Attorney is someone who gives another (his *Agent*) authority to act on his (the Principal's) behalf.

PRINCIPAL OF A TRUST The *Principal of a Trust* is the Trust property. The Trust income is the money that is earned on the Trust Principal.

PROBABLE CAUSE *Probable cause* exists if it is reasonable to believe certain facts. Mere suspicion is not enough. For probable cause to exist, there must be more evidence for the facts than against.

PROBATE *Probate* is a procedure in which a Court determines whether the decedent left a valid Will. The Court will appoint someone, a *Personal Representative* to settle the decedent's Estate by paying valid claims and expenses, and distributing whatever remains to the proper beneficiary.

PROBATE ESTATE The *Probate Estate* is that part of the decedent's Estate that is subject to a Probate procedure. It includes property that the decedent owned in his name only or as a Tenant In Common. It does not include property that was jointly held by the decedent and someone else. It does not include property held in trust for someone.

PRO BONO The term *Pro Bono* means "for the public good." When an attorney works Pro Bono, he does so voluntarily and without pay.

REAL PROPERTY *Real property*, also known as *real estate,* is land and anything permanently attached to the land such as buildings and fences.

RECEIVER A *Receiver* is a person appointed by a Court to take possession of property whenever there is a danger that in the absence of such appointment, the property will be lost or removed. The Receiver acts as a Trustee preserving and managing the property according to Court order.

REMAINDER INTEREST   A *Remainder Interest* in real property is the property that passes to a beneficiary at the end of the life interest, i.e., the property that passes to the beneficiary once the owner of the Life Estate dies.

RESIDUARY BENEFICIARY A *Residuary Beneficiary* of a Will is a beneficiary who is entitled to whatever is left of the Probate Estate once specific gifts have been distributed and the decedent's bills, taxes and costs of Probate have been paid. Unless the Will makes some other provision, Residuary Beneficiaries share equally in the Residuary Estate.

RESIDUARY ESTATE The *Residuary Estate* is whatever is left of the Probate Estate once specific gifts made in the Will have been distributed and the decedent's bills, taxes and costs of Probate have been paid.

RESOURCE A *Resource* for purposes of determining Medicaid eligibility, is an asset owned by the decedent, or his spouse, that can be converted into cash to meet their needs. Federal statute 42 U.S.C. 1382b identifies what counts (and does not count) as a Resource.

REVERSE MORTGAGE A *Reverse Mortgage* (also known as a *Reverse Annuity Mortgage)* is a mortgage whose loan proceeds are paid to the borrower incrementally over a period of time. The loan is not repaid until the borrower dies or the property is sold.

REVOCABLE TRUST   A *Revocable Trust* is a Trust which can be amended or revoked by the Grantor or Settlor during his lifetime.

REVOCABLE LIVING TRUST A *Revocable Living Trust* (also known as an *Inter Vivos Trust*) is a Revocable Trust that is created and becomes effective during the lifetime of the Grantor or Settlor.

SELF PROVED WILL A *Self Proved Will* is a Will that eliminates some of the formalities of proof in a Probate procedure. The Will is Self Proved if signed by the witnesses in the form as required by the statute.

SEPARATE PROPERTY In Texas, the term *Separate Property* refers to property that is owned by a married person in his/her own right. It includes property owned by the person prior to marriage, as well as inheritances and gifts received by the person during the marriage.

SETTLOR A *Settlor* or a *Trustor* is someone who creates a Trust.

SIBLING A *sibling* is one of two or more people born of the same parents, i.e., a brother or a sister. Unless, otherwise noted, we used the term to include those who have only one parent in common (a *half brother* or a *half sister*).

SOLE PROPRIETORSHIP A *Sole Proprietorship* is a form of business ownership in which one person owns all of the assets of the business and that person is personally liable for all of the debts of the business.

SOLEMNIZE To *solemnize* a marriage is to enter into the marriage publicly, before witnesses, in contrast to a secretive or Common Law marriage.

SPECIFIC GIFT A *Specific Gift* is a gift of a specific item of the Will maker's Estate that is made to a named beneficiary of the Will.

SPENDTHRIFT A *Spendthrift* is someone who wastes money and/or spends lavishly.

SPENDTHRIFT TRUST A *Spendthrift Trust* is a Trust created to provide monies for the living expenses of a beneficiary, and at the same time protect the monies from being taken by the creditors of the beneficiary.

SPRINGING POWER OF ATTORNEY A *Springing Power of Attorney* is a Power of Attorney that is not operational until, and unless, the Principal is incapacitated.

STATUTE OF LIMITATION A *Statute of Limitation* is a federal or state law that sets maximum time periods for taking legal action. In general, no legal action can be taken once the time set out in the statute passes.

STEPPED-UP BASIS A *stepped-up basis* is the fair market value placed on property that is purchased or inherited from another. The "step-up" refers to the increase in value from the basis of the former owner (usually what he paid for it), to the basis of the new owner (usually the market value when the transfer is made).

SUCCESSOR TRUSTEE A *Successor Trustee* is someone who takes the place of the Trustee.

SUMMARY ADMINISTRATION A *Summary Administration* is a simplified and/or shortened Probate procedure.

SURROGATE A *surrogate* is a substitute; someone who acts in place of another.

TAC *TAC* is the abbreviation for the Texas Administrative Code

TAX EXCLUSION A *Tax Exclusion* is income that is not taxed because of an Internal Revenue Code provision.

TENANCY BY THE ENTIRETY A *Tenancy by the Entirety* is the name of a form of ownership of real property held by a husband and wife. Each person is considered to be the owner of 100% of the property both before and after the death of one of the parties. Texas, being a Community Property state does not recognize this form of ownership.

TEFRA LIEN *TEFRA* is the abbreviation for the TAX EQUITY AND FISCAL RESPONSIBILITY ACT. It is a federal law that allows states to place a lien on real property owned by those who receive Medicaid benefits after age 55.

TENANCY IN COMMON *Tenancy In Common* is a form of ownership such that each tenant owns his share without any claim to that share by the other tenants. There is no right of survivorship. Should a Tenant In Common die, his share belongs to the tenant's Estate and not to the remaining owners of the property.

TERM LIFE INSURANCE POLICY A *Term Life Insurance policy* insures the life of a person for a certain period of time. No insurance proceeds are paid unless the insured person dies within the given period of time. The monies paid for the policy are not refundable, so a Term Life Insurance policy has no cash surrender value.

TESTATE *Testate* means having a Will or dying with a Will.

TITLE INSURANCE *Title Insurance* is a policy issued by a title insurance company after searching title to the property. The insurance covers losses that result from a defect of title, such as unpaid taxes, or a claim of ownership of the property.

TORT A *Tort* is a civil wrong which causes injury to someone or to his property in violation of a duty that is imposed by law. That duty could be not to harm another or not to enter onto another's property without permission.

TRADE MARK A *Trade Mark* is any word, name, symbol or devise, or combination thereof adopted and used by a person to identify goods made or sold by him and to distinguish them from goods sold by others.

TRADE NAME A *Trade Name* is any word, name, symbol or devise, or combination thereof used by a person to identify his business and distinguish it from other businesses.

TRUST AGREEMENT A *Trust Agreement* is a document in which someone (the Settlor) creates a Trust and appoints a Trustee to manage property placed into the Trust. The usual purpose of the Trust is to benefit persons or organizations named by the Settlor as beneficiaries of the Trust.

TRUSTEE A *Trustee* is a person, or institution, who accepts the duty of managing Trust property for the benefit of another.

UNASSIGNABLE ANNUITY An *unassignable annuity* is an annuity that cannot be assigned; i.e., the annuitant's benefits cannot be transferred to another.

UNDUE INFLUENCE *Undue influence* is pressure, influence or persuasion that overpowers a person's free will or judgment, so that a person acts according to the will or purpose of the dominating party.

VOID GIFT A *void gift* is one that is not legally enforceable. For example, if a Will makes a gift and the Court finds that provision to be void, the beneficiary has no legal right to receive that gift.

VOID MARRIAGE A *void marriage* is one that is not recognized legally. The couple has no legal marital rights or responsibilities to each other.

WAIVER   A *waiver* is the intentional and voluntary giving up of a known right.

A Will Is Not Enough In Texas

INDEX

WEB SITES

223 Texas Statutes and Regulations are referenced in
A Will Is Not Enough In Texas

Each state has its own set of laws relating to the control, and protection of a person's Estate. The laws of Texas relating to Guardianship, Probate and especially Medicaid are very different from the laws of other states.

The author is in the process of "translating" *A Will Is Not Enough* for the rest of the states; that is, writing state specific books that explain how to set up an Estate Plan for the given state and how to qualify for MEDICAID in that state.

A Will Is Not Enough is now available for:
ARIZONA, CALIFORNIA, CONNECTICUT
COLORADO, FLORIDA, GEORGIA, HAWAII
INDIANA, ILLINOIS, MARYLAND, MICHIGAN
MASSACHUSETTS, NEBRASKA
NEW JERSEY, NEW MEXICO, NEW YORK
OREGON, PENNSYLVANIA, TEXAS
VIRGINIA, WASHINGTON, WISCONSIN.

To check whether this book is currently available for other states call Eagle Publishing Company of Boca at
(800) 824-0823

Visit our Web site for a Publisher's discount.
http://www.eaglepublishing.com

OTHER BOOKS BY AMELIA E. POHL

How To Defend Yourself Against Your Lawyer
is a book about the unhappy experiences people have
with their lawyers, beginning with that of the author
AMELIA E. POHL. She became involved in a law suit and
found herself in the role of client, rather than lawyer. She
become concerned about lawyers who do not provide their
clients with loyalty and respect. This book is a result of
those concerns.

The book is divided into chapters that cover the most
common problems that take people to a lawyer: divorce,
probate, criminal, personal injury, starting a business,
making a Will, buying a house, etc. Each chapter tells of
the misadventures of the unwary as they sought the
services of a lawyer without a clue as to what they were
"buying." This book is funny, sad, interesting, but most of
all informative. It tells the reader how to become a savvy
consumer, i.e., how to find the right lawyer for the right
job. If you ever find the need to employ a lawyer, you will
be glad you read this book.

Copyright 2004   272 pages 6" X 9" soft cover
$20 includes Shipping and Handling

BOOK REVIEW

TED KREITER of the SATURDAY EVENING POST said "Horror fans,
forget about those tawdry tales of ghosts and vampires. Pick up Amelia E.
Pohl's *How To Defend Yourself Against Your Lawyer* to
read some really scary stuff. Like the story . . . of the grieving widow, Ethel,
whose husband died shortly after a lawyer drafted a sweetheart will for the
two of them. . . . Six months in attorney's fees later, Ethel learned that she
already had her husband's money because it never needed to go through
probate! . . Ethel then went out and found a good lawyer for $1,000 who was
able to get her $5,000 back. You do the math. . . Following Pohl's useful
advice could save a person much more than money."

Guiding Those Left Behind In . . .

Amelia E. Pohl has written a series of books explaining how to settle an Estate. Each book is state specific, telling how things are done in that state. Each book explains:

- ✧ who to notify
- ✧ how to locate the decedent's property
- ✧ how to get possession of the inheritance
- ✧ when you do, and do not, need an attorney
- ✧ the rights of a beneficiary, and much more.

Each book is written with the assistance of an experienced attorney who is licensed and is practicing in that state.

The *Guiding* series is currently available for the following states: ALABAMA, ARIZONA, ARKANSAS, CALIFORNIA
CONNECTICUT, FLORIDA, GEORGIA, HAWAII, ILLINOIS
INDIANA, IOWA, KANSAS, KENTUCKY,
LOUISIANA, MAINE, MASSACHUSETTS
MARYLAND, MICHIGAN, MINNESOTA, MISSOURI
MISSISSIPPI, NEW JERSEY, NEW YORK
NORTH CAROLINA, OHIO, OKLAHOMA
PENNSYLVANIA, SOUTH CAROLINA, TENNESSEE
TEXAS, VIRGINIA, WASHINGTON, WISCONSIN

Visit the EAGLE PUBLISHING COMPANY Web site at
http://www.eaglepublishing.com
to check whether books for other states are available at this time. See the Web site for a Publisher's Discount.

BOOK REVIEWS OF *Guiding Those Left Behind*

ARIZONA

Ben T. Traywick of the Tombstone Epitaph said "This book is an excellent reference book that simplifies all the necessary tasks that must be done when there is a death in the family. There is even an explanation as to how you can arrange your own estate so that your heirs will not be left with a multitude of nagging problems." "The reviewer has been going through probate for two years with no end yet in sight. This book at the beginning two year ago would have helped immensely."

CALIFORNIA

Margot Petit Nichols of the Carmel Pine Cone called it a ". . .TRULY RIVETING READ." " . . . I could scarcely put it down." "This is a book that we should all have, either on our book shelves or thoughtfully placed with our important papers."

OTHER BOOKS BY AMELIA E. POHL

Beyond Grief To Acceptance and Peace

AMELIA E. POHL and the noted psychologist BARBARA J. SIMMONDS, Ph.D, have written a book for those families who have suffered a loss.

- ✧ What to say to the bereaved
- ✧ How to help a child through the loss
- ✧ Strategies to adjust to a new life-style
- ✧ When and where to seek assistance.

80 pages   6" X 9" $10 includes Shipping and Handling
TO ORDER CALL (800) 824-0823.

It is the goal of EAGLE PUBLISHING COMPANY to keep our publications fresh.

As we receive information about changes to the federal or Texas law we will post an update to this edition at our Web site.

http://www.eaglepublishing.com